A License to Steal

Leonard W. Levy

A License to Steal

The Forfeiture of Property

The University of North Carolina Press

Chapel Hill and London

© 1996 The University of North Carolina Press

Manufactured in the United States of America

The paper in this book meets the guidelines for perma-
nence and durability of the Committee on Production
Guidelines for Book Longevity of the Council on Library
Resources.

Library of Congress Cataloging-in-Publication Data
Levy, Leonard Williams, 1923–
A license to steal: the forfeiture of property / Leonard W.
Levy.
    p.   cm.
Includes bibliographical references and index.
ISBN 0-8078-2242-6 (cloth: alk. paper)
1. Forfeiture—United States.   2. Searches and
seizures—United States.   3. Right of property—United
States.   I. Title.
KF9747.L48   1996
345.73'0522—dc20
[347.305522]   95-14497
                                              CIP

00 99 98 97 96   5 4 3 2 1

This book is lovingly dedicated to Elyse,

my wife of fifty years.

Contents

Preface

On February 1—not April 1—of 1995, the Associated Press ran a little story about forfeiture datelined from Helper, Utah, a town of 2,100 people. The story began, "Police officers in Helper will personally get a cut of any cash or property they seize in drug cases." Speaking for the city council that had adopted this "forfeiture incentive resolution," the mayor asked, "Why not give our guys a reason to be more aggressive?" Officers involved in seizures of drug property will get from 10 to 25 percent of the proceeds. Helper, Utah, had simply personalized the already existing state and federal laws that permitted law enforcement agencies to profit from assets forfeited in drug cases.

Forfeiture refers to the government's uncompensated confiscation of property that is implicated in a crime. The property may be used to commit the crime, be its product, or be obtained with its fruits. For example, a home bought with money from illegal drugs or a robbery is subject to forfeiture. The government may proceed against the property in a civil suit by a procedure that is at war with the Constitution, or in a criminal suit that can damage third parties. This book examines both civil and criminal forfeiture. No other book does.

Forfeiture must be distinguished from the taking of private property for a public use by the power of eminent domain. In such a case, which requires just compensation, the property is unconnected with crime; in a forfeiture case, the

ix

commission of a crime is a necessary precursor of the proceeding, whether civil or criminal. In either criminal or civil forfeiture, the forfeiture has a punishing effect. In a civil forfeiture case, the government also seeks to prevent a recurrence of a particular kind of crime and to remedy an illegal situation or condition that attends the crime or results from it. Forfeiture excludes any compensation for the confiscated property; the power of eminent domain excludes punishment.

Forfeitures are usually legitimate and possibly a majority of its victims are guilty. Most forfeiture victims do not contest the proceedings against them, although their reasons may be legitimate and by no means imply their guilt. They may, for example, be unable to afford an attorney or the cost of one is greater than the value of the assets forfeited. Moreover, more than three-fourths of the victims of forfeiture are never charged with crime. The state wants their property, not their liberty.

A "license to steal" may be an appropriate characterization of government procedures even in criminal cases that require observance of all constitutional protections as to the accused. The property might belong to an innocent third party. Innocence and victimization by forfeiture are all-too-common companions. Moreover, even the guilty are entitled to their constitutional rights, which exist in part to insure that guilt or innocence is fairly determined and that punishment is not inflicted on those not convicted. In the case of civil forfeiture, unfairness and injustice always prevail.

The topic of forfeiture provokes robust opinions, as the title of this book suggests. *A License to Steal* is in some respects a misleading title, though not as much as others that I considered. Presidents of the National Association of Criminal Defense Lawyers, quoted in this book, have spoken of forfeiture as "government thievery" and as "legalized theft." Such exaggerated characterizations of forfeiture are understandable in a constitutional system that ranks property rights with the rights to life and liberty. The Supreme Court, however, has downgraded the rights of property, thereby allowing forfeitures to thrive. Of late the Court has begun to impose some limitations on the practice, but not nearly enough. Forfeiture remains a questionable practice despite the Court. Because property rights are valuable, their violation stirs animosities. When law enforcement agencies are deservedly the butt of such animosities, forfeiture becomes a practice that undermines society.

—Leonard W. Levy
  Ashland, Oregon

Acknowledgments

Anna Beauchamp and her staff of the interlibrary loan office at Southern Oregon State College were extraordinarily helpful in filling my requests; without them this book could not have been written. I am grateful, too, for the assistance provided by Joseph Cox, formerly president of the college, and his successor, Stephen J. Reno. My friend Irwin Shapiro has my gratitude for his encouragement. Jane Garrett, Paul Schnee, and Stephen Wagley also helped in that way. Above all, I am indebted to the assistance given me by my close associate, Louis Fisher, who was an invaluable sounding board via nearly daily faxes and who provided me with copies of materials that I found difficult to get. Cheryl Anthony Epps, the legislative director of the National Association of Criminal Defense Lawyers, sent me a pile of helpful documents. Michael D. Bradbury, the district attorney of Ventura County, California, supplied an important report. Jennifer Berubee, a student at Southern Oregon State College, served as an assistant, photocopying materials for me.

A License to Steal

"We need new office furniture, boys. Declare someone a drug suspect and confiscate his house." (Cartoon by Henry Payne, reprinted by permission of UFS, Inc.)

Chapter One

Deodands:
Origins of Civil Forfeiture

Law enforcement agencies—federal, state, and local—perpetrate astonishing outrages on owners of private property through forfeitures. Although property has the same constitutional protection as life and liberty, police and drug enforcement officers seize money, cars, houses, land, and businesses of people who may be entirely innocent of criminal conduct. Officers who seize their property and seek its confiscation by the government are enforcing the law that governs forfeitures. A forfeiture is the uncompensated government confiscation of property illegally acquired or used.

Legislatures, state and national, and courts are to blame for the niggling respect shown to constitutional rights by law enforcement agencies in forfeiture cases. The law allows government to seize and confiscate the property of people suspected of some crime, though they may never be tried or, if tried, may be acquitted. The promise of forfeiture lures officers to seize what they can, because they are able to keep for law enforcement purposes most of what they seize, or they can use the assets for whatever they need—weapons, helicopters, cellular phones, salary increases, bulletproof vests, or new police cars with which to conduct the war against crime. In an era of tight public budgets, forfeiture is a seductive source of new revenue for law enforcement agencies.

Thus, when property is at stake, officers sometimes cannot resist powerful incentives to ignore the rights of citizens who are under suspicion. For example, in 1988 customs agents seized the *Atlantis II*, an $80 million research vessel owned by the Woods Hole Oceanographic Institution in Massachusetts. The pretext for confiscating the vessel was the fact that a drug-sniffing dog found about one one-hundredth of an ounce of marijuana in a crewman's shaving kit. The public outcry in this instance was exceptional, because of the trivial pretext for the seizure and because the oceanographic institution had no knowledge that a crewman used marijuana; as a result of the public response, the United States had to return the vessel.[1]

Professor Craig Klein was equally innocent but not as lucky. He bought a new sailboat for $24,000, which was being delivered to him in Jacksonville, Florida. Customs agents in Florida waters commonly suspect boats of carrying drugs. They conducted a seven-hour search of Klein's sailboat by ripping out its woodwork, smashing its engine, rupturing its fuel tank, and drilling thirty holes into its hull, many below the water line. The officers, who found no drugs, damaged the boat beyond repair. Klein sold it for scrap.[2]

Mrs. Selena Washington and Mr. Willie Jones, both of whom are black, had the misfortune of carrying a lot of cash. She was driving along Interstate 95 in eastern Florida on her way to buy construction materials to repair her home, which had been damaged by Hurricane Hugo. Interstate 95 is a pipeline for illegal drugs, and the sheriff's department of Volusia County makes a practice of stopping suspicious-looking vehicles, often those driven by blacks because a majority of people who transport drug money is in fact black. The sheriff stops cars going south—presumably those with cash to buy controlled substances—rarely those going north with caches of drugs. The sheriff's purpose is to hunt for cash. Within a few years his department confiscated about $8 million in cash believed to be narcotics moneys. When a deputy stopped Mrs. Washington late one night, his search of her purse yielded $19,000, which he confiscated as drug money. She protested vehemently and asked to be taken to the police station to clarify the matter, but he simply drove off. He did not even take her name. She had the nerve to follow him back to the police station to lodge a protest. An attorney, whom she hired to represent her, advised a settlement because of the expense of contending a forfeiture suit. The sheriff kept $4,000, the lawyer $1,200, and she got back the rest.[3]

Willie Jones was a Nashville landscaper who in 1991 bought an airline ticket to Houston with cash. That prompted an airline employee to tip off the Drug Enforcement Agency (DEA) in the hope of collecting a 10 percent commission on any drug moneys that might be seized. The Department of Justice pays out about $24 million annually to such tipsters.[4] A search of Mr. Jones revealed no drugs, but he had $9,600 in his wallet. A drug-sniffing dog supposedly detected traces of drugs on the money, a fact of slight merit because about 96 percent of all currency in circulation, whether carried by clergymen or crack dealers, has such traces.[5] Mr. Jones was not arrested but his cash, which was intended for the purchase of shrubbery, was confiscated. He was unable to post a bond for 10 percent of the money in order to mount a legal challenge to the forfeiture. It nearly drove him out of business. He lamented, "I didn't know it was against the law for a 42-year-old black man to have money in his pocket." Jones had no police record and could produce documents showing that he regularly made such trips to buy from nurseries that demanded cash. Luckily, a distinguished lawyer who heard about Jones's case volunteered to represent him. As a result a federal district court judge in Nashville tongue-lashed the conduct of the DEA officers who took Jones's money and ordered them to return it. Most such cases do not have happy endings.[6]

The Derbachers lost their Hamden, Connecticut, home as a result of forfeiture because federal agents discovered that their grandson, who lived with them, possessed controlled substances in his room. Mr. Derbacher, an honest and respected citizen, angrily denounced government greed and "Nazi justice."[7] The Sheldons of Moraga, California, fought the government when it seized their home by forfeiture. They had sold the home to another couple for $289,000 and lent them $160,435 on a second mortgage. The couple who bought the home was convicted of violating the Racketeer Influenced and Corrupt Organizations Act (RICO), and the government confiscated the home, then appraised for $325,000. As a result, the Sheldons, who had foreclosed because the purchasing couple fell behind on payments, lost control of the home and the value of the mortgage. They contested the forfeiture in the federal courts. As the case dragged on, the house was badly neglected under government control and suffered major structural damage until it was worth only $60,000. The government, Sheldon furiously charged, ran "the biggest racket since Al Capone." The Sheldons lost in the lower federal courts. In 1993, after more than a decade of expensive litigation, whose cost could not be recovered, a federal court of appeals ruled that the government had illegally taken their mortgage without the just compensation demanded by the Fifth Amendment. That decision may be appealed by the government.[8]

Billy Munnerlyn, who had an air charter service, flew a passenger from Little Rock to Ontario, California, in 1989.

DEA officers seized the passenger's luggage, finding $2.7 million in it. Although the government dropped the arrest charges against Munnerlyn, who knew nothing about the drug money, it refused to return his Lear jet. He sold three smaller planes and his office equipment to pay $80,000 in legal fees, but his attempt to force the return of his jet failed when a federal district court ruled against him. The government offered to return the plane for $66,000, which he could not afford. He finally got it back for $7,000, only to discover that government agents, having ripped the plane apart in a futile search for drugs, caused damage of at least $50,000, for which the DEA is not liable. Munnerlyn declared bankruptcy, lost his business, and became a truck driver.[9]

Robert Brewer of Irwin, Idaho, who was dying of prostate cancer, used marijuana to ease the pain and nausea. In 1990 a drug SWAT team consisting of a dozen deputies broke into his home under authority of a search warrant, never shown, that was based on an informant's misleading tip about Brewer being a major grower of the weed. The officers found eight marijuana plants in his basement growing under a special light and half a pound of marijuana, which they confiscated; they also seized his Ford van, which had allowed him to lie down while traveling the 270 miles to Salt Lake City twice a month for his cancer treatments.[10] Similarly, James Burton, who had a ninety-acre farm and a large house near Bowling Green, Kentucky, grew marijuana, on the advice of his ophthalmologist, to treat his glaucoma; Burton produced and smoked ten to fifteen joints daily to reduce the pressure in his eye. The ophthalmologist, who was authorized by the government to test marijuana in the treatment of glaucoma, testified at Burton's trial that it was the only medication that could keep him from going blind. A federal district judge found that the congressional enactment, which was the basis of prosecuting Burton, had no exemption for the medical use of marijuana. The government confiscated his farm. Burton escaped to the Netherlands to avoid federal prison.[11]

A final scandalous illustration involved Donald Scott, a multimillionaire, who owned a two-hundred-acre ranch in Ventura County, California. In the wee hours of a night in 1992, thirty-one lawmen from eight agencies, including DEA agents and Los Angeles police, occupied the ranch and smashed in the door of Scott's home with a battering ram. Five officers, guns drawn, rushed in. Scott, groggy from sleep and in a drunken stupor, grabbed his revolver and ran into the outer room. Officers ordered him to drop the weapon. As he lowered it, he was shot dead before his wife.

A search of the property yielded no drugs. Nor did the officers find marijuana growing on it, despite a tip from an informant. Indeed, before the fatal raid, the California National Guard had photographed the property from the air, and so had the DEA. The inconclusive results had led to a furtive ground scan of the Scott property by the United States Border Patrol, but no marijuana was found. Nevertheless a local judge issued a search warrant, which led to the raid on Scott's home and to his subsequent death. The search warrant later turned out to be illegal, because it lacked probable cause. A Ventura County investigation also concluded that the border patrol had illegally trespassed on the property and that the Los Angeles County Sheriff's Department had been motivated by a desire to seize and forfeit the ranch for the benefit of the various law enforcement agencies that had been involved. The property "was worth millions of dollars," said the district attorney of Ventura County, and the Ventura County sheriff "was not called because Los Angeles County did not want to split the forfeiture proceeds with that agency." The L.A. County sheriff

6

conceded that before they sought a warrant they had discussed forfeiture of the property, as they always do whenever a large amount of money or property is implicated, but denied that the interest in the forfeiture dominated concern for crime. However, the Scotts had committed no crime, and the drug experts in the law enforcement agencies appear to have confused ivy with marijuana.[12]

Miscarriages of justice, some egregious, such as those noted here, probably constitute a distinct minority of forfeiture cases. In the overwhelming number of such cases, the forfeitures are exacted from guilty individuals who used the forfeited property in the commission of a crime or who used criminal proceeds to obtain that property. Whether the individual is guilty or innocent, the procedure by which the property is confiscated tends to be appalling, devoid as it is of most of the constitutional safeguards that surround an accused person. What is the law of forfeiture that underlays forfeitures and how did it come about?

It began with deodands. The term "deodand" derives from the Latin phrase "deo dandum" and means "given to God." A deodand is a thing forfeited, presumably to God for the good of the community, but in reality to the English crown. Deodands are commonly attributed, especially by courts, to a passage in the Bible: "If an ox gore a man or a woman that they die, the ox shall be surely stoned and its flesh shall not be eaten" (Exodus 21:28). Having quoted this text, a federal district court murkily remarked, "When the ancient concept is recalled, our understanding of the law of forfeiture of chattels is more easily understood." The case in which this statement appears has the silly but revealing name of *United States v. One 1963 Cadillac Coupe de Ville Two Door*.[13] That is, the government sued the automobile as if it were personally guilty of a crime. In an especially strange case, *United States v. One 6.5 mm. Mannlicher-Carcano*

Military Rifle, the government sued the rifle that was used to assassinate President John F. Kennedy, on the theory that it was "a species of Deodands." When the courts refused to endorse the proposition that deodands are part of American law, Congress obtained possession of the weapon under the eminent domain clause of the Fifth Amendment by "taking" it for a public use with just compensation.[14]

The Supreme Court has observed that the law ascribes "to the property a certain personality, a power of complicity and guilt in the wrong. In such case there is some analogy to the law of deodand by which a personal chattel that was the immediate cause of the death of any reasonable creature was forfeited." The Court also invoked the authority of Sir William Blackstone, who, in his influential *Commentaries on the Laws of England* (1765–69), surmised that the Mosaic law inflicted the forfeiture partly because the ox's owner was somehow negligent and therefore he was punished by the loss of his ox (Exodus 21:29–30). Blackstone added to the confusion by noting that the Athenians exterminated or cast out "whatever was the cause of a man's death."[15]

In another case the Supreme Court explained: "Traditionally, forfeiture actions have proceeded upon the fiction that the inanimate objects themselves can be guilty of wrongdoing. Simply put, the theory has been that if the object is 'guilty,' it should be held forfeit. In the words of a medieval English writer, 'Where a man killeth another with the sword of John at Stile, the sword shall be forfeit as deodand, and yet no default is in the owner.' The modern forfeiture statutes are the direct descendants of this heritage."[16]

The Mosaic injunction about the ox did not, however, provide for a deodand or anything like it. Neither did the Athenians. Deodands did not derive from the Bible. In the first place the ox was not forfeited to anybody, not even the victim's family. Killing it may have signified that it was given to God as a sacrifice. But it was killed by stoning, which was the act of the entire community, a form of execution used for the most serious of crimes. In effect stoning reveals that the ox was regarded as guilty of the murder of a person. As an object of horror, its flesh was not eaten. Moreover no one in authority benefited from its value. In the case of a deodand some official must be the beneficiary of the value of the agent causing the death.

In view of the fact that the ox was an unreasoning beast, the question arises: why put it to death? The ancient Hebrews apparently attributed diabolical possession to the offending animal. When a woodchopper's ax head flew off as he was cutting down a tree, killing a person who was close by (Deuteronomy 19:5), no one considered the ax head as a deodand, subject to forfeit or destruction. Apparently his satanic majesty could inspirit living things but not inanimate objects—at least, according to the ancient Hebrews.

The sophisticated Greeks of Periclean Athens, however, did believe that inanimate objects had personalities and could be possessed by *Erinys*, the Furies. Accordingly if a boulder or piece of metal or a misthrown javelin killed a person, it had to be formally tried and if convicted would be banished to liberate Athens from pollution. Thus, Plato wrote: "And if any lifeless thing deprive a man of life, except in the case of a thunderbolt or other fatal dart sent from the gods—whether a man is killed by lifeless objects falling upon him, or his falling on them, the nearest of kin shall appoint the nearest neighbor to be a judge and thereby acquit himself and the whole family of guilt. And he shall cast forth the guilty thing beyond the border."[17] The Athenians also tried animals that killed people. The trials were solemn proceedings against beasts whose judges endowed them with personalities and solemnly condemned

9

them. Thus the Athenian practices provided a comparatively better precedent—though still a deficient one—for deodands than the Mosaic ox, but Christians of the Middle Ages knew Jerusalem better than they knew Athens.

Retribution against inanimate objects, such as the sword of John at Stile or against irrational beasts, became common in the Middle Ages. Christians fought the demons of their own theology rather than the Furies of mythology. In 864 the Council of Worms decreed that a colony of bees should be suffocated in their hive, because they had stung a person to death. The notion that they were demonically possessed or would not otherwise have committed the crime was matched by the accompanying belief that if the bees were not executed, thereby propitiating God, divine wrath in the form of floods, famine, pestilence, or other catastrophes would befall the community.[18]

Thus the ninth-century laws of Alfred the Great of England were prefaced by the Mosaic code and provided that any bull that injured a person had to be surrendered to the authorities for retribution. Similarly if a tree fell on a man or he fell out of it and died, it was given to his kin to get rid of; they revenged themselves by cutting it down and scattering its chips. A boat that capsized, causing a fisherman to die, was beached, cursed, and allowed to rot. A well in which a man drowned was filled up, and a house that collapsed on a man was torn down. In such cases as little consideration was given to the owner of the bees, the trees, the boat, or the well as was given to the owner of the Mosaic ox. The legal foundation was being built to regard the innocence of the owner of the property as an irrelevant consideration. Owners might be prosecuted if the accident occurred as a result of their negligence, but they could not retain their property if an accidental homicide occurred despite their having used reasonable care in controlling it.[19]

When the bees or trees were turned over to the deceased's relatives, the law provided a means of peaceably resolving a situation that might otherwise have erupted into blood feud and private justice. Yet guilt still attached to the thing by which a wrong had been done, and that guilt formed the basis of what ultimately became the doctrine that the object causing the accident, whether a dumb beast or a tree, was tainted with guilt instead of being possessed by a satanic spirit. Accordingly the guilty animals that had caused injury to people were judicially executed during the Middle Ages and later. Pigs, bulls, horses, snakes, and dogs were formally tried, convicted, and subjected to capital punishment for their crimes. The ecclesiastical courts of the medieval church also tried and excommunicated animals and even destructive insects such as locusts and weevils. The secular authority conducted its own trials, following the same procedures as if a rational creature were the accused, and in some cases dressed animals in people's clothing before the hangman carried out the death sentence, which might be burning at the stake or hanging. The carcasses of animals that were hanged or strangled were thrown into the river or buried. The meat and the hide were not used. Such condemnations continued well into the nineteenth century. Indeed, the last known case occurred in 1906 in Switzerland. The guilty objects constituted a symbolic ransom to appease the injured parties as well as God.[20]

As societies became more developed, the notion emerged that the guilty object required community atonement by providing compensation to someone in charge, like a chieftain or king. He was the one responsible for keeping the peace that had been shattered by the homicide, even if it was accidental. He was therefore the one who should benefit from the sacrifice.[21]

By the thirteenth century, the law of deodand had developed in England. If a headstrong horse carried a man against his will over a cliff or threw him into water, drowning him, the horse must be escheated to the king. An English jurist of the thirteenth century, Henry de Bracton (died 1267), described deodands in his *Laws and Customs of England*. After an inquest on accidental deaths, the boats from which persons were drowned or the other objects that caused their deaths were adjudged to be deodands for the crown's benefit. Near the close of the thirteenth century Parliament enacted a statute specifying the deodand procedure. A coroner's jury determined the value of the deodand, and that value rather than the things themselves was forfeited to the crown. No longer did the surviving kinsman institute suit or benefit from it. Because the king provided courts of justice and maintained the public peace, he sued for the value of the deodand. Thus, the deodand became a basis of crown property, and therefore survived so many centuries.[22]

If the king profited from the deodand, why was it called a deodand or thing given to God? The deodand or object causing the accidental death was given to God in the sense that the church had once been able to demand payment for masses to be said for the souls of the people who had been killed. Sometimes the church used the money for charitable purposes. But the crown supplanted the church as the community's sovereign representative, so that the church no longer was able to collect deodands. The king latched on to the already existing principle of deodand. Forfeitures had become an important source of revenue for the king's exchequer, not merely in cases of accidental death but even in cases of justifiable homicide, suicide, unintentional manslaughter, and murder. If the king lost a subject someone must pay into the royal coffers. Indictments for homicide had to specify the financial value of the object causing the death so as to provide for the king's interest in the deodand.

12

A jury in such a case determined the value of the deodand and would refer to the weapon used in the homicide as worth so many pence or shillings.[23]

Technically the forfeiture derived from a deodand only when the death resulted from "misadventure" or sheer accident. In the seventeenth century, Lord Chief Justice Matthew Hale wrote that a thing could not be deodand unless it caused a person's death. In effect the thing was personified as if it were the guilty culprit. The animal that killed the person, the wheel of a water mill that crushed him, and the cart that ran over him were confiscated as deodands, or their equivalent value in money was paid to the king. Although "it was not his crime," as Lord Hale said in 1688 of the property owner, "but his misfortune, yet the king hath lost his subject, and that men may be more careful, he forfeits his goods."[24]

Deodands migrated to America with the English settlers. The king's patents or land grants in America to his friends and to colonial proprietors vested all deodands in them. The patent of Lord Thomas Culpeper to the Northern Neck of Virginia, for example, granted him all the lands, woods, lakes, fish, animals, metals, minerals, fines, forfeitures, and deodands. An inquest by a coroner's jury would investigate unnatural deaths and determine whether some deodand should be forfeited. In 1626 a coroner's jury in Virginia found that John Verone had committed suicide by hanging himself with a chain, and ruled that the chain "doth fall to the kinge for a diadon." In 1638 a coroner's inquest in St. Mary's County, Maryland, having viewed the bloody corpse of a man who was crushed by a tree, ruled that the tree was responsible for his death and forfeited it as a deodand to the Lord Proprietor. A 1649 coroner's jury blamed a boat, which had capsized, for the death of a man, declared it deodand, and ordered that its appraised value of one hundred pounds of tobacco be given by the boat's owner to the sheriff for the use of the crown. Similarly, another Virginia coroner's jury, in Charles City County in 1664, ordered that a horse or its value be forfeited as a deodand to the governor for the use of the crown, after the rider of the horse fell to his death. In 1680 in New York, the high court of Governor and Council heard the case of a woman who was killed by a horse; the council declared the horse a deodand "to be knock't in the head" and its owner had to forfeit its value to the crown.[25]

Instances of deodand were not common in America, even in the eighteenth century when knowledge of English law had become widespread. The Supreme Judicial Court of Massachusetts in 1721 declared a gun as deodand after a boy playing with it accidentally killed his playmate. The court ordered the sheriff to confiscate the weapon for the use of the king. In Providence, Rhode Island, a coroner's inquest of 1724 found that a man had been accidentally killed when a cart ran over him. The jury assessed the value of the cart at five pounds payable by its owner as a deodand for the benefit of the poor of the town.[26] In this instance the deodand deserved its name.

The uncommonness of deodands in America may have resulted from the reluctance of the colonists to make the crown or its agents the beneficiary of deodands. In several colonies, for example, animals that killed people were forfeited to the survivors' next of kin. Cases like that were frequent, although even in colonies where deodands were forfeited to the crown, a royal official might allow the deodand to be used for charitable purposes. In Virginia, for example, in a 1707 case, the governor's council, having declared deodand a horse and its saddle, granted them to the wife of the deceased because the family was "extream poor." So too a coroner in Virginia, on hearing a petition from the deceased's wife, released to her a boat that had been declared deodand, because she was "an Object of Charity."[27] Whether

14

deodands were exacted for charitable purposes, for the crown's agent, or for the next of kin, the law of deodands did not flourish in America. Not even after the publication of Blackstone's *Commentaries*, which Americans knew well, did deodands flourish—perhaps because of Blackstone.

Blackstone speculated about the reasons for the law of deodands in a section of his work headed "The King's Revenue." Americans were never eager to augment the king's revenue. Blackstone began by reminding readers that all property "derived from society," so that if anyone violated the law, he forfeited his rights including his property. The king, as the "one visible person in whom the majesty of the public resides," obtained the property. Deodand was a species of forfeiture that arose from misfortune rather than from the commission of a crime. In the "blind days of popery," Blackstone wrote, the deodand was devoted to the "superstitious purpose" of saying "propitiary masses" for those "snatched away by sudden death." Thus, a deodand was an "expiation" or atonement for the benefit of their souls.

As a good Protestant, Blackstone had to explain why deodands survived the Reformation without conceding that the king sought to profit from the misfortune of his subjects. Blackstone claimed that the misfortunes leading to accidental death were partly the result of "the negligence of the owner" of the property, "and, therefore, he is properly punished by such forfeiture." Presumably the owner of the ox or well would take better care if he were liable for the loss of his offending property.[28] Lord Hale had expressed the same idea that forfeiture of the deodand induced better care.

One problem with the Hale-Blackstone explanation of deodands is that the offending property might have belonged to the victim. If his own horse threw him, or if he owned the tree that he fell from or the well in which he drowned, his death scarcely inspired him to take better care. Moreover, the very idea of accidental death implied that no negligence was involved. Deodands were unnecessary as a deterrent to carelessness, because the negligent property owner was always liable. Exodus 21:29 warned about the consequences if the owner of the ox knew that it was inclined to gore. If the vicious ox killed a person, not only would it be stoned; its owner would also be executed. English law had long punished negligence that led to injury.

The Hale-Blackstone notion that the law of deodands inspired better care and so diminished the number of accidents, however wrong, proved to be attractive to the crown as a justification for deodands. Thus, a legal institution that had begun out of religious motivation developed a completely different and false rationalization: deterrence of accident. Oliver Wendell Holmes, in his history of the common law, explained the procedure by which such a thing could happen:

> The customs, beliefs, or needs of a primitive time establish a rule or a formula. In the course of centuries the custom, belief, or necessity disappears, but the rule remains. The reason which gave rise to the rule has been forgotten, and ingenious minds set themselves to inquire how it is to be accounted for. Some ground of policy is thought of, which seems to explain it and to reconcile it with the present state of things; and then the rule adapts itself to the new reasons which have been found for it, and enters on a new career. The old form receives a new content, and in time even the form modifies itself to fit the meaning which it has received.[29]

So it was with the law of deodands.

When Blackstone analyzed deodands he did not rest solely on the explanation that they inspired better care. He also remarked that the object causing the accident was "an accursed thing," as if demonic possession justified the forfeiture to the crown. If trees, wells, and oxen could be demonically possessed, how could their owners control them to prevent accident? Blackstone, making his point about the deodands having been accursed, implied that the forfeited property lost its cursedness or taint when it reverted to the government. That implication continues in the law of forfeiture to this day. Thus an automobile or home that had been tainted by association with illegal drugs suddenly loses its taint when seized and forfeited to the government.

In any event Blackstone did little to explain deodands. Nor did he explain why a rational legal system regarded the dumb beast or the inanimate object as a guilty party deserving punishment. Still less did he explain why the punishment was visited upon the owner of the property if he or she had acted prudentially and was personally innocent. Indeed, that innocence notwithstanding, the owner was punished by the loss of the property or its equivalent value. Technically the owner was arrested and jailed until his innocence was established as a matter of law and the death pronounced *"per infortuniam,"* or a misfortune resulting from a non-negligent accident. Nevertheless, he forfeited his property.

The notion that deodands could be justified as an inducement to better care or as a deterrent to negligence continued until the frequency of deaths from accident revealed its emptiness. Industrialism, urbanization, and the development of the railroad in the nineteenth century accomplished that. But before deodands could be abolished, the law was to be altered in still another respect. A judicial ruling of 1808 had to be circumvented. In that year, in a case involving accidental death caused by a stagecoach, a man sued the stagecoach company for damages to compensate for his wife's loss. Ellenborough, the lord chief justice of England, presided at the trial and ruled that the death of a person is not a ground for an action for damages.[30]

Ellenborough gave no reason or precedent for that rule, remarking only that "in a civil court, the death of a human being cannot be complained of as an injury." That explanation invites comparison with the one offered by the judge in W. H. Auden's "Law Like Love":

> Law, says the judge as he looks down his nose
> Speaking clearly and most severely,
> Law is as I've told you before,
> Law is as you know I suppose,
> Law is but let me explain it once more,
> Law is The Law.

And Ellenborough's law became the governing rule in England and America.

The reason for the rule (that the death of a person is not the basis for a damage suit) is that when public justice superseded private retributive justice, forfeiture to the crown of the offender's property rendered wholly futile any civil actions for damages. As a result, even though the death by wrongful act injured a family by depriving its members of their legal right to the services of the deceased, the injury to the family could not legally be the basis of an action for damages. In short, death, by converting a private wrong into a public one redressable by forfeiture, had the effect of barring civil redress for the tort, that is, the wrong that caused the death.[31]

The frequency of traffic accidents and the failure of the law to provide a remedy for bereaved relatives forced Parliament to consider an alternative to deodands. They were the only price exacted of wrongdoers and scarcely sufficed to require a high standard of care. In an 1845 case, a railroad engine, having caused the deaths of four persons, was declared a deodand at an assessed value of only 125 pounds.

Moreover, the money did not assist the victims' survivors; only the crown collected when an accident caused fatalities. As a result, in 1846 Parliament enacted the "Act for the Compensation the Families of Persons Killed by Accidents," usually called Lord Campbell's Act.[32]

Campbell himself argued that "objectionable as the system of deodands was," he would not abolish it unless victims' survivors had a right to hold railroads and stagecoaches liable "for the lives and limbs of Her Majesty's subjects." He conceded that it was a "wonder that a law so extremely absurd and inconvenient should have remained in force down to the middle of the nineteenth century." The "law of deodands," he added, "was called into action weekly, as the newspapers constantly informed them." The solution was to abolish deodands and vest a right of action in the survivors.[33]

The history of deodands yields several conclusions. One is that although they were abolished in England in 1846, they did not die, because their underlying principles have endured to the present, constituting the foundations of the law of civil forfeiture in the United States. In the United States, though deodands never entered the mainstream of the law, their basic element did: a thing can be guilty and if so is forfeit to the government.

The law of deodands, like the law of civil forfeiture, was a tissue of legal fictions and contradictions. It was also unjust to its core. As early as 1373 a petition requested that even though a ship caused a man's death, it should not be forfeited as a deodand "because it is not the fault of the master of the vessel."[34] The law of deodands punished innocent people, the owners of the miscreant property that supposedly caused fatal accidents. The law made believe that they were guilty. The deodand personified the guilty thing as the defendant. The personification fiction infects the law of civil forfeiture to this day, as does the notion that the inanimate thing caused a misfortune or even a crime, for which it must be punished by forfeiture to the government. The government has superseded the king.

Another of the several legal fictions is that the law of deodands served no punitive purpose, because no person was found guilty. Only the animals or the inanimate objects in a proceeding that was considered civil rather than criminal were found guilty. Because no person was found guilty, the forfeiture did not constitute punishment. It was, rather, a remedial or regulatory action on behalf of the public, forming the foundation of the American law of civil forfeiture. That fact in no way altered the actuality: the innocent owner of the property has been deprived of it without a semblance of fair procedure. Accordingly Mr. Willie Jones, Professor Craig Klein, and Mr. Billy Munnerlyn lose their cash, their boat, and their business. The legal heritage of deodands is not only the basis of civil forfeiture in America today; it is also injustice.

Chapter Two

Felony Origins of Criminal Forfeiture

Rex Cauble, a multimillionaire Texan, masterminded and financed a huge marijuana smuggling ring called "the cowboy Mafia." Officers of the DEA seized one of his shrimp boats loaded with twenty tons of the drug and prosecuted him for violations of RICO, the Racketeer Influenced and Corrupt Organizations Act. The federal jury that convicted him returned a special verdict that forfeited his 30 percent interest in Cauble Enterprises. As a result, the United States became the owner of Cauble's share of 10,000 acres of Texas real estate, other properties in three states, an oil drilling company, at least three Texas banks, a chain of Western Wear shops, over 450,000 shares of blue-chip stock, and a welding supply company. The criminal forfeitures totalled about $75 million. The Bank of Credit and Commerce International, a multiple violator of RICO, pleaded guilty and forfeited assets of $550 million. Michael Milken, the junk-bond king, also pleaded guilty to RICO frauds, and forfeited $600 million in cash.[1]

Forfeiture results from a judgment of guilt that permits the confiscation of property used or derived from criminal conduct. But not all forfeitures are criminal in character. The deodand, we have seen, is the foundation of *civil* forfei-

21

tures in which the offending property is the defendant; the subject of the forfeiture is itself the guilty wrongdoer. Accordingly the guilt or innocence of the property owner or user is simply an extraneous matter of no legal concern. In a criminal forfeiture case, by contrast, the guilt or innocence of the alleged human perpetrator occupies the sole attention of the legal system. The prosecution directs its energies against the person who forfeits nothing unless convicted of the crime.

The legal profession, which is fond of Latin terms, speaks of criminal forfeiture cases as being *in personam*, against the person, and civil forfeiture cases as *in rem*, meaning against the thing, the inanimate and insentient property, rather than against the person. An *in rem* proceeding decides the ownership of that thing. In a criminal forfeiture case the loss of property follows as a penalty imposed after the conviction of the guilty party. The property need not have a relationship to the crime, though in a civil forfeiture case the defendant property is somehow connected to the crime regardless of the personal guilt or innocence of its owner.

The distinction between civil and criminal forfeitures reflects the distinction between civil and criminal law. Civil law determines private rights, and it provides remedies and compensation for harm done to those rights. Criminal law punishes criminal offenders. The trouble is that civil law also may punish, making the distinction between the civil and criminal law somewhat bewildering. Indeed, no principled or realistic way exists to distinguish civil and criminal cases especially concerning penalties. Civil forfeitures surely have nothing to do with private rights and remedies.

Nevertheless, the law neatly divides the legal universe into two worlds, civil and criminal. In law school, the curriculum is split into civil and criminal categories. Civil and criminal lawyers rarely practice each other's law, and they work in different courts. The Department of Justice and the offices of United States Attorneys throughout the nation have civil and criminal divisions. Civil and criminal law have different rules of evidence, standards of proof, courses of defense, and types of punishment. Fines and imprisonment are penalties exclusively associated with the criminal law, but both civil and criminal law inflict forfeitures. In criminal law the accused benefits from a presumption of innocence and a requirement that proof be demonstrated beyond a reasonable doubt. The civil law favors clear and preponderant proof, but with respect to forfeitures requires merely a showing by the government that probable cause exists to believe that some property is associated with crime.

The constitutional protections surrounding a civil defendant are severely limited compared to those enjoyed by a criminal defendant. The distinction between civil and criminal law was already ancient when the Constitution was framed, and it recognizes that difference. Over half the specific protections in the Bill of Rights apply to criminal defendants. Sixth Amendment rights to a speedy trial, trial by jury, confrontation of witness, compulsory process to obtain witnesses in one's behalf, and the assistance of counsel are guaranteed to the "accused" in "all criminal prosecutions." Although courts interpret the Fifth Amendment's self-incrimination clause so that it applies in civil as well as criminal proceedings, the words of the Constitution specify its application only in "criminal prosecutions." The world of criminal law can be keenly different from that of the civil law.[2]

Criminal forfeitures have a different origin from civil ones. The recent criminal forfeiture cases involving Rex Cauble, Michael Milken, and the Bank of Credit and Com-

23

merce International had their origins in feudal England, particularly in the practice of the king's confiscation of the properties of felons and traitors.

Criminal forfeitures began with medieval escheats or the reversion of an estate to a feudal lord. The failure of a tenant to fulfill his obligations, which was the original meaning of the word "felony," resulted in escheat. Felony came to signify the breach of the feudal bond by a significant criminal offense such as murder, rape, arson, or robbery. Conduct once regarded as warranting private retribution became public crimes. Commission of a felony was punishable by death, and the felon's lands escheated to his lord. The greatest of the feudal lords was the king, who benefited the most from the seizure of a felon's property, especially his personal property, and who, therefore, manipulated the law to augment royal benefits.[3] Blackstone said that "the true criterion of felony is forfeiture."[4]

At the time of the Norman Conquest community courts and community justice prevailed in England. The legal system was ritualistic, dependent upon oaths at most stages of litigation, and permeated by both religious and superstitious notions. Legal concepts were so primitive that no distinction existed between civil and criminal cases or between secular and ecclesiastical cases. Juries were unknown. After one party publicly accused another, the local lord, sitting as judge, decided whether the trial should be by oath or ordeal. The trial would put the accused to his "proof." If tried by oath, he would make a sworn statement to the truth of his innocence, supported by the oaths of compurgators or oath helpers who swore from their own knowledge to the truth of his remarks. Presumably no one would endanger his immortal soul by false swearing. Later the compurgators became character witnesses, swearing only to their belief that his oath was trustworthy. If he rounded up the

24

requisite number of compurgators and the swearing proceeded without a mistake, he won his case. A mistake "burst" his oath, proving guilt and resulting in punishment and forfeiture.[5]

Ordeals were usually reserved for more serious crimes, and the number of capital felonies kept increasing with time. As an invocation of immediate divine judgment, ordeals were consecrated by the Church and shrouded with solemn religious mystery. The accused underwent a physical trial in which he called upon God to witness his innocence by putting a miraculous sign upon his body. Priests administered the ordeals. The accused might have to plunge his hand into a cauldron of boiling water or carry a red-hot piece of iron a certain distance, in the hope that, three days later when the priest removed the bandages, he would find that the accused had "come clean": the wound was healing free of infection. If a person failed the ordeal, his property escheated to his lord. After 1215, when the Fourth Lateran Council forbade priests to participate in ordeals, ordeals by fire and water died out.[6]

The Normans brought to England the ordeal of battle, which gave the legal concept of "defense" or "defendant" a physical meaning. God presumably strengthened the arms of the innocent party, so that right, not might, would prevail. In any case the lord benefited by receiving the escheated lands of the convicted felon. If the king was not his lord, the king took possession of the real estate only for a year and a day, during which time he could confiscate anything on the land, whether lumber, crops, forests, minerals, or houses, and he might "waste" it by destroying whatever he pleased, before it reverted to the local lord by escheat. The king's revenues swelled from his right to "a year and a day, and waste," a right that he often sold for cash. The king always confiscated the felon's chattels or personal goods. In cases of treason, the king confiscated all properties, both real and personal. Accordingly, the king had a stake not only in convictions for felony but particularly in convictions for treason. Treason became a crime against the king's person, and he became the representative of the state, making him the injured party in cases of treason and therefore the sole beneficiary of the traitor's forfeited properties.[7]

Henry II (1154–89), a man of powerful will and administrative genius, introduced reforms intended to extend his jurisdiction and revenues. His royal courts increasingly supplanted the manorial courts of local lords, making royal justice the rule rather than the exception. The king took responsibility for maintaining law and order. Criminal conduct breached the king's peace and required punishment in his courts. The personal property of fugitives from justice and of outlaws supplemented the king's revenues. He secured exclusive royal jurisdiction over felonies and treasons, and his exchequer increased considerably. When someone was accused of a capital crime, the sheriff of the locality, acting for the king, would seize all the accused's properties, have them inventoried and their value appraised, and hold them in trust pending the outcome of the trial.[8]

From such medieval precedents come modern practices. Thus, in 1994, when CIA agent Aldrich Ames and his wife Rosario were accused of spying for Moscow, all of their assets, including their home valued at $540,000, their $65,000 Jaguar, and their six-figure stock portfolio, were "frozen" by the government, which holds them pending outcome of their trial; in the event of conviction, they will suffer not only prison terms and fines but also the forfeiture of their properties to Uncle Sam, who replaced the English king.[9]

Henry II introduced the inquest to England, radically

transforming the system of criminal justice. The inquest was the parent of our double jury system, the grand jury of accusation and the petty jury of trial. The success of the inquest, compared to older forms of proof, derived from its close ties to royal power and prosperity. The inquest consisted of a body of men from a particular locality, summoned by an official on the authority of the king; its duty was to provide a declaration of truth or verdict in response to queries put to it—who had evaded taxes, who owned certain lands, who had committed crimes, and the like.[10]

Henry II also relied on royal commissioners who periodically went on circuit throughout the country to transact the king's business. In time they undertook duties that became increasingly judicial. By their decisions, the king's judges created a law common to all his courts throughout the realm; the common law of the realm bulwarked the king's right to forfeitures. More boldly than his predecessors, Henry II regarded breaches of his peace or threats to life and property as offenses of a public nature in violation of the common law. Serious crimes required settlement in his courts by his system of justice, which relied mainly on the inquest as a way of trying crimes. Eventually all crimes, even lesser ones, were considered public crimes. The king obtained a monopoly of criminal pleas or public prosecutions against offenders, great and small, petty theft as well as grand larceny. Minor breaches of the king's peace at first were called trespasses, subsequently misdemeanors. Felonies could be roughly distinguished from misdemeanors on the basis of the gravity of the offense, but the two even today are best defined not on the basis of the character of the deed but on the punishment for it. Misdemeanors were punished by fines, not by death and forfeiture, and sometimes by imprisonment, though the purpose of jailing a petty criminal was only to force him to redeem his liberty by paying a price for it. If the culprit could not pay a fine, he might forfeit not property but his limbs, perhaps his life. He might even be outlawed for his inability to pay.[11]

The king's peace prospered while his authority increased along with his revenues, which swelled from the price of writs to be used in the king's courts and from fines, escheats, and forfeitures of every sort. The king's judges constituted a major force in the centralization of England, and the inquest, their most useful instrumentality, evolved into the grand jury and, later, also the trial jury. Trial by jury in criminal cases was still unknown at the time of Magna Carta. Its references to trials implied indictment by grand jury and judgment by the older forms—battle, ordeal, and oath taking. Nevertheless trial by jury in cases of crimes was becoming familiar by the end of the thirteenth century.[12]

Magna Carta had been exacted from King John in 1215 to limit his arbitrary extensions of the royal prerogative. John, who had become king in 1199, greedily stretched the law in his favor to increase his revenues and power. For example, he refused to relinquish the lands of felons. Consequently when the barons at Runneymede forced him to make concessions, one was: "We will not retain beyond one year and one day, the lands of those who have been convicted of felony, and the lands shall thereafter be handed over to the lords of the fiefs." This provision did not limit royal possession of lands escheated to the king by his own felonious tenants.[13]

There is no explaining why the king did not eventually get to keep escheated lands permanently in felony cases. A distinguished historian of English law has stated that "in the case of high treason the crown had a stronger claim to override the claim of the feudal lord. Treason is an offence against the king and the state."[14] But felony was also an offense against the king and the state. Further, Blackstone

28

argued: "The true reason and only substantial ground of any forfeiture for crimes" consisted in the fact that "all property is derived from society," and that if any individual abridges his fundamental obligations to society by committing a crime, he forfeits his rights including the right to possess property, which the state may repossess. But this is as true of felonies as it is of high treasons, so that one is puzzled by Blackstone's logic, especially when he concluded that "total confiscation of the moveables or personal estate" followed the commission of the crime, but if it was a felony, the king received the landed property only temporarily— for a year and a day, and then it escheated to the feudal lord. That practice seems irreconcilable with Blackstone's time, when feudalism had long since died in England.[15]

Blackstone spoke of escheats of land to the king only when he was the felon's landlord or when a defect of some sort prevented heirs from receiving their inheritance. In such cases, said Blackstone, the lands vested in the king "who is esteemed, in the eye of the law, the original proprietor of all the lands in the kingdom."[16] For precisely that reason, the law should have vested the forfeiture of lands in the king rather than the lord in felony cases. Blackstone justified forfeitures of both real and personal property in treason cases on the traitor's violation of his obligations to society, as a result of which he no longer held the right to property or "the right of transferring or transmitting property to others. . . . Such forfeitures moreover, whereby his posterity must suffer as well as himself, will help to restrain a man, not only by the sense of duty, and dread of personal punishment, but also by his passions and natural affections."[17] That reasoning helped explain corruption of blood ("whereby his posterity must suffer"), but did not explain allowing the king to hold a felon's property more than a year and a day.

Treason was wholly a common-law crime until Parliament in 1352 specified the offenses that constituted it, in order to differentiate it from other capital felonies and from petty treason, which involved treachery against a feudal lord. Adhering to the king's enemies, levying war against him, murdering any of his chief officers, counterfeiting his great seal or his money, importing false money into the realm, violating the queen or the king's eldest daughter or the wife of the eldest son—all were high treason. Later statutes broadened the crime to include fomenting a riot, allowing traitors to escape, impeding the exercise of the royal prerogative, extorting money by threatening to commit arson, and the extravagantly malleable crime of "compassing" the king's death or his deposition. To "compass" meant to grasp mentally or to imagine. Merely dreaming that the king had died sufficed to constitute the crime.

Compassing the king's death or deposition allowed convictions for treason that fell far short of having a basis in overt acts; the king and his judges had a means of effectively achieving political objectives by prosecutions for treason. Although statutory definitions of that crime extended its varieties and supposedly distinguished treason from other felonies, the elasticity of treason made it an attractive way to eliminate opponents and secure their considerable estates, real and personal, by forfeitures.

Felonies also grew substantially in number and kinds. In 1769 Blackstone counted 160 capital crimes. The king profited from all criminal convictions. He even profited from suicides, because they too resulted in criminal forfeitures.[18]

Technically, by Blackstone's time, mere conviction did not suffice to warrant forfeitures; sentence of death had to be pronounced, thereby blackening or attainting the prisoner. Before sentence he might die, receive a pardon, or be excused from the death penalty: in any such case, he might not have to forfeit his properties. Once judged to have been attainted, however, he was expelled from the protection of the law so that he was civilly dead, and execution and forfeitures followed remorselessly. Another consequence of attainder in treason cases was "corruption of blood," meaning that the individual could neither inherit any property, keep it, nor transmit it to heirs.[19]

No attainder had to be pronounced before forfeiture of goods and chattels. All personal property became forfeitable immediately upon conviction. Real estate, however, was forfeitable only after the convicted prisoner had been sentenced. The reason for this distinction impinges on contemporary forfeiture law, involving the awkwardly named "relation back" doctrine. In Blackstone's words, "The forfeiture of lands has relation to the time of the fact [crime] committed, so as to avoid all subsequent sales and incumbrances: but the forfeiture of goods and chattels has no relation backwards; so that those only which a man has at the time of conviction shall be forfeited." The explanation for this distinction—relation back for real property, no relation back for personal property—is that personal property is easily sold and might "pass through many hands in a short time." Therefore, should the government's right to the forfeiture be triggered at the moment of the commission of the crime, "no buyer could be safe, if he were liable to return the goods which he had fairly bought, provided any of the prior vendors had committed a treason or felony." A defendant might sell personal property between the commission of the crime and conviction for it, thereby benefiting his heirs. In the case of lands, however, "forfeiture relates backwards to the time of the treason committed [or felony]: so as to avoid all intermediate sales and incumbrances."[20] This reasoning, too, perplexes, because a piece of land is as saleable as a cow or a crop.

In any case, although the government's right to forfeiture

relates back to the moment of the commission of the crime, the actual forfeiture did not take effect until after judgment of attaint. The relation-back doctrine in contemporary forfeiture law ignores the distinction between personal and real property. All property derived from crime or used to commit it is subject to forfeiture at the time of the offense, though, as in England, forfeiture does not actually occur until conviction. Therefore, innocent third parties—those who might purchase the property not knowing it was subject to forfeiture—might lose it and their investment too. The relation-back doctrine, part of the American law of civil forfeiture in federal cases, was first upheld by the Supreme Court in 1814. The doctrine was made applicable to the law of criminal forfeiture by a 1984 act of Congress.[21]

Another ancient feature of our law implicating forfeiture is consent to trial. While ordeals were still in use, if an accused refused to submit himself to the proof, the law considered him to have repudiated legal norms and therefore could treat him as if he had outlawed himself. An outlaw, whose properties forfeited to the crown, was one who lived outside the law, like a wild animal, and might be killed on sight. But accused felons were treated with some consideration. Because inquests acting as a trial jury were so novel, the king's judges insisted that the defendant must voluntarily agree to accept the verdict of the jury. But he might believe that his chance of getting a verdict of not guilty was hopeless or that the jury sought his conviction. Conviction for felony meant not only death, but the forfeiture of all of one's properties, leaving one's family and heirs penniless. Some defendants therefore refused to plead to an indictment. By standing mute, they nonplussed the law. Without the defendant's agreement to put himself on his country, that is, to be tried by a jury and submit to its verdict, no way existed to try him in the king's courts.[22]

To cope with such cases a statute of 1275 provided a barbaric solution when a prisoner stood mute: extort his consent. If a felon of evil repute refused to stand trial by jury at the king's suit, he "shall be remanded to hard and strong prison as befits those who refuse to abide by the common law of the land." Significantly, trial by jury, though still called "inquest of felony," was described as the common law by 1275. Trial by jury was becoming available to anyone who had been privately challenged to ordeal by battle. But if a prisoner refused to plead to an indictment and therefore could not be tried, he was subjected to imprisonment "strong and hard" (*prison forte et dure*), which quickly degenerated into punishment strong and hard (*peine forte et dure*). At first the prisoner was stripped, put in irons on the bare ground in the worst part of the prison, and fed only a crust of stale bread one day and some water the next. When the refinement of punishment was added, he was spread-eagled on the ground and pressed with as much iron or rocks placed upon his body as he could bear "and then more." Punishment by pressing, exposure, and slow starvation continued until the prisoner put himself upon the country—pleaded to the charges—or died.[23] In America only one person, Giles Corey, a victim of the Salem witchcraft mania in 1692, was pressed to death for standing mute. He deeded his property to his sons, underwent the agony of *peine forte et dure*, and in his last gasp uttered, "More weight."[24]

What made this barbarity so peculiar is that it derived from the admirable if rigid rule that the trial by jury could not proceed without the prisoner's consent, and, moreover, that a felon even of the worst reputation should have an opportunity to prove his innocence. That is, the purpose of punishment strong and hard was not to extort a confession—and therefore it was not, in a legal sense, torture; the purpose was simply to extort a plea. The law did not care whether the prisoner pleaded guilty or not guilty, only that he plead. In 1772—that late—a new statute was enacted that a prisoner standing mute to an indictment for felony or treason should be treated as if he had been convicted by verdict or by confession, thus ending punishment strong and hard. Not until 1827 did the law command a judge to enter a plea of not guilty for a prisoner who stood mute and refused to plead for fear of the forfeitures that might follow.[25]

Time works reforms. Eventually the right of a person to bequeath his estate extinguished the lord's right to escheat. The doctrine of corruption of blood ended in England in 1834, when the Inheritance Act abolished it, and the entire law of escheat for felony, along with the king's right to a year and a day, ended with acts of Parliament adopted in 1870 and 1884.[26]

In America the English law on criminal forfeitures was known and either disliked or modified in the corporate colonies and followed in the proprietary and royal colonies without much enthusiasm or frequency. The Massachusetts Body of Liberties of 1641 provided that "all our lands and heritages shall be free from fines . . . yeare day and wast, Escheates, and forfeitures, upon the deaths of parents or Ancestors, be they naturall, casuall, or Juditiall." That provision showed familiarity with English law and a repudiation of it. Connecticut followed suit. Rhode Island allowed towns to waive forfeitures and provided that wives and children ought not bear "the iniquities of Husbands and Parents," thus rejecting corruption of blood.[27]

In New York, where the English law applied, enforcement was minimal. Leisler's Rebellion resulted in forfeitures of those convicted for treason in 1701, but the case was unique. The royal governor pocketed an escheat taken from a suicide's estate in one case, but that too was a unique incident. New York juries simply did not find that felons possessed real or personal property, so that none was forfeited, with the result that escheats and forfeitures simply died out in that colony. The historians of early New York law conclude "that most felons were so meanly circumstanced that there was nothing to forfeit." When something to forfeit existed, New York was reluctant to deprive heirs, who might then leave for other colonies; or, juries found no goods or chattels for fear that the heirs of the convict might become public wards, burdening taxpayers.[28]

From a case decided by the high court of Pennsylvania in 1784, forfeiture appears to have been the usual course of procedure in felony cases. Aaron Doan was a robber who was indicted for his capital crimes yet eluded capture and refused to surrender as ordered. As a result, the justices of the supreme court, following a procedure outline in a state statute based on English practice, declared him to be an outlaw, attainted him for his crimes, and declared forfeit all his personal and real property. After he was captured, he appealed to the supreme court, claiming that he had been denied trial by jury. The court declared that he had in effect waived jury trial by his refusal to submit, and it held that beside the forfeiture of his estate he had forfeited his life.[29]

In Maryland and Virginia, the English practice fixed a model not zealously adhered to. In seventeenth-century Maryland the proprietors sought to expand their own domains through criminal forfeitures, but the scanty records yield few examples. A statute of 1642 provided for forfeiture and corruption of blood in both treason and murder cases, but the legislature, during the same session, made forfeiture an optional punishment in cases of lesser felonies.[30] In the royal colony of Virginia the law required convicted felons to pay the price of their crimes as if they had been in

England, but the records do not show any regularity. In several cases of suicide, the heirs petitioned for relief from the forfeiture of properties to the crown, showing that the English law prevailed but that exceptions were sometimes made. In one case a coroner's jury returned a verdict of temporary insanity to avoid forfeitures. In general, though, convicted felons forfeited properties consonant with English practice. The Virginia assembly, when describing crimes of felony, included corruption of blood among the consequences, at least until the Revolution. Virginia also followed English law in treason cases, as the executions and forfeitures after Bacon's Rebellion showed in 1677.[31]

Not a single colony enforced criminal forfeitures with the inevitability and severity of England. Colonial governments probably did not relish augmenting the royal exchequer at the expense of American felons. Moreover, the experience of New York, in finding felons to be poor and in not wanting heirs to leave for another colony or to become public charities, was probably widespread.

Treason cases during the colonial period were extremely uncommon. The law, at least on the books, was English, thus ambiguous in crucial respects. Several colonies augmented English law by providing that attempts to subvert the government constituted treason, and proprietary colonies classified compassing the proprietor's death in the same way. During the American Revolution, when the patriot cause was treasonable in English eyes, some Americans, Thomas Jefferson among them, fretted about the looseness of English law. When Jefferson proposed revisions of Virginia's laws, he considerably restricted the scope of treason, and his work became the model for the provision on treason in the United States Constitution.[32]

But during the Revolution, the states tended to be unrestricted in their understandings of treason so far as it concerned provincial opponents of the American cause. Severe acts imposed forfeitures of estate, banishment, and sometimes death for supporters of the English cause who had withdrawn to English-controlled areas or joined the enemy's armed forces. In some states the refusal to take a test oath of loyalty to the patriot side or counseling support of the British constituted treason. Adhering to the enemy, giving him aid and comfort, and levying war against the state or the United States received the broadest interpretation. Eight states resorted to outlawry as a means of retaliating against traitors who could not be reached physically but whose properties were reachable. Eight states also confiscated Tory lands on the supposition that their owners were traitors. Tory estates were subject to confiscation on a widespread basis as a means of assisting the states to finance the war. Interestingly, however, although revolutionary statutes were harsh in declaring political opponents to be traitors, even accepting proof of guilt as evidenced by mere words rather than acts, the states tended to restrict forfeitures to the attainted individual and prevent the punishment of relatives. Corruption of blood began to die out in the United States even during the Revolution.[33]

In the peace that followed, American abhorrence of the worst features of the English law on treason became evident. In addition to the disappearance of corruption of blood, constructive treason, which reached just words and acts not in the nature of levying war against the states or adhering to enemies, began to die out.

The Constitution of the United States by Article III, section 3, clause 2, embodies the highly restricted American understanding of the crime: "Treason against the United States, shall consist only in levying War against them, or in adhering to their Enemies, giving them Aid and Comfort. No person shall be convicted of Treason unless on the Testimony of two Witnesses to the same overt Act, or on Confession in open Court." The next paragraph states: "The Congress shall have Power to declare the Punishment of Treason, but no Attainder of Treason shall work Corruption of Blood, or Forfeiture except during the Life of the Person attainted." By such tight definitions, the United States severely restricted criminal forfeitures. Indeed, in 1790, the First Congress enacted a statute that outrightly abolished forfeiture of estate and corruption of blood for felony as well as treason.[34]

Chancellor James Kent of New York, in his *Commentaries on American Law* (1830), observed that the forfeiture of estate "was very much reduced" in the laws of the states and that corruption of blood "was universally abolished." Maryland limited forfeiture of property to cases of treason and murder, New York to cases of treason; and several states admitted the existence of a power of forfeiture by abolishing it in cases of suicide and deodand, but remained silent as to other cases.[35] Forfeitures of specific property belonging to a convicted criminal remained possible not only in some states but even on a federal level. The 1790 act of Congress prohibited forfeiture of estate, meaning the entirety of the convict's possessions, but a limited criminal forfeiture still existed in theory. In practice, however, criminal forfeitures nearly disappeared from the United States until 1970.

Chapter Three

Forfeiture in the United States before 1970

The procedures of salt water courts, more than deodands or felony convictions, shaped the development of the American law of forfeiture. Felony convictions resulting in seizure and confiscation undergirded criminal forfeitures, which followed a finding of guilt against the felon. The law labels such proceedings as *in personam*—aimed at the individual. The proceedings that it calls *in rem* are, by contrast, directed against a thing, an insentient object. The history of deodands provides the foundation for the law's vengeance against guilty things. Similarly, *in rem* procedures against guilty vessels characterize salt water courts, which enforce admiralty law. For all practical purposes an *in rem* proceeding describes a civil forfeiture, while a criminal one is an *in personam* proceeding. The *in rem* proceeding against a guilty vessel is the paradigm of a modern civil forfeiture case.[1]

Oliver Wendell Holmes tells us that in the mid-fifteenth century if a man was killed or drowned at sea by the motion of a ship, it was forfeited to the admiral after judgment in the admiral's court.[2] That court became the source of admiralty law with its distinctive procedures, heavily influenced by Roman and canon law as well as by the peculiar needs of admiralty jurisdiction. For example, because seamen and ship captains were frequently unavailable for testimony, admiralty courts developed a system of evidence based on written interrogatories.

With one exception, admiralty or salt water courts decided cases that developed on the ocean, where the king's common law writs did not run. The exception was for most crimes that occurred on the high seas or beyond the tidewater mark; they fell within the jurisdiction of the common law, rather than admiralty law, for only common law courts could take life, limb, and liberty. Salt water courts settled disputes of tort or contract involving seamen, masters of vessels, the owners of the vessels, and businessmen who shipped cargoes. The ownership of captured enemy vessels and their cargoes, called prizes, added a wartime subject of jurisdiction.[3]

So far as the history of forfeitures is concerned, *in rem* proceedings against guilty vessels most frequently occurred in cases arising under acts of trade and navigation to protect the king's revenues, England's commercial prosperity, and the British empire's naval strength. Parliament passed acts of trade and navigation periodically during the seventeenth century, the measures of 1660 and 1696 being the most important. Their purpose was to make the British empire economically self-sufficient, by having the colonies supply the mother country with raw materials and, in turn, purchase Britain's finished goods. The economic interests of Britain and her colonies were assumed to be mutually reciprocal. English ships had a legal monopoly of imperial commerce. Goods or commodities sent to or coming from any of the imperial colonies or foreign ports had to be shipped in English owned vessels of which the master and three-fourths of the crew were English (a nationality that included colonials). Foreign vessels were pretty much excluded from colonial ports and from the coastal trade of England. Only English ships could carry the trade between the colonies and foreign nations. Foreign goods could be imported into England only on payment of customs duties. English ships, though exempt from those duties, had to give bond that they would carry goods from the colonies to England only. Foreign ships hauling goods to England from the country of origin had to be unloaded in an English port and reloaded on English ships for transportation anywhere else in the empire.[4]

Numerous colonial commodities, which the acts of trade and navigation specified or "enumerated," could be shipped only to other English colonies or to the mother country. Collectors of the customs, aided by the British navy, possessed enforcement powers. A ship's master entering England had to swear on oath answers to any questions that customs officers might put to him concerning his ship and its cargo. From the time the ship arrived in port, customs employees called tidewaiters searched it and no one could go ashore until they finished. Any infraction of regulations governing importations or exports, or any noncompliance with the labyrinthine system of red tape that bedeviled the administration of the acts of trade and navigation, could trigger forfeiture proceedings. Parliament had enacted complicated regulations to govern the importation and exportation of commodities and to establish a schedule of tariffs, bounties, and fees. Any violation meant forfeiture.[5]

In England, cases involving the acts of trade and navigation were decided by the Court of Exchequer, a common law court operating with a jury, which shared jurisdiction with the admiralty courts. The Court of Exchequer functioned as the court of the king's revenue. It too developed *in rem* proceedings, because prosecuting a thing in order to obtain royal possession of it was the most direct way of securing it when no owner was known. For example, the king had rights to property found on the high seas or stranded on beaches, including waifs and strays (lost or abandoned property or animals), beached whales and treasure troves, flotsam (goods afloat after a ship sinks) and jetsam (goods cast overboard to lighten cargoes), and goods taken from pirates. An *in rem* judgment added such properties to the royal exchequer.[6]

In England, the Court of Exchequer had jurisdiction over customs cases that might result in the forfeiture of any vessel or cargo in violation of the customs laws. However, the American colonies had no courts of exchequer and all attempts to establish such courts had failed. Prosecutions under the acts of trade and navigation, after the enactment of 1696, had to be in either the common law courts, which sat with a jury, or in vice admiralty courts, to which juries were alien. Parliament created vice admiralty courts in 1696, one for each colony, and provided that in any case arising under the various acts of trade and navigation in the colonies, the prosecutor or informer had the right to choose the court. Local American juries would not likely convict a merchant, sea captain, or vessel owner for violation of the acts of trade and navigation, especially after 1764, when the British sought to raise revenue in America by collecting customs duties in American ports. Informers and prosecutors invariably chose to make their cases in the vice admiralty courts, which earned the opprobrium of the patriot party. "The swarms of searches, tide waiters, spies, and other underlings, with which every port in America now abounds," raged a Philadelphia newspaper, "are not, it seems, quite sufficient to ruin our trade, but infamous informers, like dogs of prey thirsting after the fortunes of worthy and wealthy men, are let loose and encouraged to seize and libel in the courts of admiralty the vessels of such

42

as are advocates of the rights of America." Resort to vice admiralty courts evaded the need for grand jury indictment as well as conviction by a jury.[7]

A vessel whose guilt was suspected would be arrested and prosecuted by name; the government, acting through a collector of the customs, a naval officer, or an informer, who provided the testimony impugning the ship's records or the allegations of its officers, brought the prosecution. The law treated the ship as if it were alive, a guilty person. Holmes's engagingly explained that because a ship "is the most living of inanimate things," everyone "gives a gender to vessels." He added, "It is only by supposing the ship to have been treated as if endowed with personality, that the arbitrary seeming peculiarities of the maritime law can be made intelligible." Their peculiarities arise from the fact that other conveyances or modes of transport were not prosecuted as guilty things. If, for example, a rented wagon was involved in an accident, the rental agency was not responsible for any damage to property. But if a shipper hired a vessel to transport his cargo and the ship was involved in an accident, damaging property, the ship's owner, however innocent and unknowing, was liable for the damages and his guilty ship was forfeitable to pay for them. The law, as Holmes observed, makes believe that not only is it reasonable to deal with the ship as if it were alive but that it is also reasonable to deal with it as an "offending thing."[8]

An *in rem* proceeding was most suitable when a customs officer had possession of a ship carrying uncustomed goods or whose captain could not produce the necessary registration, manifest, bills of lading, and cockets or certificates showing that bonds had been given. In such cases the owners of the vessels were often unknown or unavailable or out of the court's jurisdiction; accordingly, the court proceeded civilly against the vessel.

43

First the vice admiralty court determined that probable cause existed for the proceeding: some violation of the acts of trade and navigation seemed apparent. The court then ordered an appraisal of the value of the properties subject to forfeiture—perhaps the cargo as well as the ship itself. Next, the court issued a proclamation calling upon those with a stake in the properties to show cause why they should not be forfeited. If the owners of the ship and cargo did not contest the seizure, the properties were summarily forfeited. If the forfeiture was contested, claimants had the legal obligation to prove that the allegations in the accusation were wrong; that is, the claimants bore the burden of proof. In effect, to escape forfeiture a claimant had to demonstrate innocence. Failure to do so proved nonconformity with regulations, resulting in the forfeiture of ships and cargoes. The government sold them at public auction to the highest bidders. The judges of the vice admiralty court received commissions of 5 percent for convictions, plus payment of a variety of fees. The remainder was divided one-third each to the informer, the governor, and the king, unless the guilty vessel had been captured by the navy; in that case the navy received half of the proceeds and the royal exchequer the other half.[9]

The vice admiralty courts imposed the strictest liability on Americans who engaged in salt water activity. The act of an ordinary crew member could cause the forfeiture of a vessel, despite the ignorance of the vessel's captain or owner concerning the crew member's illegal conduct. The situation was the same in England under the Court of Exchequer, whose chief baron in 1776 explained that a ship's owner was responsible for whatever his ship did, because otherwise the acts of trade and navigation could scarcely be enforced; to have required the knowledge or consent of the vessel's officers would have "opened a door for perpetual evasion, and the provisions of this excellent act for the increase of navigation would have been defeated."[10] Such was the *in rem* civil proceeding that exercised so great an influence on American law. Property employed to commit a crime was subject to forfeiture, a proposition that profoundly affected the development of forfeiture proceedings in the United States.

After independence, most of the states established their own admiralty courts or vested admiralty jurisdiction in their own courts, notwithstanding the recent denunciations of admiralty procedure. During the revolution there were prizes to be adjudicated and state revenue measures to be enforced.[11] In one of the earliest reported state admiralty cases, decided by the Court of Common Pleas of Philadelphia County, Pennsylvania, in 1787, informers revealed that the ship *Anna*, having docked at the port of Philadelphia, unloaded a large quantity of wine without first checking at the collector's office. The captain of the vessel was unaware of his mate's transgression, and the owners of the vessel were victims in the affair, but a Pennsylvania statute, copied from an English navigation act, had provided that "every vessel from which any goods, wares, or merchandise, shall be unloaded, before due entry thereof, etc. shall be forfeited." An informer prosecuted the *Anna*. Counsel for her owners argued that the case raised a question "of the greatest importance to the commercial interests of the country, as it was now to be determined whether an innocent owner of a ship, was responsible for all the unwarrantable actions" of her officers or crew and whether the ship itself could be the subject of forfeiture.

Judge Edward Shippen observed that revenue laws were necessarily harsh. If the case had involved a minor bit of property that had been illegally unloaded, confiscation of the ship would not follow. But the wine was part of the cargo on which duties had not been paid. This was a civil case involving fraud, not a criminal one in which innocence could be exculpatory. The state often "punished" a person "in his pocket" for the acts of others. In this instance the law required forfeiture of the ship.[12] Thus, forfeiture of the guilty vessel followed, though the court acknowledged that forfeiture was a punishment. That is, even though forfeiture was a punishment, the *in rem* civil proceeding, which was quite summary in character, sufficed to satisfy the requirements of law; if the case had been a criminal one, all the rights of the criminally accused would have come into play. Here they were irrelevant. Interestingly, the court's harshness was mitigated by its concession that forfeiture would have been unjustified if the transgression had involved a "small matter" not part of the cargo. In modern America, a tiny trace of marijuana suffices to justify forfeiture of a vessel.[13]

In 1787, the same year as the case of the *Anna*, the new federal Constitution provided that the judicial power of the United States shall extend to "all cases of admiralty and maritime jurisdiction." The First Congress enacted a statute subjecting to forfeiture any ships and cargoes violating customs legislation, and that statute became a model for others in cases involving smuggling, piracy, and the slave trade, as well as revenue measures.[14] The statutes passed by early Congresses read as if Britain had been implementing the enforcement powers of the vice-admiralty courts. Thus, an act of 1799 for levying and collecting duties on imports was eighty-two pages long and provided for fifty-six different forms, eleven different bonds, fourteen different schedules, and nineteen different oaths.[15] Port collectors and even naval officers were empowered to board ships, examine their manifests, and even to break open and inspect any part of their cargoes or property in sealed containers.

Any property suspected of indicating an intent to defraud the United States was subject to forfeiture. Congress authorized *in rem* forfeiture proceedings to convict ships and cargoes implicated in the violation of federal law, and by the Judiciary Act of 1789 authorized the federal courts to exercise "exclusive original cognizance of all civil causes of admiralty and maritime jurisdiction, including all seizures under the laws of impost, navigation or trade of the United States."[16] When the Judiciary Act was being drafted, a Massachusetts judge, writing to a member of the Senate drafting committee, urged "seizures of property for breach of the acts of Trade and Revenue where the process is in rem."[17] In time any kind of property could be confiscated if it was used in the commission of a federal crime or derived from the commission of such a crime.

The seventeenth-century English acts of trade and navigation have had an enduring influence to this day, when over one hundred fifty federal statutes mandate forfeiture of property, including property as discrepant as illegal firearms, uninspected meat, conveyances for the transport of illegal aliens or of contraband, animals used for fighting, diseased poultry, equipment unlawfully used in national parks, laundered money, corporations acquired in violation of antitrust laws, unreported cash in excess of $10,000 crossing the border, and unlawfully imported pre-Columbian art.[18]

The *in rem* proceeding that leads to civil forfeiture is attractive to the nation's lawmakers because it is swift, cheap, productive, and much more likely to be successful than a criminal forfeiture proceeding. If the government prosecutes not the property, civilly, but the individual accused of crime, criminally, the defendant has the benefit of all the rights of the criminally accused guaranteed by the Constitution. A jury is instructed to assume his innocence until the government proves his guilt beyond a reasonable doubt to the jury's satisfaction. In a civil forfeiture case the government doesn't have to establish guilt; its obligation is merely to show probable cause—enough facts to support a reasonable belief that a connection exists between the property and the commission of a crime, or that the confiscation was made under circumstances that warranted suspicion. Hearsay, circumstantial evidence, and anything more than a hunch can be used to establish probable cause. That done, the burden of proof shifts to the owner of the property or its claimant who must establish by a preponderance of evidence that the property was unconnected to a crime. In effect he must prove the innocence of the property.

Victory in a civil forfeiture case allows the government to claim the advantages of the "relation back" doctrine, meaning that the government's right to the property relates back to the time of its illegal use; the property purportedly reverts to the government from the moment of the offense, thus wiping out or disadvantaging any subsequent transactions involving that property. The owner, facing its forfeiture, has difficulty dumping it. Civil forfeiture allows the government to confiscate the offender's property even if evidence might be lacking or be too tainted to prove his guilt; indeed, although an individual may be acquitted in a criminal prosecution, the government may still attack and acquire his guilty property by an *in rem* proceeding. That proceeding is a prosecutor's legal Eden.

The federal courts from the beginning were as committed as vice admiralty courts had been, before the Revolution, to the rigorous enforcement of civil forfeiture prosecutions. *The United States v. "La Vengeance,"* decided by the Supreme Court in 1796, was a precedent-setting case. The schooner was a French privateer that had illegally exported arms and ammunition, with the result that the United

States seized her. Counsel for the ship claimed the case was a criminal one, not an admiralty suit, requiring a criminal process including trial by jury. Chief Justice Oliver Ellsworth, for the Court, tersely held otherwise, ruling that the case was definitely one of admiralty jurisdiction; the export of arms and ammunition was merely the offense that may have begun on land but consisted of a water transaction. The Court unanimously agreed, said Ellsworth, that "it is a civil cause. It is a process of the nature of a libel [accusation] *in rem*; and does not, in any degree, touch the person of the offender." Therefore the case did not require a jury trial.[19]

The decision in the case of *La Vengeance* seemed almost un-American to owners and shippers. "It was one of our serious grievances, and of which we complained against Great Britain in our remonstrances to the king, and in our addresses to the people of Great Britain, while we were colonies, that the jurisdiction of the courts of vice-admiralty was not extended to cases of revenue," counsel argued in an 1808 case. In England, he pointed out, a seizure for violation of a revenue law or an act of trade and navigation was tried by a jury in the Court of Exchequer, according to the course of the common law. Nothing required that such cases should be tried in a court of admiralty, and the acts of Congress creating forfeitures for breaches of revenue laws "seem to refer to the exchequer practice, rather than to that of admiralty." To hold otherwise violated the Fifth Amendment's guarantee that property shall not be deprived without due process of law. To that argument, Chief Justice John Marshall, for a unanimous Court, curtly replied that the case of *La Vengeance* had "completely settled" the question. The law prescribed admiralty proceedings in such cases, without trial by jury. The forfeiture of the schooner and her cargo stood.[20]

In 1827 *The Palmyra*, a Spanish privateer that engaged in piracy, excited reconsideration of the use of *in rem* proceedings to effectuate civil forfeiture. Counsel for the privateer contended that forfeiture was illegal except on conviction of the offender. The Supreme Court repudiated that view. Justice Joseph Story for the Court ruled that that view had never been applied "to seizures and forfeitures created by statute, in rem, cognizable on the revenue side of the exchequer." An *in rem* civil proceeding stood independently of any criminal proceeding *in personam*. In an *in rem* proceeding, the "thing," that is, the ship, was considered the offender, not its owner or master, "or rather the offense is attached primarily to the thing." That was the personification fiction, which Story regarded as a settled principle of admiralty law. It applied to seizures of vessels that violated the act of Congress against piracy. There were *in rem* cases where forfeiture followed exclusively for outlawed conduct without an accompanying criminal penalty. There were cases in which both a forfeiture *in rem* and a sentence for personal punishment existed; but no court had ever decided that the prosecutions were dependent on each other. "No personal conviction of the offender is necessary," Story concluded, "to enforce a forfeiture in rem."[21]

Story spoke again for the Court in another piracy case that arose seventeen years later involving the brig *Malek Adhel*. Its owner was completely innocent of the ship's wrongdoings. Could he lose his ship because of the conduct of its captain? Even if he should be liable for the negligence of the captain, binding him *in rem* for the captain's crimes was "contrary to reason and justice" given the fact that the owner neither knew of nor authorized the piracies. Story replied that the act of Congress punishing piracy made no exceptions for the innocence of ship owners. "The vessel which commits the aggression is treated as the offender, as the guilty instrument or thing to which the forfeiture attaches," Story ruled, "without any reference whatsoever to the character of conduct of the owner." He justified that harsh rule on grounds of policy: "And this is done from the necessity of the case, as the only adequate means of suppressing the offense or wrong." That was equally true in cases of smuggling and other violations under the revenue laws. The acts of master and crew bound the owner whether he was innocent or guilty. In support of that proposition, Story quoted an 1818 circuit opinion of Marshall: "This is not a proceeding against the owner; it is a proceeding against the vessel for an offense committed by the vessel."[22]

In sum Parliament's 1696 act of trade and navigation, creating the vice admiralty courts, once regarded as an instrument of oppression, animated American civil forfeiture law. The personification fiction rationalized punishment of the vessel as a means of diverting attention from the practical fact that in the real world criminal punishment had been summarily inflicted on the innocent owner without allowing him the rights enjoyed by a common felon. *In rem* proceedings against things, like the deodands to which they were analogous, were make-believe prosecutions of property in order to deprive the owners of their constitutional rights, thereby enabling the government to make a confiscation not otherwise likely.

In 1862 Congress abandoned the make-believe about forfeiture not being a personal punishment and the pretense about constitutional rights not having been willfully abandoned. The Confiscation Act of 1862 authorized the use of *in rem* civil proceedings to inflict punishment on rebels who possessed property in the North. The act was a reply to a Confederate law that confiscated the southern properties of adherents of the Union.[23] If the Union and the Confederacy had merely been wartime enemies, these forfeiture acts would have raised no problem, because enemy property possesses no immunities or rights. Taking enemy property was an exercise of the war powers, transcending normal constitutional limitations, to impose damage on the enemy.[24] But adherents of the Confederacy were not just enemies; they were also American citizens. The Union, having denied the states a right of secession, insisted that the Confederacy was not an enemy nation. As Senator Jacob M. Howard of Michigan declared, the United States was not waging war against "foreign enemies . . . but against persons who owe obedience to this government and are rightfully subject to it." He added, however, that the lawful government during a rebellion could inflict on the rebels *punitive* burdens as the government might think best fitted to repel their violence.[25]

Nevertheless, the rebels were also citizens of the United States entitled to all constitutional rights, including a right to just compensation if the government seized their property for a public use. They could not be treated merely as enemies; their property could not be subject to confiscation as enemy property. Accordingly, the United States, supported by its Supreme Court, considered the Civil War as having an extraordinary dual character. Justice Robert Grier would say in the 1863 *Prize Cases* that "insurgents who have risen in rebellion against their sovereign . . . are not *enemies* because they are *traitors*; and a war levied on the Government by traitors, in order to dismember and destroy it, is not a *war* because it is an *'insurrection.'*"[26] But the Court was ambivalent, because Lincoln's blockade of southern ports could be sustained only if the Confederacy were an enemy belligerent. So the Court ruled that a war existed, even though it was also a rebellion. So too, the Court observed, in an opinion upholding the constitutionality of the Confiscation Act of 1862, "in the war of rebellion the United States sustained the double character of a belligerent and a sovereign, and had the rights of both."[27] Lyman Trumball of Illinois, chairman of the Senate Judiciary Committee, made the point crudely when he announced, "We may treat them as traitors and we may treat them as enemies, and we have the right of both, belligerent and sovereign."[28]

As a result of such theories, which enabled Congress to do as it pleased, Congress deemed the enemies of the Union as traitors and enacted a draconian measure against them, the Confiscation Act of 1862. It bore the title, "An Act to Suppress Insurrection; to punish Treason and Rebellion, to seize and confiscate the Property of Rebels, and for other purposes." The first several sections described the rebels as persons engaged in treason; anyone adhering to the Confederacy was a traitor. By way of penalizing traitors, the next sections imposed upon them the punishment of forfeiture of all properties, real and personal: "to insure the speedy termination of the present rebellion, it shall be the duty of the President of the United States to cause the seizure of all the estate and property, money, stocks, credits, and effects of the persons hereinafter named" and to use those properties for the Union cause. Judicial proceedings against those adhering to the Confederacy were to conform to the *in rem* suits characteristic of admiralty cases.[29] Forfeiture had nothing to do with conviction for treason or even rebellion. As a matter of fact the *in rem* proceedings, which the statute authorized, were not even aimed at the property of traitors; the forfeiture sections referred rather to the property of "persons in armed rebellion, or abetting it."

Congress debated this punitive measure throughout the spring of 1862. Opponents insisted that confiscation would be lawful only if the rebel owners of property had been found guilty of treason in conventional criminal prosecutions.[30] Senator Orville H. Browning of Illinois, a friend of Lincoln, declared that "confiscation of property for the crime of the owner can be effected by proceedings *in rem*, but can follow only upon the personal conviction of the offender, in punishment of his crime." The fact that the statute called for *in rem* proceedings without a criminal prosecution was no more than "hocus pocus" whose objective was to shun the constitutional rights of criminally accused persons in regular trials. Senator John B. Henderson of Missouri ridiculed the notion that Congress was providing civil forfeitures, because no one could reasonably believe that the measure was directed against guilty property. Browning predicted that if the measure were enacted, "a total revolution [will be] wrought in our criminal jurisprudence, and, in despite of all the safeguards of the Constitution, proceedings *in personam* for the punishment of crime may be totally ignored, and punishment inflicted against the property alone."[31]

Supporters of the Confiscation Act argued that the forfeiture proceedings *in rem* denoted a civil proceeding, even though forfeiture, admittedly, was intended as a punishment. Opponents excoriated that argument, asserting that a punitive measure required the protection of the Fifth and Sixth amendments governing criminal trials. Supporters replied that the measure did not suppress traitors; rather, it suppressed rebellion. In the end supporters lamely resorted to *force majeure*: without *in rem* forfeiture, they claimed, the traitors would escape with impunity or "go forever unwhipped of justice."[32] The bill passed by margins of two to one in both houses.

President Lincoln objected to some of the bill's features and submitted to Congress the draft of a veto message. The first of two unconstitutional features, he asserted, was that the bill's forfeiture provisions seemed to divest title to property "forever," because it declared forfeiture "beyond the lives of the guilty parties; whereas the Constitution of the United States declares that 'no attainder of treason shall work corruption of blood, or forfeiture, except during the life of the person attainted.'" Significantly Lincoln accurately spoke of the "punishment" inflicted by the measure, showing in effect that he read it as a criminal measure. Second, he objected to the fact that "by proceedings in rem," the measure "forfeits property, for the ingredients of treason, without a conviction of the supposed criminal, or a personal hearing given him in any proceeding." By joint resolution Congress remedied the bill to accommodate part of Lincoln's first objection. Acts done prior to the adoption of the measure were exempted from its provisions; "nor shall any *punishment* or proceedings under said act be so construed as to work a forfeiture of the real estate of an offender beyond his natural life."[33] Congress failed utterly to address Lincoln's second objection, in effect that the act unconstitutionally inflicted punishment without due process of law. It constituted a prohibited bill of attainder, a legislative finding of guilt of a distinct class of persons without judicial proceedings. For reasons unknown, Lincoln signed the bill into law.

The Confiscation Act of 1862 was spottily enforced, but only a single enforcement would have sufficed to provoke a court test. It did not reach the Supreme Court, however, until long after, in 1871. By a 7–2 vote the Court sustained the constitutionality of the statute on the simplistic grounds that it was an exercise of the war power rather than a criminal measure for the punishment of crime. Justice William Strong, for the majority, observed that although the first several sections of the act dealing with treason did aim at individual offenders, the forfeiture sections revealed a different objective. Their avowed purpose was not to punish treason or rebellion but to seize and confiscate the property of rebels in order to insure a speedier termination of the rebellion. Thus, the forfeiture provisions did not "reach any criminal personally," but sought only to terminate the war. And the rebellion was, indeed, a war. Confiscation of the property of wartime enemies posed no constitutional problems. The Constitution imposed no restriction on the power to prosecute war or confiscate enemy property, including the property of domestic enemies and their aiders and abettors.[34]

Justice Stephen Field wrote a powerful dissenting opinion. As he read the act it was directed not against enemies but against persons guilty of treason. The forfeiture provisions applied to persons guilty, after passage of the act, of certain acts of treason. Those provisions were not aimed at enemies. Accordingly the act was not passed as an exercise of the war powers but in the exercise of the ordinary power of punishing offenses against the United States. If the act had been intended to confiscate the property of enemies, it would not have had a merely prosecutorial character. The act imposed forfeiture as a punishment for future treasonous offenses, not for past offenses by an enemy. The Joint Resolution of Congress declared that the forfeiture provisions did not apply to any acts done prior to passage of the measure. Moreover, the terms used in it, "forfeiture" of the estate of the "offender," had no application to the confiscation of enemy property under international law.

Field then asked whether proceedings *in rem* under the statute could be maintained without the previous conviction of persons charged with treason. *In rem* proceedings as authorized by the statute were directed against the offending thing, which was forfeited because of the unlawful use made of it or its unlawful condition. The *in rem* proceedings were independent of any criminal proceedings against individuals. However, if the confiscation of property were made not for a use to which it had been put but, rather, was inflicted for the personal delinquency of the owner, then the confiscation was punitive and punishment might be imposed only upon conviction of the owner for his personal guilt. To hold otherwise, Field maintained, as did the majority of the Court, meant that "all the safeguards provided by the Constitution for the protection of the citizen against punishment without previous trial and conviction . . . would be broken down and swept away." He concluded: "It seems to me that the reasoning which upholds the proceedings in this case, works a complete revolution in our criminal jurisprudence, and establishes the doctrine that proceedings for the punishment of crime against the person of the offender may be disregarded, and proceedings for such punishment be taken against his property alone."[35]

Time proved the accuracy of Field's concern. *In rem* forfeiture proceedings became common after the Civil War. Punitive sanctions, once thought to be possible only after the criminal conviction of an individual, became a routine accompaniment of civil forfeiture cases. Therefore the need for criminal forfeitures simply disappeared. *In personam* forfeiture prosecutions had never been common before the Civil War. Indeed, there had been but one federal case and just a few state cases.[36] After the Supreme Court sustained the Confiscation Act of 1862, there were no more criminal forfeitures following an adjudication of personal guilt.

Dobbins v. United States, decided in 1878, illustrated what Field called a "revolution in our criminal jurisprudence." In this case the government seized a distillery that had defrauded the United States by keeping false books and failing to pay taxes. The distiller had built his business on land leased from its owner; the owner protested against the forfeiture of his land, swearing that he knew nothing of the fraudulent use to which the distillery had been put.

Unanimously the Supreme Court held that because the owner had permitted the land to be used as the site for the distillery, the distiller's fraud forfeited the owner's land. Admiralty cases involving *in rem* proceedings against vessels constituted the Court's precedents, though none of the mystical properties of vessels clothed the distillery or the land. The offense, the Court declared, "attached primarily to the distillery . . . without any regard whatsoever to the personal misconduct or responsibility of the owner" beyond the fact that he had leased the property to the distiller, and "it was that property and not the claimant [owner] that was put to trial"; therefore that property was "inculpated." By such reasoning the Court decided that the unlawful acts of the distiller bound the owner of the property "as much as if they were committed by the owner himself," even though he was innocent of the distiller's fraud.[37] Not without some poignance, the owner believed himself to have been the accused party in a criminal trial. He was punished as if convicted but only his land had been tried, without any of the constitutional protections that would have surrounded him had he been the accused. Presumably the personification fiction gave life to the land, the distillery, and the related property including the whiskey, the barrels, and the bottles.

In a later case a distiller was sentenced to a fine and imprisonment following his conviction in a criminal prosecution, and he lost his distillery through forfeiture by a civil suit *in rem*. After the United States "arrested the property," the Court decided that "the proceedings to enforce the forfeiture against the *res* [thing] named must be in a proceeding *in rem* and a civil action."[38] The Court apparently meant to prove that criminal forfeiture proceedings were no more than fossil remains of the past.

Nevertheless, only two years later a forfeiture victim, unable to believe that he could lose his properties without having been criminally convicted, challenged the new doctrine. The Court resolutely insisted that the offending merchandise was forfeitable by civil proceedings independent of a criminal prosecution aimed at punishing the guilty party. In effect the Court ruled that the fraudulently imported merchandise had committed an offense separate from any criminal liability of its owners.[39]

In 1886 the Court was overwhelmed by a fit of sanity when it handed down an opinion that "will be remembered as long as civil liberty lives in the United States," as Justice Louis D. Brandeis later said.[40] The case was *Boyd v. United States*, in which the government sought to prove its case for forfeiture by demanding that a property-owner produce his records. The demand complied with an 1874 act of Congress whose purpose was to enforce the revenue laws. Justice Joseph Bradley for the Court held the statute unconstitutional as a violation of both the Fourth and Fifth Amendments. Congress had sought to extort from individuals private books and papers that would make them liable to penalties and to the forfeiture of their property. The compulsory production of one's records constituted an unreasonable search and seizure as well as a violation of the protection against being compelled to be a witness against oneself criminally.

Said Bradley: "We are clearly of the opinion that proceedings instituted for the purpose of declaring the forfeiture of a man's property by reason of offenses committed by him, though they may be civil in form, are in the nature criminal." In the case before the Court, the ground of forfeiture consisted of acts of fraud against the public revenues, punishable by fine and imprisonment; moreover, Bradley said, if an indictment had been brought, "upon conviction the forfeiture of the goods could have been included in the judgment." The civil suit brought against the property, "though technically a civil proceeding, is in substance and effect a criminal one."[41] Two justices concurred in the judgment but believed that the case showed no Fourth Amendment issue. The *Boyd* Court unanimously agreed that a forfeiture proceeding, being tantamount to a criminal one, required the protection of the right against self-incrimination; a seven-member majority further held that in a civil forfeiture case, the owner of the property also had the benefit of the right against unreasonable searches and seizures.

Boyd cannot be reconciled with the decades of precedents involving vessels and distilleries. It stands like a civil liberties sapling missed by a judicial bulldozer, a freak in a row of decisions hailing *in rem* civil proceedings, even if punitive, as constitutionally perfect. There is no explaining the realism of Bradley's *Boyd* opinion or the fact that though it remained law it was long unique.[42] In an 1896 case, for example, the Court, having returned to its usual fictive mode, unanimously limited the safeguards available to property owners in a punitive civil forfeiture case by holding that the Sixth Amendment's guarantees did not apply; that amendment, the Court ruled, related to criminal prosecutions, not to an *in rem* proceeding.[43] Yet the same case would be a criminal one with respect to Fourth and Fifth Amendment rights. And, the Court has never repudiated its view that an *in rem* proceeding in a punitive forfeiture case is at least quasi-criminal in character.

Nevertheless, for scores of years after *Boyd*, civil forfeiture cases routinely resembled a 1921 case, decided 8–1, involving the forfeiture of an automobile. An auto dealer retained title of the car on which the purchase price had not been paid off. Without the dealer's knowledge the car was used to conceal liquor on which federal taxes had not been paid. The government sued the car, which a jury found guilty. On appeal, the dealer alleged that confiscation of his car deprived him of property without due process of law. The Court acknowledged that victimization of the innocent dealer "seems to violate that justice which should be the foundation of the due process of law required by the Constitution," but other militating considerations prevailed. Congress had ascribed to the car "a certain personality, a power of complicity and guilt in the wrong," reminiscent of the law of deodands. In fact the personification fiction, making the thing guilty, was "too firmly fixed in the punitive and remedial jurisprudence of the country to be now displaced."[44]

The Court failed to remember *Boyd* and the criminal character of punitive proceedings even if civil in form. The personification fiction, supreme again, extinguished all constitutional considerations including due process of law. Only people have rights, not things. The innocent auto dealer, having had no day in court, lost his property through forfeiture because of the criminal conduct of someone else. With *in rem* judgments like this, criminal forfeiture proceedings languished as if nonexistent. The government scarcely wished to shoulder the burden of proof of guilt beyond reasonable doubt or to contend with the multiple rights of the criminally accused, as it would have had to do in criminal prosecutions. And so remained American constitutional law with respect to forfeitures until Congress in 1970 suddenly rediscovered virtues in criminal forfeiture.

Chapter Four

The Rediscovery of Criminal Forfeiture

Crime *does* pay, extraordinarily well, even beyond the imagination. Not street crime, but organized crime and especially white-collar crime. White-collar crime often refers to violations of the law by persons of high status or by corporations, such as chemical companies that pollute the environment or building contractors who transgress safety rules and housing codes, or executives who conspire against the antitrust laws, or bankers who speculate with their depositors' funds, or brokers who engage in insider trading or who market fraudulent stocks. White-collar crime also refers to crimes such as embezzlement or fraud conducted by middle class people such as bank clerks or accountants. White-collar criminals include them as well as major malefactors like Michael Milken, numerous traders at the Chicago Mercantile Exchange, Ivan Boesky, the Drexel Burnham Lambert Group, Inc., Hooker Chemical, and most notoriously Charles Keating, who bilked the depositors of his Lincoln Savings and Loan Association out of $2.5 billion. In 1980, white-collar crime cost the nation an estimated $200 billion a year, an amount that utterly befuddles comprehension.[1]

"Organized crime" as of 1970 referred to the criminal cartels that were operated by about two dozen "families" known as the Mafia or La Cosa Nostra, sometimes as the mob or the syndicate. It was virtually a governmental sys-

62

tem, organized on military lines, that specialized in illegal gambling, narcotics trafficking, loan sharking, and other services demanded by certain elements of the American public. In 1970, Congress enacted special legislation aimed at economically crippling organized crime, which probably constituted the world's largest business.[2] Illegal gambling alone then produced an annual income estimated at anywhere from $7 billion to $50 billion.[3] President Richard M. Nixon estimated the "take" as totaling "from $20 billion, which is over 2% of the gross national product, to $50 billion."[4] An expert told the House Committee on the Judiciary in 1970, "If U.S. Steel, American Telephone & Telegraph, General Motors, Standard Oil of New Jersey, General Electric, Ford Motor Co., IBM, Chrysler, and RCA all joined together into one conglomerate merger, they would still be in second place. That's how big organized crime is today."[5] Senator John L. McClellan of Arkansas, who sponsored the Organized Crime Control Act of 1970, retailed the same statement in Congress.[6] Just the narcotics traffic in 1970 was estimated at $50 billion.[7] The untaxed gambling profits of organized crime, according to the IRS, amounted in 1970 to more than $600,000 every hour. As indicated, the profits from white-collar crime vastly exceed those of organized crime.[8]

The intellect cannot grasp the enormity of these figures. A stack of $1,000 bills about four inches high equals $1 million. The stack would have to go three-fourths of the way up the Washington Monument to reach $1 billion. Fifty billion dollars in $1,000 bills would go thirteen times higher than the Empire State Building. Money in such magnitude can corrupt governments, especially at the local and state levels, though not even the federal government escapes its influence. Organized crime flourishes especially where it has bought local officials in the police department, the prosecutor's office, the city council, and even the bench. If the IRS could collect taxes on all the business transactions of organized crime, the government could balance its budget and reduce taxes, perhaps even erase the national deficit. White-collar crime is about four times as great as organized crime, though organized crime engages most of the public's attention.

Organized crime robs the nation of untold billions not only by unlawful activities but also because of its control over selected areas of the economy. The dangers to the entire economy are multiplied by the infiltration of legitimate business by mobsters who understand that the most stupendous profits are in white-collar or corporate crime. Michael Corleone, in Mario Puzo's *The Godfather*, reflected the growing sophistication of organized crime when he decided to buy a Las Vegas hotel. An American Bar Association committee found clear evidence "that organized crime which takes billions of dollars—mostly in cash and mostly untaxed—from the American public has broadened its operations by infiltrating and taking over legitimate businesses."[9] Profits from illegal activities buy many legitimate businesses, especially in service industries and the entertainment world; those profits also buy seats on boards of directors. The Senate Judiciary Committee found that "a host" of legitimate businesses and unions had been "invaded and taken over."[10]

The evolution of the 1970 legislation fixing on criminal forfeiture as a penalty is clear, though the forfeiture provision's antecedents are not. Indeed, Congress does not seem to have adopted criminal forfeiture as a result of reflective deliberation. Criminal forfeiture had had a notorious history, which is the reason that the First Congress in 1790 banned forfeiture of estate. Congress's deliberate reliance on criminal forfeiture in 1970 seems perplexing, although the history of the events culminating in the 1970 legislation climaxed almost twenty years of concern about the malevolent influence of the Mafia on the American economy.

As long ago as the Kefauver Committee of 1951, the Senate found that the following businesses had been penetrated: advertising, amusement, appliances, automobiles, baking, ballrooms, bowling alleys, banking, basketball, boxing, cigarette distribution, coal, communications, construction, drugstores, electrical equipment, florists, food, football, garments, gas, hotels, import-export, insurance, jukebox, laundry, liquor, loans, news services, newspapers, oil, paper products, radio, real estate, restaurants, scrap, shipping, steel surplus, television, theaters, and transportation.[11] Yet the Kefauver Committee did not recommend criminal forfeiture, not even civil forfeiture, as a means of combating what apparently was massive criminal infiltration of so many businesses. Indeed, it proposed nothing to deal with such infiltration. In 1960, a Senate committee chaired by John L. McClellan of Arkansas, who would later sponsor the Racketeer Influenced and Corrupt Organizations Act (RICO), exposed the criminal infiltration of trade unions and in 1965 focused on the Mafia. McClellan's committee did not mention criminal forfeiture.[12]

The next step toward the enactment of the 1970 legislation was the publication in 1967 of the report of President Lyndon Johnson's Committee on Law Enforcement and the Administration of Justice. Its recommendations were extremely influential in producing what eventually became the Organized Crime Control Act of 1970, of which RICO was a part. The report of the President's commission stressed the Mafia's infiltration of legitimate business and labor and the "illegitimate methods—monopolization, terrorism, extortion, tax evasion—to drive out of control lawful ownership and leadership and to exact illegal profits from the public."[13] The commission dealt with several matters that subsequently became part of the Organized Crime Control Act; its recommendations provided the stimulus for the 1970 legislation. Yet the commission made no recommendations for any alterations in the substantive criminal law, said nothing to suggest RICO, and did not treat the subject of forfeiture. The old law of criminal conspiracy seemed quite adequate for the commission's purposes, plus measures expanding the use of grand juries to investigate crime, extending prison terms, enacting a general witness immunity statute to deal with the Fifth Amendment problem, adding special intelligence units to police departments, enhancing prosecutorial manpower, altering rules of perjury, establishing a witness protection program, and strengthening electronic surveillance. The commission had no recommendation on infiltration except the wishy-washy proposal that state and federal departments of justice "ought" to "develop strategies and enlist regulatory action against businesses infiltrated by organized crime."[14]

Members of Congress responded by introducing a variety of bills, holding extensive hearings, and issuing reports that led to the 1970 enactments. Senator Roman Hruska of Nebraska introduced the earliest measures. One proposed that the civil remedies of antitrust be applied to organized crime, and another punished investing in a business any moneys that came from criminal activities. Hruska's proposals did not refer to forfeiture. McClellan's proposals were closer antecedents to RICO, but even he was slow to fix on forfeiture as a penalty. His first bill, introduced in January 1969, made no reference to forfeiture but contained many of the recommendations of the President's Crime Commission.[15] McClellan declared that his bill was "designed to attack the infiltration of legitimate business" by removing "the cancer" of organized crime from the economy "by direct attack."[16]

When Attorney General John N. Mitchell first testified before the Senate committee that was considering measures against organized crime, his main point was that as long as the flow of money continued, imprisonment of the leaders of Mafia families stimulated the promotions of new people to take the places of those convicted. Nevertheless, Mitchell supported McClellan's bill. When McClellan asked how Mitchell would attack the source of organized crime's revenues, Mitchell vaguely promised to answer at some future time.[17]

McClellan's "Corrupt Organizations Act," introduced April 18, 1969, recommended a maximum sentence of twenty years imprisonment, a fine, which became a paltry $25,000, and criminal forfeiture of "all" the violator's "interest in the enterprise engaged in, or the activities of which affect interstate or foreign commerce."[18] McClellan believed that the solution to the problem of organized crime lay in attacking its sources of economic power everywhere possible.

When President Nixon addressed the Congress on organized crime a few days later, he said that Attorney General Mitchell had concluded that "new weapons and tools" were needed to strike at the Mafia and "the sources of revenue" that fed its coffers. When he spoke of criminal infiltration of business, he observed that the imprisonment of its lieutenants did not put the Mafia out of business. "As long as the property of organized crime remains, new leaders will step forward to take the place of those we jail." His solution was application of the civil remedies of antitrust and "the powers of a forfeiture proceeding."[19] He did not amplify the point.

In the summer of 1969 Richard G. Kleindienst, the deputy attorney general, sent a letter to McClellan outlining the Justice Department's views on his proposed Corrupt Organizations Act. Kleindienst noted that the concept of forfeiture as a criminal penalty, which was embodied in the

McClellan bill, differed from "existing forfeiture provisions under Federal statutes where the proceeding is *in rem* against the property," which is used unlawfully and "is considered the offender, and the forfeiture is no part of the punishment for the criminal offense." Kleindienst referred to the forfeiture provisions of customs, narcotics, and revenue statutes, which the courts had sustained as constitutional, against the objection that they violated due process, "on the grounds that they are wholly preventive and remedial" and were designed to aid the enforcement of laws in question.

But, Kleindienst continued, the criminal forfeiture provision of McClellan's proposal required a proceeding *in personam* against the defendant, if he was convicted for having violated the measure; he would be subject not only to fine and imprisonment, but also to forfeiture of all interest in the enterprise. That concept of forfeiture, Kleindienst said, had originated in the English practice "whereupon conviction of treason and certain other felonies the party forfeited his goods and chattels to the crown." The First Congress had abolished forfeiture of estate and corruption of blood, including in cases of treason. "From that date to the present, therefore, no Federal statute has provided for a penalty of forfeiture as a punishment for violation of a criminal statute of the United States." He concluded that the McClellan bill "would repeal" the act of 1790 "by implication." That was incorrect, because forfeiture of estate meant loss of all properties, real and personal. Accurately, however, Kleindienst ended with the evasive remark, "It is felt that this revival of the concept of forfeiture as a criminal penalty, limited as it is in Section 1963(a) to one's interest in the enterprise which is the subject of the specific offense involved here, and not extending to any other property of the convicted offender, is a matter of congressional wisdom rather than of Constitutional power."[20]

Thus the Justice Department failed to endorse criminal forfeiture, leaving it up to Congress. Moreover the department was not quite right in asserting that Congress had never passed an act fixing criminal forfeiture as a penalty. Justice Story, when on circuit duty, had ruled that confiscation of property under the Embargo Acts first required the criminal conviction of the offender; and Congress in 1866, when authorizing the forfeiture of smuggled merchandise, had made smuggling a felony. The sponsor of the 1866 act noted that Congress had earlier provided for the civil forfeiture of smuggled goods and now sought a criminal remedy against the offender. The Supreme Court ruled that forfeitures under the act of 1866 were "strictly penal" and that the "act denounces a forfeiture of the goods concealed."[21] That, perhaps, is arcane antiquarianism; yet the Department of Justice should have known it. More important, Kleindienst rightly regarded criminal forfeiture as a novel policy, which the Nixon administration did not urge. Rather, it merely acquiesced in whatever decision Congress might make. Moreover, the department's opinion was that although the criminal penalties of McClellan's bill would have a "deterrent effect on racketeer infiltration of legitimate business enterprises, the principal utility of S. 1861 [McClellan's bill] may well be found to exist in its civil remedies provisions—injunctions, divestiture and dissolution," provisions that were "substantially identical to existing provisions of the antitrust laws."[22] So, the Department of Justice did not promote criminal forfeiture.

In the hearings that led to the 1970 legislation, criminal forfeiture did not loom as a major consideration. Most witnesses did not even address the issue. Lawrence Speiser, the director of the Washington office of the American Civil Liberties Union, was the only person who expressed reservations about reviving criminal forfeiture, and he scarcely spoke of it. He opposed the legislation because it was too broad and therefore might reach unintended victims—an acute insight in light of what subsequently happened. Although RICO aimed at organized crime, "there is nothing contained in it which would necessarily limit it to such." That observation governed Speiser's objections to criminal forfeiture. He did not oppose it because it was nefarious, only because it might punish the wrong people. Norman Mailer, Speiser hypothesized, might have to forfeit money from a book or lectures denouncing the Vietnam War; Mailer's lawyer might lose his fee, because "arguably such fee was indirectly derived from a pattern of racketeering activity," given the breadth of the measure's language. Equally bad, a corner grocer might accept money for food from people whom he knew to have been involved with the Mafia. "Must he refuse to sell his wares, or inquire specifically as to where his customer got the money, on pain of subjecting himself to forfeiture or fine or imprisonment when he subsequently invests that money?" Speiser had no principled objection to criminal forfeiture.[23] Notwithstanding Speiser's objections about loose language, the Senate Judiciary Committee did nothing to tighten the language of the bill and reported it favorably to the Senate as the year closed.

The Senate report, urging adoption of the Organized Crime Control Act, declared that the objective of RICO, its Title IX, was "the elimination of the infiltration of organized crime and racketeering into legitimate organizations operating in interstate commerce."[24] The measure sought this objective by "the fashioning of new criminal and civil remedies." Criminal forfeiture, of course, was the only new criminal remedy. The Senate report regarded it as a means of assaulting the economic power of the Mafia. Fine and imprisonment had proved to be insufficient. "The use of criminal forfeiture, however, represents an innovative attempt to call on our common law heritage to meet an essentially modern problem." The report, having quoted at length from Kleindienst's letter, concluded its exposition of criminal forfeiture by saying that it was the means of removing "the leaders of organized crime from their sources of economic power." When the report reviewed the provisions of the bill, it explained that the criminal forfeiture clause was "designed to accomplish a forfeiture of any 'interest' of any type in the enterprise acquired by the defendant or in which the defendant has participated in violation" of the statute.[25] No witness, no senator, and no report mentioned civil forfeiture or explained why criminal forfeiture was better than civil.

The Senate debated the bill for three days in early 1970. No one opposed the forfeiture provision. When McClellan explained it, he stressed that it "would forfeit the ill-gotten gains of criminals where they enter or operate an organization through a pattern of racketeering activity." He also said that RICO would result in the "wholesale removal of organized crime from our organizations" as well as strip them of those "ill-gotten gains"—a term McClellan liked to repeat. Senator Ralph Yarborough of Texas approvingly declared, "Along with severe penalties, a unique criminal forfeiture provision will make it possible to divest the racketeer of any interest he may have obtained in the organization or business." Senator Hruska, who cosponsored the measure, repeated the common refrain that the purpose of the bill was "to remove the influence of organized crime from legitimate business by attacking its property interests and removing its members from control of legitimate businesses which had been acquired or operated by unlawful racketeering methods."[26] But Hruska did not mean forfeiture, which he did not mention; he spoke of the civil anti-

71

trust provisions. The "debate" compels no respect. As a matter of fact, since all speakers over a period of three days probably devoted less than two minutes to forfeiture, the debate was pathetic. The Senate passed the bill 73–1.[27]

Its name had been the Corrupt Organizations Act, part of which was called "Racketeer Influenced Organizations." That part contained the criminal forfeiture provision. The two names were to be joined as Title IX of the final version of the Organized Crime Control Act of 1970. Title IX of that act was RICO, the acronym resulting from the fact that it reached legitimate organizations that were racketeer influenced (RI) and also corrupt organizations (CO) that were illegitimate.

During the summer of 1970 the House considered the measure. Senator McClellan, the most important witness before the House Committee on the Judiciary, explained why the usual criminal penalties had been inadequate to dislodge criminal infiltration of businesses and unions. He added that the criminal process suffered from a major limitation as a means of protecting our economic institutions from infiltration. The limitation consisted in the procedural handicaps confronted by the government in any criminal prosecution. "This one-sided character of the criminal process has been a handicap in the use of the criminal law as a means of avoiding infiltration of legitimate business by organized crime, just as it has hindered the use of the criminal law to curb other aspects of organized crime." The requirement of proof beyond reasonable doubt and the various constitutional rights secured to the accused by the Bill of Rights made the criminal law "a limited tool for dealing with organized crime infiltration of legitimate business."[28] One would think McClellan should have concluded that because criminal forfeiture was a "limited tool," civil forfeiture was by far the more preferable, but he never considered civil forfeiture. He never explained why he put his faith in criminal forfeiture despite the lack of experience with it in American national history. Rather, he said that criminal forfeiture

> would provide an effective adjunct to a criminal prosecution: it would punish the criminal appropriately by forfeiting to the government his ill-acquired interests in a legitimate business, and directly aid the business community by expelling him from the legitimate business he had abused. The government would have to dispose of the forfeited interest as soon as reasonably possible, and could sell the property in such a manner as to ensure that the enterprise was not again infiltrated by the convict or his criminal associates. Since the convict would not be compensated for the forfeited interest, the forfeiture would be a criminal one, and could be applied only if the individual's guilt were proven beyond a reasonable doubt in a criminal trial.[29]

McClellan might have more easily praised the virtues of civil forfeiture as an even more efficient instrument of government. Of course, any civil libertarian should have applauded his choice of criminal forfeiture, precisely because of the constitutional protections that enveloped criminal procedure—the very limitation that McClellan inconsistently regretted.

Attorney General Mitchell repeated the stale information that his deputy, Kleindienst, had earlier provided the Senate and again placed greater stress on antitrust techniques. No one thought to ask him why criminal forfeiture was preferable to civil forfeiture. The subject of forfeiture was simply not a topic that absorbed the House committee's interest, nor that of its witnesses.[30]

The Association of the Bar of the City of New York sub-

mitted a lengthy analysis of Title IX of RICO, found enough
wrong with it to oppose the measure, yet had not a word to
say against or about criminal forfeiture.[31] Only the New
York County Lawyers Association offered a statement on
Title IX that addressed the forfeiture issue, erroneously:
"Regrettably, the proposed statute goes beyond its stated
objective by seeking forfeiture of the racketeer's estate." It
did not; on that point, Kleindienst had correctly noted that
the bill "limited" criminal forfeiture to "the offender's interest." It did not require forfeiture of all his property, real and
personal, which is what forfeiture of "estate" meant. The
county bar was not only inaccurate; it was insistent. It de-
plored the provision that made criminal the investment
of dirty money in a legitimate enterprise, either as a result
of income from a pattern of racketeering or from taking
control of a legitimate business in payment of a gambling
or loan-sharking debt. Forfeiting such investments, the
county bar repeated, constituted an "*in personam* proceeding against the racketeer's estate," which was untrue.

The county bar was also naive. Claiming that the provision defining racketeering was overbroad, it asked, "Is it
philosophically sound to deny to racketeers, their widows,
children, and grandchildren the opportunity to get into legitimate business?" The question showed a failure to understand that the objection to criminal infiltration was that the
Mafia corrupted business, stole its assets, sought profits
from arson frauds, engaged in illicit bankruptcy, and used
criminal tactics against competition. The county bar acknowledged that other RICO provisions did relate racketeering activity closely enough to the infiltrated enterprise
to treat it as an instrumentality or product of crime. But
the county bar explicitly censured the provision (section
1961a) as a violation of the 1790 statute banning forfeiture of estate. A far better point made by the county bar

was that the provision in Title IX for the protection of the "rights of innocent persons" was too vague and insufficiently protective.[32]

The House Committee on the Judiciary favorably reported the bill with some alterations that did not affect the forfeiture provisions of Title IX. The House report asserted that the penalties of that title fixed punishment "by forfeiture to the United States of all property and interests, as broadly described, which are related to the violations."[33] Three members of the Judiciary Committee wrote an adverse report—Congressmen John Conyers, Abner Mikva, and Sylvester Ryan. They agreed with some witnesses that overbroad language exposed to forfeiture even those interests "indirectly" acquired through racketeering. They wanted stronger protections against forfeiture for innocent third parties who had an interest in the property subject to forfeiture. They accurately predicted that the forfeiture of property used as collateral by the wrongdoer for a legitimate loan might leave an unsecured creditor without protection. (That is how an innocent banker later lost his business.)[34] The dissenters also promiscuously claimed that the revival of criminal forfeiture after 180 years of dormancy was fighting corruption of business with corruption of blood, which simply was inaccurate. Corruption of blood meant that offspring and their descendants were incapable of inheriting or transmitting property. The dissenters did not mention whether civil forfeiture, without the freight of constitutional protections associated with criminal forfeiture, was preferable.[35]

In the House debate on RICO, no one stated anything new or convincing about forfeiture. The dissenters opposed throwing out deep-seated traditions in favor of protecting private property and stood squarely against corruption of blood, while the supporters of the measure, a majority of

431 to 26, represented themselves as using criminal forfeiture to make war on the profits of racketeering.[36] President
Nixon signed the bill into law on October 15, 1970. Nothing
in the legislative history of the act fortifies confidence in the
belief that Congress adopted criminal forfeiture for good
reasons. Granted, the belief was widespread that criminal
forfeiture would allow the government for the first time to
strike at the profits of organized crime and wipe out its hold
on legitimate organizations. But staggering fines might
have done much in that direction, as well as systematic
prosecution of organized crime leaders. It is not true that
imprisoning them is ineffective. And, surely civil forfeiture
would have been as effective as criminal forfeiture, in some
ways more so. The one advantage that criminal forfeiture
possibly had over its civil counterpart is that the scope of
confiscation could be greater. Yet not one congressman or
witness mentioned that. And whether civil or criminal forfeiture had the broader reach depended on statutory language. Indeed, when the government in 1980 for the first
time studied the subject, the conclusion was that civil forfeiture at that time had the broader reach.[37] But Congress
in 1970 knew nearly nothing about the subject. No one connected with the RICO forfeiture provision seemed to be
quite sure of what he was doing or, if he spoke positively but
generally about criminal forfeiture being a novel weapon to
cripple the economic foundation of organized crime, he had
no basis other than wishful thinking for knowing what he
was saying.

What property, according to the language of RICO rather
than its supporters' wishful thinking, was actually exposed
to forfeiture? And what activities jeopardized that property? Section 1962 of RICO prohibited three sorts of activities: (1) the investment of income in the acquisition of any
interest in any enterprise affecting interstate commerce, if

that income derived from "a pattern of racketeering" or the collection of an unlawful debt; (2) the acquisition or maintenance of any interest in any such enterprise by means of racketeering acts; and (3) the operation of the affairs of an enterprise by a pattern of racketeering activity or the collection of unlawful debt. RICO defined "racketeering activity" to mean acts or threats in violation of state or federal law; dozens were specified, including, significantly, bribery, various kinds of fraud, embezzlement, and other white-collar crimes. A "pattern of racketeering activity" meant the commission of at least two outlawed crimes, one of which was committed after the enactment of the statute. "Enterprise" meant, as broadly as possible, any individual, partnership, corporation, association, or group of associated individuals even if not a "legal entity." "Unlawful debt" meant a debt that was unenforceable because of laws against gambling or usury.[38]

The criminal penalties under RICO consisted of a fine of not more than $25,000—peanuts for organized crime; imprisonment of not more than twenty years; and forfeiture of the property involved in the commission of the crime or acquired from it. RICO defined that property as any interest obtained or maintained in violation of the statute, and any interest in an enterprise, or property of any sort affording a source of influence over an enterprise that is established, controlled, or operated in violation of the statute. No forfeiture could occur until after the conviction of a person, but conviction made forfeiture mandatory. The statute authorized disposal of all forfeited properties, "making due provision for the rights of innocent persons," meaning persons who innocently came into possession of forfeited properties prior to the party's conviction.[39]

Without doubt, RICO reached the white-collar criminal, not just the Mafioso. Any business executive who engaged in a pattern of fraud, for example, or who tampered with pension funds, was a candidate for RICO prosecution. RICO's critics had stressed overbreadth and a resultant danger to civil liberties, but, as Senator McClellan pointed out in a law review article, unless a person not only commits a RICO crime "but engages in a pattern of such violation, and used that pattern to obtain or operate an interest in an interstate business, he is not made subject to proceedings" under RICO. Thus, the ACLU's grocer was safe from the RICO prosecutor. On the other hand, McClellan acknowledged, "It is impossible to draw an effective statute which reaches most of the commercial activities of organized crime, yet does not include offenses commonly committed by persons outside organized crime as well."[40] One RICO provision would prove particularly tempting to prosecutors seeking ingenious ways of bringing down unexpected victims. Because Title IX applied to any person or group and banned any use of criminal tactics in running an organization, it had a potential use against unsuspecting people—an anti-Semitic hate group that murdered a Jewish talk-show host, environmentalists who spiked old-growth trees to deter their being cut down, or right-to-lifers who used violence against abortion clinics—as well as against people who took criminal risks but hardly expected to be subject to criminal forfeiture, such as politicians who succumbed to bribery.[41] A statute conceived as having the rather express purpose of driving organized crime out of unions and businesses would turn out to be an all-purpose prosecutorial tool usable against almost any kind of criminal conduct.

Eight days after RICO became law, Congress enacted a comprehensive drug control act, one section of which was named the Continuing Criminal Enterprise Act. CCE applied the criminal forfeiture penalty to drug "kingpins," the big shots who organized or managed drug rings of five or more people and who made substantial profits from repeated commissions of federal drug felonies—"repeated" meaning three or more times. The purpose of CCE was to make the cost of doing business too high for the professional drug criminal or kingpin to remain in operation. Upon conviction he faced a minimum of ten years in prison to a maximum of life imprisonment, a fine of up to $100,000 for the first conviction and up to $200,000 thereafter, and forfeiture of the "profits" as well as the "interest" in his continuing criminal enterprise.[42] As in the case of RICO, criminal forfeiture supposedly targeted the economic base of the felon's operations.

The legislative history of the criminal forfeiture provision in CCE is as vague, brief, and shallow as its counterpart in RICO. On the floor of Congress, Senator Strom Thurmond of South Carolina, the bill's sponsor, discussed the criminal penalties provision without mentioning forfeiture. Only a senator who merely read the provision verbatim mentioned it; no one discussed it. Nor did anyone discuss whether either of the 1970 criminal forfeiture statutes could be enforced by procedures that did not defeat their purposes.

Procedural obstacles would eventually cripple the forfeiture provisions. If, for example, enforcement procedures allowed felons to dispose of their property before the government could seize it, the forfeiture provisions would be abortive.[43]

Aside from procedural problems that time and experience would quickly reveal, Congress made the CCE act unnecessarily limited in scope and cumbersome in a substantive sense. No sound reason existed for requiring the prosecution to prove that the defendant had not only committed a federal drug felony but that the felony was part of a continuing series of federal drug felonies committed in concert with five or more persons who took orders from the offender; and the offender had to commit a continuing series of violations from his managerial position and obtain "a substantial" income from the criminal enterprise. Moreover the statute unnecessarily used language that created serious legal problems: what was an offender's "interest" in an enterprise? What indeed was an "enterprise"? And why did the statute make "profits" forfeitable instead of proceeds? Congress did not know what it was doing when it enacted the 1970 legislation providing for criminal forfeiture.[44]

Civil forfeiture did not disappear simply because that legislation fixed a new remedy. Indeed, Congress never abandoned civil forfeiture, not even as to narcotics trafficking, despite the CCE act. Another statute enacted by the same Congress in 1970 subjected to civil forfeiture all controlled substances produced or obtained in violation of various statutes, as well as all raw materials, products, and equipment used or usable for the making, handling, or conveying of illegal drugs and any containers for them. Conveyances used to transport or conceal such drugs were also forfeitable.[45] And, in a major amendment of 1978, Congress made not just profits but all proceeds civilly forfeitable by the old *in rem* proceeding, including moneys, negotiable instruments, and other valuables used or usable for buying the illegal drugs or facilitating a violation of laws involving illegal drugs.[46] That 1978 legislation placed in the hands of federal law enforcement a powerful weapon, which eventually was put to vigorous use. But before that, all forfeitures, especially RICO and CCE forfeitures, lagged miserably. A decade after the resort to criminal forfeiture, a drug agents' manual published by the Drug Enforcement Agency declared that forfeiture normally meant civil forfeiture: "Forfeitures are civil actions against property," unless a statute explicitly requires a criminal conviction.[47] Criminal forfeitures, as a matter of fact, proved to be a failure, a ludicrous failure for at least a decade, as a government study revealed.

Chapter Five

A Decade of Failure:
The 1970s

For a decade criminal forfeiture was a flop. During that time, in the 1970s, the government utilized civil forfeiture to confiscate vehicles and cash used in the trafficking of controlled substances. However, the government did not even glancingly dent the economic basis of organized crime or look at white-collar crime. The federal courts had slight opportunity to interpret the 1970 legislation, because of the paucity of criminal forfeiture cases until the closing years of the decade. But one Supreme Court case on civil forfeiture looms above the forfeiture landscape like a giraffe among pygmies. It was the Pearson Yacht case in 1974.[1]

State authorities searched for illicit drugs on a vessel that Pearson Yacht Leasing Company had rented. On finding the remains of one marijuana cigarette, the state confiscated the yacht under a statute subjecting to forfeiture any vessel used to transport controlled substances. The seizure was made without notice to Pearson Yacht or even to those who leased the yacht, and no hearing was held either. Pearson Yacht, having failed to receive rent for the yacht, sought to repossess it, only to learn that it had been forfeited. Because Pearson Yacht had no previous knowledge that the yacht had been used in violation of state law, a federal district court understandably upheld the company's objection that it had been denied due process of law and had been deprived of property without just compensation. The Supreme Court, however, in its leading decision in a civil forfeiture case, ruled in favor of the forfeiture.

Justice William J. Brennan, one of the Court's most capable members and normally a civil libertarian, spoke for a 7–2 majority, holding that the innocence of the yacht company mattered not a speck. Brennan saw no violation of due process because of a special need in the case for the state to act promptly. The yacht, he explained, might have sped away if the state had a constitutional obligation to give notice of its intent to seize or to give a hearing. Seizure without notice enabled the state to assert *in rem* jurisdiction over the property in order to effectuate the forfeiture. So Brennan reasoned. However, the fact that the yacht might have sped away merely justified its prompt seizure without a warrant, not its forfeiture. Brennan failed to consider the fundamental distinction between seizure and confiscation.

Justice William O. Douglas, dissenting, also attacked this part of Brennan's opinion by observing that no special need for prompt action had existed here, because the forfeiture proceeding occurred more than two months after the discovery of the marijuana. The various exigent circumstances instanced by Brennan were, said Douglas, "inapt."[2]

Brennan's argument that the yacht company was not entitled to just compensation for the loss of its property rang somewhat truer, in view of the precedents. He offered a splendid brief history of forfeitures to prove that the property interests of innocent parties had never received consideration in civil forfeiture cases. He reviewed deodands, the goring ox, and Holmes; forfeitures for felony and treason, which were extremely inapt because they involved criminal forfeiture after due process convictions of the guilty; and *in rem* statutory proceedings against goods and vessels used in violation of customs and revenue laws, which were quite to the point. Contemporary state and federal forfeiture statutes reached "virtually any type of property that might be used in the conduct of a criminal enterprise," Brennan noted. The owner's innocence simply did not matter because the law proceeded not against him but against the guilty thing, the tainted object, here the yacht. Thus, the modern Supreme Court reinvigorated the personification fiction of civil forfeiture cases. In addition to precedents, Brennan had another string to his bow: forfeiture might have the salutary effect of inducing property owners "to exercise greater care in transferring possession of their property."[3]

In connection with that point, Brennan conceded that cases might arise posing serious constitutional questions. A forfeiture might be unduly oppressive, he thought, and serve no legitimate purposes, if the owner "proved not only that he was uninvolved in and unaware of the wrongful activity, but also that he had done all that reasonably could be expected to prevent the proscribed use of his property."[4] In those words the Court created its own innocent owner test, but it failed to explain what the Pearson Yacht Company might have reasonably been expected to do to prevent the use of marijuana by its lessees. The Court's test imposed a severe and nearly insurmountable burden on property owners. Presumably, searching those who rented the yacht and their effects or demanding a urinalysis test might be more than could reasonably be expected, just as a warning— "Don't use any sort of drugs aboard"—might be insufficient. Congress, in its 1970 legislation, had merely provided "due provision for the rights of innocent persons." The yacht company's innocence, however, meant nothing to the Court, despite its concession that some innocent owners might have constitutional relief. Moreover, the Court's refusal to consider the yacht company's claim to just compensation for property taken for a public use did not confront a serious contradiction always implicit in such cases. No compensation is provided in a criminal case, because the property is taken as a penalty for the personal guilt of its owner. However, in a civil forfeiture case, where the proceeding is directed against the guilty object, punishment of the owner is not a factor, because punishment in an *in rem* proceeding does not exist. Punishment requires a criminal proceeding. Therefore no compensation is due if the penalty is a punishment. An *in rem* proceeding involves a penalty that is supposedly only a regulatory or remedial matter. But ever since the *Boyd* case of 1886 the Court has now and then acknowledged the obvious: civil forfeiture is at least "quasi-criminal" in character, because the penalty of confiscation is in fact a punishment.[5]

Even in the Pearson Yacht case, the Court conceded that civil forfeiture "fosters the purposes served by the underlying criminal statutes, both by preventing further illicit use of the conveyance and by imposing an economic penalty, thereby rendering illegal behavior unprofitable."[6] But the same Court failed to consider that the yacht company had not engaged in illegal behavior and, too, failed to consider that the taking of the yacht was tantamount to punishment of the yacht company for the careless rental of its property. Accordingly, the Court's holding, that no compensation was due, lacked merit.

How, then, is the Court's decision to be explained, and why did the liberal justices, led by Brennan, engage in such intellectual flimflammery? The explanation requires a digression. In 1976, on the bicentennial anniversary of the founding document, the Declaration of Independence, which celebrated life, liberty, and the pursuit of happiness, the Court decided the case of *New Orleans v. Dukes*.[7] One might think that liberty and the pursuit of happiness include one's right to a livelihood, but no such right exists under the Constitution, according to *Dukes*. The Constitution does not mention a right to livelihood, but it does not mention a great many other rights that the Court has been ingenious enough to discover: a right to abortion, a right to pornography, a right to travel, a right to association, a right to free counsel for indigents, a right to spew hatred, a right to flag burning, and a right to corporate free speech. A Court that is so imaginative should be able to find a right to pursue a livelihood in the same Constitution. That right seems fundamental to liberty, and it should be accepted as a protected property right, too.

Consider the facts in *Dukes*. They involve a woman who sold hot dogs from a pushcart in the French Quarter of New Orleans. If Nancy Dukes had been a nude dancer in one of the strip joints in the French Quarter and the City Council had put her out of business, she might have pleaded freedom of expression under the First Amendment.[8] Nude dancing can be symbolic free speech but selling hot dogs is just commerce and therefore, like forfeitable property, is subject to little constitutional respect even if it involves one's livelihood.

Dukes had operated a licensed pushcart in the French Quarter for two years when the City Council banned all pushcarts except those operated by their owners for at least eight years. This ordinance put only Dukes out of business but allowed two other pushcart owners to operate. The Fifth Circuit thought that the exclusion of Dukes denied her the equal protection of the laws, but the Supreme Court unanimously reversed. In an unsigned opinion the Court said that the ordinance was "solely an economic regulation" designed for safeguarding the tourist charm of the French Quarter and thereby aiding the city's economy. The Court did not explain why a third pushcart would offend tourists or hurt the city's economy, but the point of its decision was that no such explanation is required when a mere economic right is at stake. "When local economic regulation is challenged solely as violating the Equal Protection Clause, this Court consistently defers to legislative determinations as to the desirability of particular statutory discriminations."[9] The government regulation need only have some rational basis as a means of achieving some police power end. If an economic right is involved, the Court never questions the reasonableness of the government's means. Economic rights, especially those of individuals, are inferior rights.

By contrast, if some regulation seems to threaten First Amendment rights or any of the rights of the criminally accused, or any of the rights that the Court has invented, such as the right to an abortion or the right to travel, the Court subjects the regulation to strict scrutiny, reverses the presumption of constitutionality, and places upon the defender of the regulation the obligation of proving its constitutional validity. In *Dukes*, however, the Court said that it will "not sit as a superlegislature to judge the wisdom or desirability of legislative policy determination made in areas that neither affect fundamental rights nor proceed along suspect lines." The Court does not regard property rights as fundamental ones. Only once in the past half century had the Court held unconstitutional an economic regulation as a denial of the equal protection of the laws,[10] and in *Dukes* the Court overruled that sole precedent as a needlessly intrusive judicial infringement on the state's economic powers. In the same half century, not one state or local act of economic regulation was held unconstitutional based on a violation of due process of law. Like the corpse of John Randolph's mackerel, shining and stinking in the moonlight, economic due process of law, the old substantive due process, is dead even as to personal rights in property. The Court has abdicated the responsibility of judicial review in such cases, although it has not done so in any other Bill of Rights case.

That point necessitates a reminder that a property rights case is a Bill of Rights case. The Fifth Amendment, like the Fourteenth, protects equally "life, liberty, and property" against deprivation without due process of law. The just compensation clause of the Fifth Amendment also protects property. Indeed, the Fourth and Seventh Amendments also protect property as does the contract clause and other provisions of Article I, section 10. The Constitution does not grade rights or suggest that they have any hierarchical order. The Court does that, however. It employs a rational basis test only when property rights are concerned, never for other rights. Accordingly, the states can impose regulations on the entry of citizens into all sorts of jobs, requiring licenses from those who wish to be barbers, plumbers, masons, morticians, beekeepers, lawyers, bartenders, taxidermists, and doctors, to name a few. Those who judge their qualifications are members of the guild or occupation who prefer to keep competition down as well as standards up. About the only people who are unlicensed in some states are clergymen and university professors, apparently because no one takes them seriously.[11]

Pearson Yacht, therefore, is part of a fairly consistent pattern of cases involving property rights. In any civil forfeiture case, the Court will not seriously scrutinize the injury to property rights, because it does not regard such rights as worthy of the same respect as the rights of an accused felon, a member of a minority race, or a First Amendment dissident. The rights of property rank far lower than civil rights or civil liberties in the Court's scale of constitutional values. As a leader of the Court's liberals, Justice Brennan has been in the vanguard of those who downgrade property rights. His opinion in *Pearson Yacht*, the most significant of the Court's civil forfeiture cases, is merely evidence of the systematic unconcern that characterizes the Court's property rights decisions. The Court would have to see property rights as human rights, as did the framers of the Constitution, to reach different results.[12]

Decisions in forfeiture cases are by no means against the property owner if the government has proceeded against him criminally. In criminal forfeiture cases, other federal courts made decisions that handicapped the government, not consistently but with enough frequency to hurt the confiscation of assets. Because RICO failed to mention "profits," the courts rejected the government's attempts to reach the proceeds of enterprises conducted in violation of RICO. And because the CCE act mentioned profits but not proceeds, the courts rejected government attempts to secure the forfeiture of cash transactions that exceeded net gains.[13] According to several federal courts, profits meant the amount left after deductions of all costs, including the drug trafficker's purchase of controlled substances. The forfeiture provisions of RICO did not extend to "fruits or profits generated from the enterprise."[14]

In one RICO case the federal circuit court ruled that the amount of forfeiture money sought by the government for rigged bidding represented profits from the enterprise rather than an interest in it. The statute did not cover forfeiture of racketeering income, according to the court. It applied only to "interests in an enterprise" that had been illegally acquired or maintained, excluding income derived from the enterprise and excluding also the assets of enterprises that were illegal per se.[15] Some courts read congressional intent to mean that only legitimate organizations that had been infiltrated by organized crime were subject to the legislation, not organized crime itself, while others ruled that RICO encompassed the Mafia.[16] Thus, in one case a federal court held that the insurance proceeds of $300,000 obtained from an arson-for-profit scheme, prosecuted under RICO, were not subject to forfeiture, because they did not constitute an interest "in an enterprise."[17] That meant that profits generated by illegal activities were not forfeitable unless they were reinvested in an enterprise or used to acquire or control another enterprise. But racketeers usually bled legitimate businesses of their assets until the company went bankrupt, leaving little if anything of a forfeitable interest. Lower court rulings could have severely limited the applicability of the 1970 legislation by denying the extension of RICO to racketeering profits. However, the Supreme Court resolved the conflict between federal courts in 1981 by deciding in favor of the government, so that RICO finally applied to illegitimate as well legitimate organizations.[18]

The Fifth Circuit Court of Appeals also supported the government in its 1982 review of the case involving the arson scheme to collect insurance moneys. The court sustained the government's position that the insurance constituted "interests" acquired in violation of RICO, which extended to the forfeiture of income or proceeds of racketeering activity.[19] The Supreme Court addressed the issue that had split the federal courts, ruling in 1983 on behalf of the Fifth Circuit's position in favor of the government. Justice Harry Blackmun for the unanimous Court declared that the legislative history of RICO "clearly demonstrates that the RICO statute was intended to provide new weapons of unprecedented scope for an assault upon organized crime and its economic roots." Blackmun added that Congress's intent to authorize forfeiture of racketeering profits seemed "obvious."[20] Other courts had read the same evidence differently, especially when construing the many congressional statements about the need to expunge organized crime from legitimate businesses. Lower federal court decisions against the government's criminal forfeiture operations would not have been so numerous and hindering, if Congress had not been guilty of slovenly draftsmanship as well as ambiguous, if not poor, policies in 1970.

In 1980, Senator Joseph R. Biden, chairman of the Senate Judiciary Subcommittee on Criminal Justice, held hearings to investigate the degree to which the 1970 forfeiture legislation had succeeded. He was appalled by the "dismal record" of the Department of Justice. Its attack on the financial foundations of organized crime had been "very nearly nonexistent." He learned, to his dismay, that the department did not even have records on which to base a response to his queries. No one in the department knew the number or outcomes of forfeiture cases.[21] Biden asked the General Accounting Office to conduct a study of the problem. In 1981 the GAO published its account of asset forfeiture as "A Seldom Used Tool in Combatting Drug Trafficking," describing the extent to which the government had used forfeiture in narcotics cases. Despite RICO and CCE, both enacted in 1970 to combat organized crime by attacking its economic base, the GAO found that the "assets obtained through forfeiture have been miniscule." It castigated the government for not exercising the leadership and management necessary to make asset forfeiture a widely used law-enforcement method.[22]

In the decade of the 1970s, the government had prosecuted only ninety-eight narcotics cases, some under RICO, most under CCE. Those cases yielded a potential of only $2 million in forfeitures at a time when the proceeds from drug trafficking were estimated at $60 billion annually. The discrepancy was ridiculous, and the $2 million amounted to "little more than incidental operating expenses" of a major narcotics dealer, leaving the illicit profits as well as the assets derived from those profits "virtually untouched." The criminal forfeiture legislation of 1970, once envisaged as a major method of diminishing the financial resources of organized crime, proved to be a failure during the 1970s. In the same decade, the Drug Enforcement Agency had arrested over 5,000 "major" violators of RICO and CCE statutes. A major violator was a person trafficking in at least $4 million a month in heroin or $2.8 million monthly in cocaine. That is, a major violator did far more business in a month than the $2 million in criminal forfeitures exacted by the United States government for the entire decade. GAO found not a single case of forfeiture of significant derivative proceeds or business interests acquired with illegal moneys.

"Zilch" describes the progress made under the 1970 criminal forfeiture legislation to diminish the infiltration of organized crime into legitimate businesses and unions. Successful criminal forfeitures had affected only vehicles and homes used in crime but not at all the types of property that constituted the economic assets of organized crime. The fines exacted in criminal prosecutions amounted to far more, a total of $13.4 million, although only a tiny fraction of that had been actually collected. Violators of drug laws could be fined up to $25,000 for illegal sales and up to $100,000 for conducting a continuing criminal enterprise. The amount that had actually been collected in fines of criminal-enterprise members was merely $5,330.[23] It bears repeating that organized crime's estimated revenues from narcotics trafficking in 1980 was $60 billion, an amount that trivializes the government's criminal forfeitures during the 1970s.

Civil forfeiture cases had yielded far more than criminal forfeiture prosecutions, a gross—much of it still uncollected at the time of the GAO study—of $7.1 million in cash that had been direct proceeds of dealing in controlled substances. The U.S. Customs Service and the DEA together had also managed to achieve the civil forfeiture of almost $30 million worth of properties used in the commission of narcotics crimes. The amount, repeated the GAO, represented "mere incidental operating expenses" for a large narcotics organization.[24]

Why had forfeiture, especially criminal forfeiture, been such a failure? The Black Tuna case vividly illustrates some of the problems the government confronted when prosecuting under the criminal forfeiture statutes. That case of 1979–80 involved a Florida-based drug organization that imported over one million pounds of Colombia marijuana and grossed about $300 million over a sixteen-month period. The Department of Justice spent about a year submitting thousands of documents to a grand jury and presenting over a hundred witnesses, before bringing fourteen ringleaders to trial. The indictment, which was 100 pages long, charged both RICO and CCE counts. Using tactics of organized crime to escape conviction, the defendants had one of the government's key witnesses severely beaten as a warning to others, bribed a juror, and plotted the murder of a federal judge to cause a mistrial. The FBI uncovered the bribe and the plot during its wiretaps of the principals.

The government put on its case before a jury for over four months. Evidence showed that at least sixty people worked for the defendants, including airline pilots, ship captains, businessmen, and a doctor. The organization lived in a world of private Lear jets, a four-bedroom duplex apartment at the Fontainbleau Hotel in Miami Beach, yachts that cost up to half a million, and $60,000 in restaurant bills.[25] Proof of guilt was conclusive; proof that the organization's assets derived from criminal proceeds was not.

The law required that no judgment of forfeiture could be entered in a criminal proceeding unless the indictment specified the criminal interest or property subject to forfeiture. This obligation to name the forfeitable assets in the indictment signified several difficulties confronted by the government. First, it had to know in advance of the indictment which properties were subject to forfeiture. Second, it had to reveal that fact prior to trial, by listing those properties in the indictment; without a forfeiture count in the indictment, criminal forfeiture ceases to be possible. Third, the government could do nothing to prevent the dissipation or concealment of those properties. Only properties that were connected to crime were subject to forfeiture, and the government had to prove their relationship to crime. Moreover, it could not seize the properties until after a jury returned a verdict of guilty. In a civil forfeiture case the government can seize assets at the moment it initiates the forfeiture proceeding, but in a criminal forfeiture case the assets remain in the defendant's custody until the jury finds him guilty and returns a special verdict authorizing the forfeiture as a penalty beyond imprisonment or a fine. Consequently defendants have ample opportunity, as well as incentive, to dispose of their assets and so avoid the possibility of losing them to forfeiture in the event of conviction. Drug assets are extremely liquid and can be laundered; they can also be sold or assigned to dummy holders.

In the Black Tuna case, the indictment sought RICO forfeiture of three valuable homes, an auto business, two expensive yachts, a houseboat, and three airplanes; additionally, the indictment sought CCE forfeiture of all profits obtained in violation of the statute. Attorneys' fees consumed $559,000. The auto business turned out to be worthless by the time the government latched onto it; the planes, yachts, and houseboat had all disappeared; and the government was unable to trace the profits of the organization. The defendants received extremely heavy prison sentences, but the criminal forfeiture was an unmitigated failure in the Black Tuna case: the government ended up with a mere $16,000.[26]

The government might have sought an injunction against the transfer or sale of any of the Black Tuna properties that were forfeitable. An injunction was the government's sole mechanism for keeping the forfeitable properties intact and their whereabouts fixed, but it was an extremely unsatisfactory mechanism. The RICO and CCE acts did not provide any standard for the issuance of restraining orders by a federal district court. The procedure remained unsettled. Was the government's application in a one-sided, ex parte hearing sufficient, or was an adversarial hearing necessary? An adversarial hearing, at which the defendants could counter the government's application, required the government to satisfy rather stringent standards. On no other issue involving the interpretation of the 1970 criminal-forfeiture legislation had the federal courts so consistently thwarted the government.[27] As a result of decisions against it on restraining orders, the government virtually had to demonstrate its case in order to get an injunction that would freeze the defendant's assets. Indeed, the government would have to show that it would likely prevail on the merits at the trial. That would not only be burdensome; it would force disclosure of the government's prosecutorial strategy prematurely and so injure its trial case.

Even if the government was prepared for that, it could not secure restraining orders unless it acted immediately after the indictment was returned; no way existed to obtain an injunction prior to the issuance of formal charges against the owners of the forfeitable properties. Once an indictment was returned, swift action was essential, because delay could be fatal to the freezing of the forfeitable assets. Moreover, even if a court issued the restraining orders, the penalty for defying them was merely the penalty for contempt of court—one year in jail or a $2,000 fine, which was less than chicken feed to major narcotics traffickers who dealt in millions, not thousands.[28]

Most discouraging was an extraordinary federal district court ruling that restraining orders would be unconstitutional. If issued, that court reasoned, a restraining order would prejudice the defendant's case by assuming his guilt, deprive him of property without due process of law, and violate the presumption of innocence.[29]

The hoards of cash as well as planes, boats, cars, and stash houses that some kingpin narcotic traffickers need can be physically seized and forfeited, but the Black Tuna case reveals the substantial difficulties even of doing that. Worse, the fact that the CCE statute subjected "profits" to forfeiture created special legal problems. Some federal courts would actually rule that profits were the net gain after deducting the criminal's costs.[30] Moreover, defining the criminal's "interest" in his enterprise would pose another conundrum. Drug dealers, unlike racketeers, do not always conduct an "enterprise" in which they have a forfeitable "interest." And, like RICO, CCE involved prosecutors in an intricate tracing problem. Only the assets utilized to commit the crime, or derived from it, or constituting an interest in a criminal enterprise could be subjected to forfeiture, and the connection of those assets to the crime must be established. Forfeiture is not possible unless the assets to be forfeited were bought or maintained with illegally derived moneys. Also, the assets themselves had to be found before they could be forfeited.

Once money has been "laundered" abroad by having passed through several banks, and has been converted into real estate, certificates of deposit, securities, and other forms of property, finding it can be difficult or impossible. The Cayman Islands, Hong Kong, and Panama, as well as other international financial centers and tax havens, attract launderers of illegal moneys and have bank secrecy laws that prohibit disclosure of names, amounts, and sources of funds. Multiple wire-transfers of moneys by complex laundering schemes constitute sham transactions designed to conceal the origin of property. Phony names, fictitious corporations, and foreign bank accounts make tracing a financial nightmare. When the money returns to the United States in the bank account of some front company, sometimes in the form of an alleged loan to avoid taxation, tracing a nexus to crime can outwit a prosecutor's ingenuity and technical competence. Moreover the laundered money can be mingled with legitimate money and be used to purchase capital assets, further compounding the problem of proving the nexus between criminally derived moneys and the crimes.

Four different kinds of property are subject to forfeiture. Illegal drugs, as a form of contraband, constitute a type of property that no one is entitled to keep. Contraband consists of property deemed by statute to be inherently dangerous. Because possession of it is a crime, its destruction—as in the image of Elliot Ness smashing barrels of illegal whiskey—raises no constitutional problems. Certain foods as well as drugs fit the category of contraband, as do certain gambling devices and weapons. Derivative contraband is a related form of property, used to hold, move, or facilitate the exchange of contraband. Thus, conveyances of any kind—aircraft, autos, vessels—can also be seized and forfeited without much legal hassle. Congress in 1939 had enacted a Transportation of Contraband Act that penalized and made forfeitable the use of vehicles to transport controlled substances, counterfeit coins, and certain firearms. Forfeiture must always rest on statutory authorization.

A third type of property is money or direct proceeds, which can be more difficult to prove forfeitable in court, although in civil cases the task is simpler because the government's burden of proof is so much lighter than in criminal cases; and in some cases involving police excesses, as when DEA agents or deputy sheriffs simply confiscate cash suspected of being the product of a drug transaction, legal hurdles are altogether bypassed. A fourth type of forfeitable property is derivative proceeds, which may be property of any sort—an entire business, a bank account, land, stocks and bonds, houses, or rare stamps and coins—bought directly or indirectly with the proceeds from trading in controlled substances. Income from narcotics can be direct or indirect proceeds; indirect proceeds in the form of capital assets purchased with criminal profits are the hardest to trace to the felony. No property is forfeitable unless it is connected to the activities prohibited by statute. Tracing the appropriate connection might require considerable financial know-how as well as information from tipsters. Without proof of the connection between property and crime, the hope of attacking the economic base of racketeering or trafficking in drugs may be baseless. CCE and RICO raised many hopes skyward without anyone's having considered the quicksands of poorly conceived legislation. Congress's naivete was stunning, and it also ignored the real world in which the proceeds from narcotics and racketeering were laundered abroad and transferred anywhere almost instantaneously by computerized instructions.

Problems concerning the narcotics trade were even knottier than those of racketeering. Attempts to prevent the exportation of drugs from their country of origin failed. Attempts at physical destruction of drug crops—coca, poppies, and marijuana—in their countries of origins failed. Attempts to subsidize the growth of substitute crops in the countries of origin also failed. Attempts to prevent the importation of illicit drugs into the United States have failed, too. And the domestic war against drug trafficking and drug abuse has failed as well. The enormity of our drug problem and its dangers to our economy, our safety, and our national health pass understanding. Each year the estimated size of the narcotics traffic in the United States increases. By 1980 it reached $60 billion and by 1990 over $100 billion. Civil and criminal forfeiture combined had scarcely nicked drug profits.[31]

Neither the shortcomings of the criminal forfeiture statutes nor adverse court rulings were the prime reason that criminal forfeiture did not fulfill its expectations as a daring innovation that would gobble the assets of organized crime. The GAO in its report on the failure of asset forfeiture declared that "the primary reason has been the lack of leadership by the Department of Justice."[32]

A decade after the enactment of the 1970 legislation the department lacked "the most rudimentary information needed to manage the forfeiture effort." It did not know how many forfeiture cases had been attempted, or how many succeeded and how many failed, and it did not know the reasons for success or failure. Indeed it had no record of the disposition of cases, and its investigators and prosecutors were fairly ignorant of the elements of criminal forfeiture. The GAO immediately added that considerable efforts were being made by the department to remedy its inadequacies. But for a decade, when the department did not compile data on forfeiture cases, its investigators and prosecutors "lacked the incentive and expertise to pursue forfeiture." The department did not require a statement of reasons why forfeiture was not even attempted in most prosecutions under the 1970 legislation. Forfeiture had simply not been a departmental goal.

DEA agents were not at all trained to conduct the sophisticated financial investigations necessary to implement the legislation, particularly with respect to derivative proceeds with which organized crime accumulated its economic assets. The department rewarded its investigators for the number of arrests of major drug traffickers, not for the forfeiture of their assets. Agents had virtually no incentive to develop a case for forfeiture before arresting violators; prosecutors too sought their conviction, not the forfeiture of their assets. Almost every prosecutor in the department questioned by GAO admitted his inadequacies in the area of criminal forfeiture. They regarded the subject as one of unusual complications, because the RICO and CCE acts were booby-trapped with difficulties. To obtain a criminal conviction, a prosecutor had only to show a specific criminal incident; to obtain a criminal forfeiture, one had to demonstrate a pattern of crime and had to trace laundered proceeds. The difficulties were, in fact, so great that prosecutors believed that attempting forfeiture might jeopardize securing convictions and would be an inefficient expenditure of their time. They preferred to use the time to put other violators in prison. Prosecutors, like agents, measured success in convictions, not forfeitures.[33]

The Department of Justice admitted most of the charges against it in the GAO study of asset forfeiture. In a long letter to GAO, Justice whined about the novelties and special problems connected with criminal forfeiture, especially the tracing problem; ambiguities, gaps, and deficiencies of the 1970 legislation received a thorough shellacking. Also, the department correctly insisted that "notable progress" was being swiftly made. DEA was recruiting new agents with special financial knowledge and skills to arm a newly

100

created Financial Investigation Section. The Justice Department bragged that forfeitures in fiscal 1980 amounted to over $90 million, a twenty-fold increase over the preceding year, but they were seizures, not forfeitures, in civil, not criminal, cases; the amount forfeited was $46 million—a substantial increase indeed. And, assets from derivative proceeds were at last being attacked, even if very modestly.

The department boasted, too, that it had introduced new, detailed courses on criminal forfeiture, including the tracing problem, and over 60 percent of DEA's agents had taken the courses to assist them in their financial investigations. IRS agents, who were even better skilled, were cooperating in many investigations. DEA had also revised its evaluation of agents and prosecutors so that their success with asset forfeiture counted. A 350-page Drug Agents Manual, which was about to be published, would significantly guide agents and prosecutors, as had the criminal division's new instruction manual for the use of U.S. Attorneys in criminal forfeiture cases throughout the country.[34] The department also made recommendations for alterations in the 1970 legislation, as had GAO. Those recommendations and the failures of the 1970s combined to produce new congressional studies and, eventually, legislation adopted in 1984, which vitalized criminal forfeiture.

Chapter Six

New Legislation: 1980–1984

A comparison of civil and criminal forfeitures as of 1984, before the enactment of a new forfeiture statute of that year, reveals not only relative advantages and problems; it also illuminates the need for the new statute. Civil forfeiture started with a wallop: without advance warning, the government seizes assets. The seizure is not lawful unless the government has probable cause to believe that the particular property is either an instrumentality of crime that assists its commission, or is a fruit of the crime, meaning a product of its commission. Probable cause is the Fourth Amendment's opaque standard for an independent magistrate's decision whether to issue a warrant for search or seizure. Probable cause is also the standard that should guide an officer's judgment that he must conduct a search or seizure without a warrant because circumstances leave him no opportunity to seek one. The same standard for search in cases of crime applies to seizure in forfeiture cases, which are triggered by crime.

Theoretically the Fourth Amendment would have slight meaning if the police, rather than a magistrate, had the authority to decide that evidence in a given instance suffices to establish probable cause to justify the search of a particular place for evidence of a crime and the seizure of that evidence or of the individual who committed the crime. Freedom from unreasonable search and seizure, which the Fourth Amendment protects, would be paltry if it depended only on the discretion of the police. Nevertheless, there are circumstances that justify warrantless seizures. As a matter of fact, warrants are the basis for seizure only in a minority of cases. An officer may conduct a warrantless search and make a seizure if the search is incident to a lawful arrest, or is conducted under emergency conditions, or has the voluntary consent of the party searched. When making an arrest an officer may seize evidence of the crime. He may also seize evidence if the opportunity for the seizure will be lost without his swift action. Thus a vehicle or vessel that can speed off may be seized if the officer has probable cause to believe that it was used to commit a crime or facilitate one. However, a delayed seizure is usually invalid if made at leisure, well after an arrest.[1]

Courts make believe that "probable cause" for a seizure is not a technical concept, and they say it is only the judgment of a reasonable or prudent person that a crime has been committed in a particular place or that the evidence of it is there. The prudent person is not much assisted by the judicial declaration that probable cause is more than mere suspicion but less than a prima facie case of guilt or enough evidence to convict. Probable cause to seize property exists when an officer has personal knowledge or trustworthy information to justify his belief or the belief of a reasonable man that the property is evidence of crime, because it was used to commit it or results from having committed it. In any event, either a warrant based on probable cause justifies seizure or an experienced officer's judgment tells him he can find evidence of a crime that might be lost if he does not act without a warrant.

In reality probable cause is fairly easy to establish. It can rely on an informer's tip, circumstantial evidence, and hearsay. If the officer proceeds on his own determination of probable cause, a magistrate must back him up in order for the seizure to be sustained. A court must, sooner or later, be the final determinant assessing the existence of probable cause. On the other hand, courts rarely refuse to agree with law enforcement in making that assessment.[2]

If the seized evidence of the crime is worth more than $10,000, the government must seek forfeiture before a court. A claimant of the property may contest forfeiture by filing a bond that also ensures a judicial proceeding. The bond costs 10 percent of the appraised value of the property, but no less than $250 and no more than $5,000. It helps pay for costs and deters frivolous suits. If the property is worth less than $10,000 and no one files a bond, forfeiture proceeds administratively.

In an administrative forfeiture case, all parties receive written notice of the proposed forfeiture, which is also publicly reported in local newspapers. Claimants to the forfeitable property may be represented by counsel and argue against the forfeiture. Their claims will be investigated by the Department of Justice, and a departmental attorney, who receives the records of the case, listens to their argument and determines its outcome. His written statement explaining his decision may be challenged by an appeal to a federal judge.[3]

If judicial proceedings follow seizure of the property, the federal district court that has jurisdiction is the one in the district where the property is located. Judicial proceedings mean a civil trial by jury, unless the assets were seized at sea. In that case the judge tries the case without a jury. The property in a civil forfeiture is the defendant, of course, but those claiming title to the property may seek to prove that law enforcement erred in believing that the property is evidence of crime. The government needs only to show that it had probable cause to make the seizure. If the judge agrees that probable cause existed, the entire burden of proof shifts to the claimant to prove by a preponderance of evidence that the government was mistaken and that the property was guiltless. A preponderance of evidence is enough to establish probable truth. The claimant loses the assets if the court rules that he failed to make his case. The claimant's innocence of crime does not matter. The property is on trial in a proceeding *in rem*, not the person claiming the assets.[4]

In a civil forfeiture case, the government benefits from the relation-back doctrine: its claim to the property originates at the time of the commission of the crime. Accordingly, although a guilty party may wish to dispose of the property in order to defeat the forfeiture, he cannot because the government, on seizing it with probable cause, has taken physical possession of it. Civil forfeiture cases start with forfeiture because the relation-back doctrine gives the government title to the property at the moment it was used for criminal purposes—if a court subsequently agrees. That doctrine thwarts the transfer of the property to a third party. Of course, the owner may anticipate seizure and defeat the government by speedy laundering of the proceeds or hiding ownership in sham corporations. But if the government was able to seize the assets, civil forfeiture prevents the owner's efforts to dispose of them.[5]

Criminal forfeiture has far fewer complications than civil forfeiture. It follows a standard criminal prosecution against an accused person; the person, not the property, is on trial, and he or she has all the constitutional protections of any accused person. The distinctive dimension of criminal forfeiture consists in the fact that it is an additional punishment of the guilty party, supplementing prison time and fines. The prosecution must name the forfeitable properties in the indictment, and the jury must return a special verdict on the question of forfeiture. The seizure of the property, until 1984, was delayed until after the jury returned a guilty verdict. The grave weakness of criminal forfeiture was the fact that the party received such early notice of the intended forfeiture and retained possession of the property until a verdict of guilt. Accordingly he had ample opportunity to dispose of it by transferring ownership or hiding his assets. The relation-back doctrine had no operation in criminal forfeiture cases, and the difficulties of the government with securing restraining orders to prevent disposition of the forfeitable properties riddled criminal forfeiture with loopholes.[6]

Thus, civil forfeiture required only the government's showing of probable cause to warrant seizure without notice of forfeitable properties, while criminal forfeiture required indictment, notice of forfeiture at the time of indictment, proof beyond reasonable doubt, and the full panoply of constitutional protections. Civil forfeiture made the claimant's culpability irrelevant, while criminal forfeiture made forfeiture dependent on his conviction. Civil forfeiture, because of the relation-back doctrine, terminated third-party interests, while criminal forfeiture allowed someone to claim that innocence mattered especially if he were a legitimate purchaser of forfeited assets who knew nothing about their involvement in crime.

Whether under civil or criminal forfeiture, the properties forfeitable depended on statute. A lunkheaded Congress in 1970 failed to make cash proceeds from drug transactions forfeitable, thereby handcuffing the government in drug transaction cases under the CCE statute, even though the proceeds in most such transactions were in cash. That deficiency was not rectified until 1978, and not until 1984 were several other shortcomings of the RICO and CCE acts remedied. A serious deficiency in civil forfeitures dealt with real property. It was forfeitable in criminal forfeitures but in civil cases only such real property as may have been part of the profits of a narcotics deal was forfeitable. A dealer might lose his vehicle or helicopter or yacht if he used it to transport drugs; he might lose equipment employed to manufacture illegal drugs. But if he used a building or any real estate for the purpose of making or storing drugs, it was not forfeitable under the civil forfeiture statutes.

After the GAO Report of 1981 revealed the fiascoes of the 1970s, the need for new legislation was as clear as the image of Lincoln on a penny. Both substantive limitations and procedural deficiencies had eviscerated criminal forfeitures. The Subcommittee on Crime of the House Judiciary Committee held hearings in 1981, at which witnesses recommended revisions in the forfeiture acts of 1970. The House intended to make clear that forfeiture under the RICO Act reaches "all profits and proceeds" of illegal activity covered by the RICO statute "regardless of the form in which they are held, and whether such assets are held directly or indirectly by the violator."[7] Accordingly the House understood that forfeiture must cover all proceeds, not just profits, and that ways had to be found to prevent the transfer of assets prior to conviction. The GAO Report earlier that year had made such recommendations, and the Department of Justice proposed an elaborate bill that went still further. A spokesman for the department declared:

The major changes in RICO forfeiture provisions that are incorporated in our proposal address two problem areas. The first is our present inability to obtain the forfeiture of proceeds of racketeering because of court

107

decisions that have held that such proceeds do not constitute a forfeitable interest under the RICO statute since they are not interests in an enterprise. These decisions have severely inhibited realization of the intended purpose of the RICO criminal forfeiture provisions, which was to separate racketeers from their sources of economic power.[8]

The Justice Department spokesman urged various means of defeating the transfer or concealment of forfeitable property. One means was to extend to criminal forfeitures the relation-back principle so familiar in civil forfeitures, vesting the government's right to the property at the moment the crime was committed and thereby voiding any subsequent changes in the status of the property. Another was authorizing the federal district courts to issue restraining orders before the indictment; still another was the notion that in the event that the property's owners somehow outwitted the government by managing to transfer the forfeitable property or get it out of the court's jurisdiction, the court should be able to order the forfeiture of other assets as a substitute for those missing.[9]

A private attorney, William W. Taylor, opposed reinforcement of the criminal forfeiture acts. He wrongly opposed criminal forfeiture as forfeiture of estate and corruption of blood. What bothered him most was the application of criminal forfeiture to business corporations. RICO, he believed, should be restricted to organized crime, not white-collar crime; the statute should not be permitted to curtail a corporation's capacity to function in the marketplace. Forfeiture, he believed, was "a greater threat to the white collar criminal that it is to the underworld figure."[10]

A former deputy assistant attorney general, Irving B. Nathan, believed that fears about criminal forfeiture involving white-collar crime had been much exaggerated. He defended RICO prosecutions of legitimate but rapacious businesses should they violate the statute. One legitimate company that had been properly prosecuted, he said, had bribed public officials to get government contracts from which it made enormous profits. RICO, as the Supreme Court had recently ruled, applied to legitimate as well as illegitimate enterprises.[11]

The Senate too worked on revision of the forfeiture laws. In 1982 Senator Strom Thurmond reported the Judiciary Committee's recommendation for a Comprehensive Criminal Forfeiture Act. The report reexpressed confidence in forfeiture as the way "to remove the wealth generated by and used to maintain organized criminal activity," but sought to mend defects in the existing legislation.[12] In addition to making the proceeds of racketeering forfeitable, the proposed bill made civil forfeiture extend to real property so that the government might take "a secluded barn used to store tons of marihuana" or a house "used as a manufacturing laboratory for amphetamines."[13] The bill also proposed to authorize courts to issue injunctions that would freeze forfeitable assets, thereby preventing their concealment or transfer or diminution. Additionally, the bill proposed to assure that in case the defendant somehow managed to outwit the government by hiding or getting rid of his forfeitable assets, he would have gained nothing. If tracing the assets became impossible or even too difficult, substitute assets, not named in the indictment, could be forfeited instead, if ordered by a court. That proposal went far to make the economic impact of forfeiture an inevitability.

An equally drastic provision extended the relation-back doctrine to criminal forfeitures; historically, the doctrine applied only to civil forfeitures.[14] If the change became law, it would give the government lawful possession of the property at the moment that the defendant engaged in crime. However, the relation-back doctrine could go into effect only after conviction of the defendant under the reasonable doubt standard. After conviction, no transaction assigning forfeitable assets to third parties would be legal unless the third party could prove, at a subsequent hearing, that he innocently bought the property in good faith for a fair price and had no reason to believe that it was forfeitable. The third party could petition for "remission" (or the cancellation of the forfeiture) in order to secure its return, or he might petition for its "mitigation" (or reduction). But remission and mitigation were acts of executive mercy to which the third party had no right. This provision, if enacted, would have guaranteed against sham transfers to third parties such as friends, relatives, or lawyers; only "arms' length" transactions would survive scrutiny.[15]

The bill also contained a provision that improved civil forfeiture. Although criminal forfeiture had multiple shortcomings, civil forfeiture had worked rather successfully and, as a result, the government had relied on it especially in drug-related cases. As such cases considerably increased because of the increase in drug trafficking, the dockets of some federal courts became logjammed. The proposed bill suggested a way of unburdening the backlog of civil forfeiture cases by permitting federal prosecutors to pursue criminal forfeitures in drug cases. The Continuing Criminal Enterprise Act of 1970, which focused on drug cases, applied only to kingpins and was permeated with numerous complications. For example, the kingpin had to control or act in concert with five or more followers when committing a federal drug felony, and the felony had to be part of a continuing series of three or more federal drug crimes that added substantially to his income. The proposed bill would simply have subjected to criminal forfeiture the properties involved in any federal drug crime. Those properties included proceeds derived directly or indirectly as a result of the crime or used in any manner to commit it or facilitate its commission. The bill, therefore, considerably expanded the scope of criminal forfeiture in drug cases.

The bill also streamlined forfeiture proceedings by extending criminal forfeiture to drug-related properties previously subject only to civil forfeiture. Because civil forfeiture is an *in rem* proceeding against property itself, a court trying such a proceeding had to have jurisdiction over the property. If the property was located in more than one district, the same case had to be tried civilly in each of those districts. Separate but parallel civil cases in different districts drained prosecutorial resources and added to the judicial logjam of civil forfeiture cases. The solution to this problem lay in a proposal that authorized criminal forfeiture in drug cases, thereby allowing the consolidation into one prosecution of cases involving properties spread out in various districts. Prosecutors, judges, and juries could efficiently hear and decide one case against an individual instead of more than one against his widespread property. Both houses passed the proposed legislation by overwhelming majorities, but President Reagan pocket-vetoed an anti-crime bill, of which the forfeiture provisions were a part, for reasons irrelevant to forfeiture.[16]

A year later, in 1983, Senators Biden and Thurmond introduced similar bills. During the hearings, the American Bar Association's Section on Criminal Justice submitted noteworthy objections on the possible impact of forfeiture in the area of managerial crime. The concerns expressed in this document reflected a growing unease about forfeiture in corporate America. "RICO and its forfeiture provisions are being applied to a wide range of commercial behavior," said the ABA document. "RICO prosecutions are being brought not only against individuals associated with inherently criminal activity, e.g. narcotics, arson, murder for hire and loan sharking, but also against persons charged with corporate misbehavior and commercial frauds." Because illegal activities were "usually intertwined with those of legal activity," the ABA warned that statutory overbreadth might raise problems about the "disproportionality of punishment" under the Eighth Amendment; denying due process of law to third parties who bought forfeitable properties also vexed the ABA.[17] In addition, it preferred the 1970 provision that made only "profits" rather than "proceeds" forfeitable, because profits enabled businesses to deduct costs in cases involving fraudulent contracts. The ABA also disliked the substitute assets provision, arguing: "A RICO offense may span many years. Property obtained during it may increase or decrease in value and businesses may fall on hard times. In short, this section would result in orders of forfeiture far in excess of property actually available to the defendant at the time of his indictment, or it might result in forfeiture so disproportionate to the amounts attributable to the illegal conduct as to raise eighth amendment considerations."[18] The ABA also objected to making injunctions any easier for the government to obtain. Despite such objections, the Senate committee strongly endorsed a bill to revise the forfeiture laws similar in ways to the bill that had failed the year before.

The new bill retained the proposed provision on substituting proceeds for profits, extended RICO to obscenity, and expanded the CCE act to cover all federal drug felonies that previously could be proceeded against only in an *in rem* proceeding. Also, civil forfeiture applied to all property, real as well as personal. But most of the provisions of the bill focused "primarily on improving the procedures applicable in forfeiture cases," especially in order to prevent pre-

conviction transfers of assets in criminal forfeiture cases
and to allow substitute assets when forfeited assets had
been transferred or concealed to prevent government confiscation.[19]

Accordingly, the bill applied the relation-back doctrine to
criminal forfeiture cases, thereby closing loopholes in the
1970 legislation. Post-conviction hearings would be available to provide innocent and bona fide purchasers of forfeited properties a chance to prove their claims. Remission
of forfeiture remained a matter of executive grace for those
with merely a hardship or some other equitable claim, but
for those who could demonstrate that they were without
cause to believe that the property in question was forfeitable, the right to a judicial hearing was guaranteed.[20] That
right represented a major procedural change benefiting innocent third parties. Nevertheless, the rights of the innocent still received much less in the way of procedural safeguards than the interests of criminal defendants.

The substitute assets proposal of 1982 remained in the
1983 bill. It provided that if property subject to forfeiture
was no longer available after conviction, a court could require defendants to forfeit other assets of comparable value.
The court must find one of five conditions to exist before authorizing substitute assets to be forfeited: the assets specified in the indictment cannot be located, or have been transferred, or have been placed beyond the court's jurisdiction
as in a foreign bank, or have been substantially diminished
in value by the defendant, or have been commingled with
other property that cannot be easily divided.[21]

The committee report also analyzed the problem of injunctions, another vital consideration in preserving the
availability of forfeitable assets until the conclusion of the
criminal trial. First the report sought to simplify the existing method of securing restraining orders against a defen-

dant after the filing of an indictment. Instead of an elaborate evidentiary hearing, as some courts had required, the report recommended a bill providing that the indictment itself constituted probable cause that the property would be forfeited; accordingly a swift judicial response to the government's request for an injunction became possible. In effect, the committee admonished courts not to look behind the probable-cause finding implicit in the indictment. The 1993 bill went still further. It made pre-indictment injunctions a possibility for the first time, with and without notice. After due notice and a hearing, the bill authorized a court to decide that a substantial probability existed that the government would prevail on the forfeiture issue; also, the court might believe that a failure to issue an injunction would result in the property's transfer or concealment. In such a case, an injunction might issue before the filing of an indictment.

The court might also issue an injunction even without notice and hearing, because the committee report urged a provision in the bill authorizing a temporary ex parte or one-sided injunction. If the government established probable cause for a forfeiture and satisfied a court that notice would jeopardize the availability of the property, the court could issue an injunction restraining the defendant. Such a case would most likely arise if cash proceeds were at issue; their liquidity made speed a necessity and required the sacrifice of notice and hearing. This provision conflicted with arguments made unsuccessfully by several defendants to the effect that pre-trial restraining orders violated the presumption of innocence. The report disagreed.[22] In effect the committee sought to bring criminal forfeitures into line with the Supreme Court's ruling in the 1974 Pearson Yacht case, to the effect that seizure in civil forfeiture cases could be achieved without previous notice when the government needed to secure an important public interest or needed to act swiftly.[23] But considerations that justified seizure in civil cases did not necessarily apply in criminal ones.

The 1983 bill also addressed the problem of disposing of forfeited properties. The attorney general was empowered to control them; he was obligated to sell them, making due provision for the rights of any accused persons. Previously moneys went into the general treasury and were not available to pay the expenses of forfeiture prosecutions or for the care of forfeited properties. The attorney general now might transfer forfeited drug-related properties to another federal agency or to an assisting state or local agency. State and local law enforcement agencies sometimes significantly assisted in drug cases that resulted in forfeitures for the United States. No mechanism previously existed to allow their getting a cut of the proceeds in order to reward them for cooperation. Furthermore, the recommended bill authorized the creation of a Department of Justice Forfeiture Fund and a comparable fund in the Customs Service. These funds could be used to cover the costs of forfeiture cases and of maintaining seized properties that might otherwise deteriorate and lose value. The funds could also be used in cases of remission and mitigation as well as to reward informers.[24]

In addition, the bill included a provision raising to $100,000 the amount involved to warrant a judicial forfeiture. The existing law required judicial forfeiture if the amount exceeded $10,000 or even less than that if a claimant contested the forfeiture. Administrative forfeiture, by comparison, was swift and cheap, taking only two to three months rather than a year or more as in judicial forfeiture cases. In order to ease crowded dockets, the bill raised to $100,000 the amount that could be settled by an uncontested administrative forfeiture.[25] Property owners frequently failed to contest forfeiture proceedings for the reason given by a court: "In this case the owner of $321,470 in cash turned his back on what must have been pin money to him compared with the value of preserving his anonymity."[26] In the case of *United States v. $5,644,540 in U.S. Currency*, the government found all that cash in the rear end of an abandoned rental car, together with another quarter of a million dollars worth of precious metals; it was all taken to be drug proceeds. DEA showed no surprise when no one contested the forfeiture.[27]

No legislation was enacted in 1983 but Congress persisted in attacking the forfeiture problem. In 1984 the House Committee on the Judiciary reported a bill, after having conducted additional hearings.[28] A majority of the committee recommended against the substitute assets provisions that had been part of the bills of 1982 and 1983. The majority believed that if a defendant could get rid of the assets specified in an indictment, he might also get rid of substitute assets. Apart from the belief that the substitute-assets idea would not be effective, the majority preferred a tenfold increase in fines, from $25,000 to $250,000 or, alternatively, in drug cases, a fine limited only by "twice the proceeds." The majority also believed that forfeiture of substitute assets raised Eighth Amendment problems and might even violate the constitutional provision against forfeiture of estate. In one case, as the committee observed, a court had warned that an honest shopkeeper might forfeit his entire business if he got mixed up in a single fraudulent scheme.[29] More to the point the committee quoted another case in which a court had noted that forfeiture might threaten "disproportionately to reach untainted property," invoking the specter of the Eighth Amendment.[30]

The committee's majority concluded that the need for the substitute asset provision appeared to be unsubstantiated, and the idea itself "ill-advised" and "unworkable." "Any attempt to forfeit 'substitute assets' which has no 'nexus' to the crime in 'in personam' forfeiture is a giant step in the direction of 'forfeiture of estate.'"[31] That was the viewpoint of the majority of seventeen voting against substitute assets.

A minority of twelve members filed a separate report, observing that criminal forfeiture was a punitive measure against a convicted felon, making forfeiture of substitute assets a necessity if the punishment was not to be illusory. The minority endorsed the tenfold increase in the amount of possible fines, but noted that the unpaid balance of criminal fines was "immense." In more than 21,000 cases criminal fines had not been fully paid; the aggregate amount of unpaid fines was then $131,917,602. One-fourth derived from cases over ten years old, in most of which the debtor's location was unknown or he had no assets. The minority argued too that the majority misunderstood the forfeiture of estate provision in the Constitution. Forfeiture of substitute assets could not violate it, because the ability of the defendant to own other property during his lifetime was unaffected. As for the Eighth Amendment, the minority agreed that disproportionate forfeitures might violate it, but the forfeiture of assets equal in amount to criminal proceeds, or no greater than the amount originally forfeitable, did not constitute disproportionate forfeitures.[32] Congress accepted the majority view by deleting the substitute assets provision from the bill, and the Comprehensive Forfeiture Act became law in 1984. Two years later Congress quietly adopted the substitute assets provision.[33] The legislation of 1984 and 1986 empowered the government with potentially draconian forfeiture weapons.

Chapter Seven

Enforcement and Victims

Forfeiture proceedings invariably have a human element that the law often obscures. In one criminal case, for example, the defendant won an acquittal on money-laundering and conspiracy charges involving drug proceeds, yet confronted tragic consequences. He was Harlan Vander Zee of the Stone Oak National Bank, who had been a San Antonio banker for nearly thirty years. In 1991 and again in 1992 federal judges presiding over his trials stopped the proceedings and dismissed the indictments because the evidence against Vander Zee was so flimsy. Nevertheless Vander Zee lost everything that counted—his banking position, home, savings, and good name.[1] The cause of his downfall was his relationship with Mario Salinas, a Mexican citizen, vouched for by a director of Vander Zee's bank. Salinas and some associates wanted to move money out of Mexico, put it into U.S. banks, and buy certificates of deposit. When Vander Zee heard that the money was in U.S. currency, he called the chairman of the bank's board, who told him to go ahead after he had checked with the proper authorities.

Vander Zee twice called the U.S. Treasury Department in Washington and asked for advice. He was told, "No problem. Take the money. All you've got to do is fill out the form." Vander Zee played safely by making other calls, locally and in Washington, to the Criminal Investigation Division of

118

the IRS, the FBI, the U.S. Secret Service, and the Office of the Comptroller of the Currency. He learned about counterfeit bills and proper reporting requirements. In effect, he was told, "Just fill out the CTRs"—the cash transaction reports, which are the prescribed government forms for reporting currency transactions involving more than $10,000. Federal authorities told him, "You're not policemen; we are. Banks are not responsible for determining the source of the funds. Their only responsibility is to report those funds." An officer of the Treasury Department said on tape that the bank officers were "covered" so far as the Bank Secrecy Act was concerned, because their obligation was simply to complete the forms.

Vander Zee took Salinas's money, sold him the certificates of deposit, and filled out the CTRs on behalf of Stone Oak National Bank. A deputy assistant secretary of the Treasury Department, Division of Law Enforcement, sent the forms to IRS's Criminal Division with a note saying that apparently the bank "is alerting us to what they consider unusual currency transactions." Altogether Vander Zee accepted $700,000 from Salinas on behalf of the bank. Over a two-year period, no government officer or agency said anything critical or became involved until the Justice Department instituted a criminal prosecution against Vander Zee for his involvement in money laundering.

Salinas turned out to be a kingpin drug trafficker. A year after his conviction he escaped from a minimum security facility and remains a fugitive from justice. Different federal district judges stopped the trial against Vander Zee and granted verdicts of acquittal. But he was a ruined man, $60,000 in debt to legal counsel. When he told his story in 1992 to the House Committee on Government Operations, he insistently asked why his government had ruined him. Why had they prosecuted him, twice, though he was innocent? He blamed it on "the forfeiture laws" for allowing forfeiture proceeds to be kept by prosecutors.

"This reward," he declared, "might well impair or distort the detached judgment that is so necessary of the government agencies and individuals who are charged with the responsibility of administration and enforcement of these forfeiture laws. It might well turn some into the likes of a bounty hunter of the late 1800s." The alleged conspiracy, Vander Zee claimed, was "not hatched within the walls of the Stone Oak National Bank. The real conspiracy was hatched and nurtured within the halls of justice, the U.S. Department of Justice. And I continue to remain their hostage. My life, my reputation, my job, my security, they've all been destroyed by the unconscionable acts of an unscrupulous few. This is my reward for cooperating with my government."[2]

By chance Cary H. Copeland, the director and chief counsel of the Department of Justice's Executive Office for Asset Forfeiture, happened to be present when Vander Zee testified. Copeland, the next witness, laconically remarked of Vander Zee's case that it did not involve forfeiture at all, because he had been prosecuted for money laundering.[3] Technically that was true. But it did not answer the question of why the Department of Justice had prosecuted him at all. In the overwhelming majority of forfeiture cases, which involve civil forfeitures, no one is prosecuted. Moreover, the fact that Vander Zee was prosecuted for money laundering did not make erroneous his complaint about forfeiture practices. The Money Laundering Control Act of 1986, one authority has observed, "as a practical matter made forfeiture available for almost every federal crime, including most white collar crimes, since the deposit in a financial institution of money derived from criminal activity renders the money forfeitable."[4] Copeland himself on a different occasion remarked, "And through money laundering, we are able to do forfeitures for a whole host of crimes, white collar crimes, to the extent that we show fraud plus a financial transaction."[5] Vander Zee's case reflected no fraud.

In 1986 the DEA captured the Air America ring, headquartered in Scranton, Pennsylvania. No other ring had smuggled as much cocaine into the United States, at least ten tons with a street value of about $2 billion. The members of the Air America ring were pilots who neither bought nor sold drugs. Rather, they transported cocaine for the Medellin cartel of Columbia. The pilots regarded themselves as professionals who operated an efficient air freight business at considerable profit. The founder and head of Air America cleared about $20 million, most of which had disappeared in foreign banks or the DEA could not locate. The indictment against him and his pilots charged a "continuing criminal enterprise" that involved money laundering and income tax evasion as well as drug trafficking. The defendants had accumulated about $45 million in profits while operating their business from 1980 to 1985. One pilot had hidden over $3 million in a friend's home, and another had buried over $4 million in the sewer pipes under his house. The government found cash and properties valued at $20 million, a considerable forfeiture total when measured against the government's cost of about half a million dollars in expenses. Of the twelve defendants, one who was wholly uncooperative was sentenced to a prison term of twenty-four years. The others received prison sentences ranging from one year to ten. The DEA never recovered a single ounce of the more than ten tons of cocaine that Air America had smuggled into the country over a five-year period before being caught.[6]

In the first federal case against a bank that involved the laundering of drug money, the government in 1990 won a

$15 million forfeiture judgment, the largest at that time ever assessed against a bank. The bank was BCCI, or Bank of Credit and Commerce International, one of the world's largest, operating in seventy-three countries. BCCI, which was controlled by Pakistanis, Persian Gulf emirs, and Saudi Arabs, was crooked throughout. Officers of the bank in Tampa admitted that they had disguised transactions involving funds that they knew were proceeds from cocaine sales.[7] Two years later the government initiated and won a RICO prosecution against BCCI for bribery, terrorism, laundering cocaine proceeds, and frauds—"the largest bank fraud in world financial history," according to one prosecutor. When BCCI pleaded guilty in the Washington, D.C., district court, the government won the largest criminal forfeiture ever, $550 million. That was the total of the bank's assets in the United States. The government planned on using half the money to repay depositors who were BCCI victims and the other half to shore up two financially ailing American banks that BCCI had fleeced.[8]

Another major RICO prosecution involved James Regan and four other officers of the Princeton/Newport Partnership, a multibillion-dollar arbitrage business that took its name from its dual centers in Princeton, New Jersey, and Newport Beach, California. All the charges were based on a series of security trades that supposedly carried no risk. The government had tape-recorded conversations in which the defendants had agreed to "park" securities at Drexel Burnham Lambert, pretending to sell them for the purpose of creating fake tax losses. Regan and the others had also committed a variety of other frauds, including mail fraud, securities fraud, and wire fraud, as well as numerous other RICO violations. The government sought the forfeiture not only of all racketeering proceeds but also the salaries of the individuals and their twenty percent "interest" in Drexel, whose assets totaled about $1 billion. The jury convicted them but refused to accommodate the government by wiping out the interest of the partners in the firm. The district court agreed, ruling that the government had sought forfeitures that would be grossly disproportionate, contrary to the Eighth Amendment's injunction against excessive fines. However, the government sought a RICO prosecution against Drexel Burnham Lambert independently of the prosecution against its partners. In the end, the district judge returned forfeiture verdicts of only $1.6 million against the Drexel defendants and sentenced them to prison time from three to six months. The government's victory came when the company itself pleaded guilty in 1989 and agreed to a forfeiture of the titanic sum of $650 million.[9]

At the same time that the government targeted Drexel Burnham Lambert, it initiated its suit against Michael Milken and his associates as conspirators in a racketeering enterprise that violated RICO. Milken was the wizard of high-risk, high-yield junk bonds, the instruments of corporate warfare that did so much to fuel and stagger the national economy in the 1970s and 1980s. He financed some of the greatest corporate takeovers in history and was history's highest-paid financier. In 1987 his compensation for the year was $550 million. He committed a variety of financial crimes. The government obtained a ninety-eight count indictment that sought the staggering sum of forfeitures in the amount of $1.8 billion. Milken and the government eventually compromised in a plea bargain. On his confession of guilt to several felony counts, he was sentenced to a prison term of 10 years (he served 22 months) and agreed to forfeitures amounting to $600 million.[10]

In 1992 Steven D. Wymer, a money manager of International Treasury Management of Irvine, California, was accused of cheating about sixty-five municipal governments of

$100 million. He pleaded guilty to a RICO indictment and agreed to the forfeiture of his assets, as well as a prison term and steep fines. The government traced $75 million of his business assets and personal assets estimated at $10 to $15 million.[11]

A still bigger violator of RICO was James McNamara, a Long Island auto dealer who bilked General Motors out of $422 million. The government charged him with various frauds and money laundering over a period of a decade, linking his empire of real estate, mining, and commodities investment to racketeering. Federal forfeiture laws allowed the government to seize all the property used to commit crimes as well as the proceeds of the crimes. McNamara agreed to turn over close to $400 million in civil forfeitures in a special deal. Although it was one of the largest forfeitures of business assets ever approved by a civil court, McNamara managed to avoid criminal forfeitures. The government prosecutor nevertheless classified the case with that of Michael Milken and BCCI.[12]

Civil forfeiture remains the foremost device for confiscating properties used in crime or the products of it. The attractions, as always, continue to be the much lower burden of proof for the government and the fact that owners or claimants of seized property have no way to enforce their constitutional rights. In civil forfeitures, the property, which has no rights, is accused of crime and convicted on the basis of a showing of probable cause. If the claimant cannot prove the innocence of his property, he loses it. Civil forfeiture remains, as always, swift and cheap—and pretty much a sure thing.

Abuses of civil forfeiture are daily occurrences across the nation. In Suffolk County, New York, the district attorney, who presided over local forfeitures that augmented his budget by more than $3 million in a couple of years, drove a swanky BMW as his official car instead of a county car; he had seized the BMW from a drug dealer and made it his own. The *New York Times* commented, "The fact that it's legal doesn't make it right."[13] An obvious temptation to capitalize on some drug baron's holdings could corrupt. Critics find it easy to characterize such prosecutors as bounty hunters. An ACLU officer observed that the Suffolk DA was "benefiting personally from the forfeiture procedures. There is a bounty phenomenon, because the more the District Attorney seizes, the more he benefits from it." In the case of this prosecutor, James M. Catterson, the exposé revealed that he maintained sole control over the seized funds, and he alone decided how they should be used. Since the money did not consist of tax dollars, he did not feel himself to be accountable to the public. He spent the forfeiture money as he thought best for law enforcement: $300 for a gold watch for a secretary who was retiring, $3,412 for servicing the BMW, and thousands of dollars for computers and office furniture. The case revealed the existence of a fundamental constitutional problem concerning public control of public agencies and moneys that go into public tills from forfeitures. On the other hand, no moneys had to be budgeted for cars in Suffolk County after Mr. Catterson became prosecutor. He confiscated thirty-five to forty cars and turned them over to staff members and detectives for work cars.[14]

In a similar case in Somerset County, New Jersey, the prosecutor, Nicholas L. Bissell, attracted criticism for his aggressive use of forfeiture laws and the way he spent seized assets. He paid about $6,000 out of forfeiture funds for a corporate membership in a private tennis and health club for the benefit of his seventeen assistant prosecutors and fifty detectives. Bissell, like his counterpart in Suffolk County, New York, maintained complete control over the disposition and auditing of the forfeiture seizures of his county. He received some bad publicity when a local contractor, James Giuffre, went public with his story. Giuffre had been arrested on a drug charge; he was a cocaine user who got caught with half an ounce in his home. He claimed that Bissell threatened to confiscate his home and prosecute him for a felony that would result in his imprisonment for ten years and the loss of his professional license if he, Giuffre, did not agree to a deal he was offered. Giuffre had to consent to the forfeiture of some real estate lots for which he had paid $174,000 and stipulate that he had bought that property with drug moneys. When he asked to consult with a lawyer before consenting to the deal, Bissell's chief of detectives told him there would be no deal if he involved a lawyer.

Bissell's version is that Giuffre waived his right to counsel and begged for a deal that would keep him out of jail and save his home. In any case, Giuffre agreed to the forfeiture of his real estate a day after his arrest, without a formal complaint against him having been filed and without the aid of a lawyer. Bissell confiscated the real estate and then sold it for the benefit of the county to a lone bidder at a public sale for only $20,000; it soon wound up in the possession of friends of Bissell's chief of detectives, the person who made the deal with Giuffre. A licensed appraiser in the area stated that the lots should have sold for ten times the amount; a county assessor listed their market value at $147,000; and a bank made a $150,000 loan to the purchaser who put up one of the lots as collateral.[15]

Thanks to Bissell, Somerset County, which ranked thirteenth in population out of twenty-one counties in the state, ranked first in seized cash.[16] John Penn, a New Jersey legislator from Bissell's county, advocated vainly that no property can be forfeited unless its owner has first been criminally convicted. "What concerns me," he declared, "is that the police can arrest someone, and, without due process, plea-bargain someone out of his property by saying, 'Give us your property and we won't send you away to prison.'"[17]

In one case, a defendant balked when presented with a deal by Bissell's office. Gregory Fuhs, a first-time offender who was arrested for growing marijuana on his property for personal use, was held in lieu of $100,000 cash bail and threatened with the loss of his home. If he had agreed to sign over to the county $65,000 in his business and savings accounts, he could have gone free and saved his home. Believing that the $65,000 was an excessive price, Fuhs declined the offer. Bissell then seized both the $65,000 and the home, and won a conviction. Apart from the forfeitures, Fuhs spent a year in jail and paid a fine of $3,500.[18]

Civil forfeiture was supposed to be the instrument for bankrupting Mafiosi and drug kingpins. State imitations of the federal civil forfeiture laws had the same objective. But it often did not work that way. In California, for example, local prosecutors conducted over 6,000 forfeiture cases in 1992, and over 94 percent of them involved the seizure of $5,000 or less.[19] As a Seattle defense attorney said of his state's forfeiture statute, "The minute they got it in place they started applying it to the little people."[20] The Department of Justice, acting through DEA, had time and resources to fight little people, too. In a study that took ten months, two reporters for the *Pittsburgh Press* reviewed 25,000 seizures made by the DEA and examined the court documents from 510 cases. Eighty percent of the people who lost property to the federal government, they found, were never charged, and "most of the seized items weren't the luxurious playthings of drug barons, but modest homes and simple cars and hardearned savings of ordinary people."[21] The DEA's own database, wrote the reporters, conflicts with the official line that DEA targets drug barons or kingpins. Only 17 percent of the total 25,297 items seized by the DEA during an eighteen-month period ending in 1991 were valued at more than $50,000.[22]

Kevin Perry of Ossipee, New Hampshire, for example, was a gravel pit laborer and his wife was a waitress. They pleaded guilty to the misdemeanor of growing four marijuana plants behind their mobile home and paid a small fine. A month later, however, Perry received a registered letter informing him that the United States was seizing his mobile home, which was located on a dirt road and worth $22,000. It was forfeitable because it was used for "facilitating a drug crime." Perry could not believe that the government would make his family homeless for a misdemeanor for which he had already paid the penalty. He fought for his home against the United States in a fifteen-month battle, which was possible only because he found a big-hearted lawyer in Manchester. The lawyer represented Perry for a total of $400 instead of his usual $125 an hour, which would have brought the bill to $6,000. The government finally agreed to return the house for $2,500. "I took out a loan to buy back my own damn house!" Perry exclaimed. "I'm paying $155.63 a month. . . . It seemed like extortion. I thought, 'This is America?'"[23]

In a small Oregon town, police raided a residence where Debra V. Hill and her family were guests and discovered a small amount of methamphetamine in a box of clothing that she claimed did not belong to her. She had $550 in her possession from a welfare check, and the police confiscated it as drug money. She was so desperate for cash that she agreed to forfeit $250 to the district attorney in return for the remaining $300. She did not get anything back when the police dropped the drug charge.[24]

Donald A. Regan of Montvale, New Jersey, lost his new

Camaro, $40,000 in legal fees, and his good name, because he gave a lift to someone, known to the police, who had cocaine. The police arrested Regan as well as his passenger, who swore that Regan was innocent of any drug involvement. The police dropped the charges against him but kept his car. When he protested its loss, the police agreed to return it if he would pay them half the bluebook value. He refused, fought the forfeiture in court, and lost because under the law the car was an instrumentality of an intended drug deal.[25]

In another case, the FBI seized a priest's Mercury Grand Marquis on the suspicion that it belonged to a drug trafficker because the priest bought it from a car dealer involved in drug smuggling. The priest got his car back only after he hired a lawyer and proved that he had bought the car; but he had to sign an agreement not to sue the FBI.[26]

Dick Kaster, a retiree from Ventura, Iowa, was convicted of illegally catching fish, for which he was fined. Then state wildlife agents seized his $6,000 boat. He sold a bait shop and a hatchery business in order to finance a suit to recover the boat. The state "stole" it, he says with outrage. Though he fought the case to the state supreme court, he hasn't received his boat back.[27]

Therese Cheung-Seekit, a Vietnamese woman with poor English skills, tried to leave the United States in 1988 on a humanitarian trip, carrying $113,000 that she did not report to customs in Seattle. She paid a $5,000 fine. The federal government then confiscated the remainder of the money because she violated the Trading with the Enemy Act. She told a federal judge that the money was "not dirty." She had collected it from more than one hundred Vietnamese families in Seattle to take back to needy relatives. The judge castigated the federal officers but sustained the forfeiture, because the law clearly supported the government.[28]

The Weavers of Lockhart, Alabama, also had a distressing experience. Fred Weaver hired an attorney to defend him against marijuana charges. The Weavers paid him with their most valuable asset, two shacks on a vacant lot worth $18,000. The government's seizure of the shacks "chilled me out of the case," said the attorney. Weaver then gave another lawyer an old fishing boat worth less than $3,000 to challenge the seizure of the shacks. Then the government seized the boat, chilling the second lawyer out of the case. "It's sad," he said, "but I can't work for nothing. Even if we won, it wouldn't be worth it. The Weavers don't have much to begin with. They're poor people." Mrs. Weaver, who was on welfare, said, "We've had all our rights taken away. We've lost everything we ever worked for. We're down to nothing."[29] No right to an attorney exists in forfeiture cases, not even for indigents. The Weaver case starkly illustrates how the government can use forfeiture to deny people the ability to pay lawyers to defend themselves against seizure, civil or criminal. An Oregon newspaper declared that getting a lawyer might be "impossible, because if you have enough money to pay him, the government may confiscate the money as the fruits of crime."[30]

About 80 percent of all civil forfeiture cases are uncontested, quite likely because most of the suspects are in fact guilty. As Cary Copeland of the Asset Forfeiture Office said, "The last thing these people want to do is play 20 questions with the cops."[31] On the other hand, many people simply cannot afford to contest a case because of the high cost of lawyers. Legal fees in a federal case easily run to $25,000, considerably more than the value of most forfeitures. One Oakland defense attorney declared, "Sue to get your car back? Forget it. If they take your car, it's gone. Unless I get pissed off and take a case for the sweet pleasure of revenge, I'm not going to handle anything less than $75,000 in assets, from which I'd get one-third."[32]

130

Richard Apfelbaum, a Florida cosmetics salesman, also learned about the high cost of fighting a forfeiture to recover his property. He had $9,460 in a carry-on bag and was on his way to Las Vegas to gamble. DEA agents thought he acted suspiciously and asked if they could search him. Having nothing to hide, he consented; they took his money, leaving him $30 to get home. Apfelbaum spent $2,000 on legal fees and posted a bond costing 10 percent of the seizure. The government dragged out the case, forcing him to give up. "I'm not in a position to spend $10,000 in legal fees trying to get $9,000 back," he remarked.[33]

Cary Copeland asserted that no one needed a lawyer to defend against a forfeiture proceeding. "It's not that complex. It's easy enough to represent yourself."[34] In San Jose, California, however, the local newspaper found dozens of cases in which claimants without lawyers had to complete a questionnaire fourteen pages long with almost two hundred questions. They were asked for bank statements, canceled checks, and documents proving purchases, and they were obligated to endure lengthy cross-examination by prosecutors. A defense attorney remarked that seizing the money of people who never were intended to be targets of forfeiture is like "shooting fish in a barrel." The burden of proof is on the claimant to demonstrate that he obtained the seized asset legally, he said, and without the right receipt the claimant has no chance. The lawyer added that if the amount in dispute is not worth at least a couple of thousand dollars, or if the claimant does not have ironclad proof of ownership, he ought not even bother trying to make a recovery. If the property seized is cash, claimants are out of luck. They have only ten days from the time of seizure to file a claim. A day beyond that washes out one's right to contest a forfeiture. A mistake in filling out a form has the same result. One woman lost over $1,000 because she signed a form in only one rather than in both required places.[35]

Most people lose cash because no practical way exists to fight the police who simply take it in the belief or on the pretext that it is drug money. Some defense attorneys become apoplectic on the issue. "Civil forfeiture," declared the president of the National Association of Criminal Defense Attorneys, "is essentially government thievery." If the civil forfeiture laws are a license to steal, the cops are the robbers. In Washington, D.C., police shake down black men, taking their cash, even small amounts—$4 in one instance—and, of course, no arrests are made. Most often, the so-called police theft is technically legal as when the cops confiscated an $18,000 automobile as a getaway vehicle belonging to a woman who was accused of shoplifting. At airports, law enforcement officers, federal and local, routinely seize cash from travelers who supposedly fit a drug profile or look suspicious.[36]

In this connection, Congressman Henry J. Hyde of Illinois testified before a House Government Operations Committee:[37]

Please enter with me the Kafkaesque world of civil asset forfeiture. I advise you never to buy an airplane ticket at an airport for cash. This behavior will likely cause the ticket agent to alert police as to a possible "drug dealer." [The agent hopes to receive a government reward for his information.] You will be searched, and if you are carrying large amounts of cash it will be confiscated. Unfortunately for you, you fit a "drug profile." And be very careful how you leave a plane. As the *Pittsburgh Press* reported, "[DEA] agents in Illinois are told it's suspicious if their subjects are among the first people off a plane, because it shows they're in a hurry. In Michigan, the DEA says that being the last person off the plane is suspicious because the suspect is trying to appear unconcerned. And in Ohio, agents are told suspicions should surface when suspects deplane in the middle of a group because they may be trying to lose themselves in a crowd."

If you are not carrying drugs, Hyde continued, and mean to use the money at an auction where business is done only in cash, "It doesn't matter. Agents can seize your money based on probable cause that it is intended for use in a drug transaction." If you want to get the cash back, Hyde remarked, "your troubles have just begun."[38]

Archie Glasgow of St. Louis, like Willie Jones and Richard Apfelbaum, had such troubles because he carried a lot of cash in an airport. DEA agents took $66,700 from him on the supposition that it was drug money, despite his insistence that he possessed it legitimately. The agents did not press any charges against him and let him continue on his trip without the cash. They weren't trying to get criminals off the streets, only the money in the pockets of suspects. Glasgow fought the seizure in the courts and won, when a U.S. Court of Appeals ruled that the DEA acted in bad faith. Within a week of the seizure the agency knew that he meant to contest the forfeiture; they simply sought to con him by saying that he could institute his claims process when he received notification that the DEA had gotten a forfeiture ruling against his cash. The notification appeared in a newspaper some weeks later in a list of hundreds of DEA seizures. Although a federal district court ruled against Glasgow for not having filed a timely claim to recover his money, the court of appeals reversed, reasoning that Glasgow's constitutional right to property was too significant to be satisfied with the DEA's newspaper notice.[39] Either the DEA was wrong in believing that Glasgow was a suspicious character or its profile of drug agents misled it.

In Florida, the profile has a racist bias. More than 90 percent of the southbound drivers stopped on Interstate 95 in Volusia County are black or Hispanic, like Selena Washington, whose case was mentioned previously. Even if it is true that most people in Florida who engage in drug trafficking are nonwhite, the practices of Sheriff Bob Vogel and his five-man drug team in Volusia have given a new meaning to the term "highway robbery" and also provoked a suit for violation of civil rights. A Florida state representative, Elvin Martinez, informed the House Committee on Government Operations that what was happening in Volusia was "typical" in Florida "everywhere you have traffic going north and south."[40] In 76 percent of the cases in Volusia County, or 199 stops out of 262, Sheriff Bob Vogel's deputies made traffic stops and subjected drivers to searches resulting in confiscations of cash, but not of drugs. The drivers were not charged with any crime.[41] The deputies collected almost $8 million from three years of traffic stops. In a more extended study involving 1,084 drivers, only nine received traffic tickets, although all the stops were supposedly for traffic violations of some kind, such as having a dirty license tag or a burned-out light, going over the speed limit, following too closely, or making lane changes without signaling. Obviously the deputies had more in mind than traffic violations.

Nevertheless, even so hostile a critic as the *Orlando Sentinel* conceded that "it's clear that most of the $8 million seized was drug money. In a quarter of the cases, arrests were made, mostly involving drugs. Many drivers had previous drug convictions. Some didn't even argue over the seizures." Indeed, one-fourth of the drivers whose money was seized but who were not arrested were never heard from again. They were probably, as the sheriff suspected, drug couriers. The people stopped by Vogel's deputies often fit a profile of such couriers: young minority men who dress flashily, travel alone in cars with out-of-state licenses or in rented cars, drive a few miles over the speed limit, act nervously when stopped, and don't have much luggage. At night the deputies use floodlights across the highway so they can see the drivers and their cars; a lawyer said that they did not want to stop an elderly white couple with Disneyland stickers. Despite the profile, the deputies did not find drugs in three-quarters of the cases nor in any of the 199 cases in which they confiscated money but made no arrest and gave no ticket. Those cases yielded $3.8 million.[42]

All were consent searches. Innocent people are either intimidated by the police or believe they have nothing to fear from them; in either case, they agree to a search of their car and become victims. In other cases, if a driver refused consent, a suspicious deputy radioed to another deputy to bring a dog to sniff the car and establish probable cause for a search. The *Orlando Sentinel* proved that the presence of cocaine odor on currency means nothing. Reporters gave fresh money to distinguished citizens such as a police chief, college president, minister, and newspaper editor, in exchange for the bills in their wallets, and then had a lab test those bills. Sheriff Vogel refused to allow his dogs to repeat their sniff tests: "We're not going to call into question the credibility of our dogs," he said. But a toxicologist who tested the money with a gas chromatograph and then confirmed his results with a mass spectrometer discovered that except for brand new, uncirculated bills, 90 percent of the money in circulation actually tests positive for cocaine, as previously indicated. The fact that a drug-sniffing dog wags his tail or barks proves nothing.[43]

Another toxicologist arrived at similar results in broader tests. He covered many areas over a seven-year period, testing American currency. "An average of 96% of the bills we analyzed from the eleven cities tested positive for cocaine," he reported. Scientists report that they can identify the presence of narcotics on currency down to the nanogram level—one billionth of a gram, which is the same level a dog can detect with a sniff. Still another toxicologist, who spent eleven years directing the police crime laboratory in Philadelphia, cautioned against reliance on dog-sniffing because it did not prove that the owner of the money had ever been in contact with drugs. An agent of the Virginia State Police, who supervised the training of drug dogs, said that the odor from a single suitcase filled with marijuana and placed with a hundred other bags in a closed baggage car in Miami could permeate all the other bags in the baggage car by the time the train reached Richmond.[44]

Ethel Hylton, a forty-six-year-old black woman from New York City, was dog-sniffed at the Houston airport. As a result a DEA agent relieved her of the $39,110 found in her purse. She said she was in Houston to buy a house and that the money came from insurance proceeds and her savings over a twenty-year period of working as a housekeeper and janitor. She had no criminal record, and the *Pittsburgh Press*, which investigated the case, substantiated her claims. The newspaper examined 121 cases in various airports, train stations, and bus terminals in which police found no dope, made no arrests, but seized cash anyway, and in over three-quarters of the cases the victims were nonwhite.[45]

One of the Florida I-95 victims was Jose Raposa of New Bedford, Massachusetts, from whom a deputy took $19,000. Raposa hired an attorney, fought the case, proved that the money had been borrowed from a bank, and finally accepted a settlement: the sheriff retained 25 percent, the lawyer received $1,000, and Raposa got the rest. "They should have given all my money back," he said, "but the lawyer said go for the deal." Sheriff Vogel's staff included a lawyer whose full-time job was to negotiate such deals. In a similar case, Edwin Johnson, a forty-eight-year-old black businessman, was outraged by the seizure of $38,923, money from a business he had just sold. The deputy did not believe his statement that he carried cash because he didn't trust banks after having been victimized by a wage garnishment. Johnson's lawyer produced all the documents proving that the money was his and after six months persuaded him to accept a settlement, because the sheriff could "outlast" him. The sheriff's office kept $10,000 and of the rest the lawyer took one-third. Johnson was another of the sheriff's innocent victims.[46]

The entire budget for Vogel's office derives from such victims. Vogel operates without tax dollars. Moreover, he runs an expensive department at no cost to taxpayers. Able to keep all moneys that end up forfeited, he has millions to spend, and with forfeited funds has purchased high-tech narcotics equipment, computers, new cars, cellular phones and other communications devices, detectors of electronic bugs, two planes, spy cameras, new uniforms with snappy Stetsons, the best weapons, and other goodies for over $3.5 million.[47] Giving the police a financial stake in law enforcement is one of the results of our forfeiture laws. Whether police should be out raising money for their department rather than catching criminals is a fundamental question posed by these laws. No good arguments exist to justify the sort of windfalls that enrich Vogel's department or the forfeiture of money by innocent victims, regardless of race.

In Oregon, there is a joke that "driving while Hispanic is against the law." In a study made in 1991 of 6,400 highway stops made by Oregon state troopers, over a thousand drivers—a disproportionate number—were Hispanic, and in more than three-fourths of the cases in which the police seized cash yet found no drugs on the driver, the drivers were Hispanic. The state police acknowledge that Hispanic ethnicity is a factor in their profile of a drug courier but it is only one of twenty-five to thirty, they say. In that year, 1991, the state troopers seized almost $1 million in cash. That's not much compared to the forfeiture fantasyland of Los Angeles, where the police scoop up thirty times that amount annually.[48]

Oregon's state troopers, to their credit, have confiscated not only cash but large quantities of drugs. Oregon also has a state law that allows localities to enact ordinances subjecting to forfeiture automobiles used not only in the commission of drug crimes but almost any crime, including driving without a license, drunk driving, and driving to solicit prostitution. In Portland, the police seized 569 cars in one year. One man lost a $40,000 car when he stopped it to pick up a prostitute. Had he picked her up on foot, he might have lost $100 in a fine; using an automobile to violate the law disproportionately intensifies the penalty. The police must go through a civil forfeiture hearing in order to get the car forfeited, but it is not difficult. After an officer testifies that he had probable cause to make the seizure, the judge then requires the car's owner to establish innocence by proving that the car was not involved in the commission of the offense. It is the innocence of the car that must be established, because in civil forfeiture, the owner's guilt or innocence is irrelevant.[49]

At any given moment an astounding number of forfeited automobiles, thousands of them, as well as planes, jewels, boats, office buildings, houses, and all sorts of valuables are in parking lots, marinas, airfields, bank vaults, and warehouses around the nation, taken from people charged with crimes or taken because the property was somehow involved in crime whether their owners were innocent or not.

Some $2 billion in forfeited properties await disposition and the amount increases annually. Does that enormous amount and the even vaster amount that has been forfeited and utilized by the public justify the forfeiture program? Like the bread that is impossible to slice so thinly that it has only one side, there are two sides to the forfeiture problem: the official and the critical.

Cary Copeland, when the director of the Justice Department's forfeiture office, would not even grudgingly concede that some cases show injustice. He blamed critics and criminals for distorting the facts. "Allegations that there are many innocent victims of forfeiture are simply untrue," he wrote in 1993. "The Department of Justice has conducted more than 170,000 seizures since 1985, and fewer than one in 5,000 of those cases have even been criticized." Copeland's position was that not even those few should have been criticized. "In that handful of cases," he wrote, "the government's side of the cases was never presented because a balanced presentation is not sensational. Only by accepting the allegations of criminals as truthful," he added, "and failing to give the government's side can forfeiture be portrayed as harsh."[50] In public addresses, testimony before congressional committees, and letters to editors, he relished pointing out that the First Congress, which framed the Bill of Rights, initiated civil forfeiture, and the Supreme Court has often sustained its constitutionality. He regarded forfeiture as "particularly effective against the intricate financial structures developed by drug traffickers, money launderers, organized crime groups, and other complex criminal organizations." Asset forfeiture, he insisted, works well as a device of law enforcement at all levels against drug trafficking and organized crime. Forfeiture attacks criminal syndicates and their enterprises and for that reason is an "absolutely vital weapon" against them. With good reason

Congress has enacted over two hundred statutes authorizing civil forfeiture for items ranging from contaminated foods to the pelts of endangered species. Thus, "asset forfeiture has become the principal legal mechanism by which the Government recovers money and property derived from or used to facilitate designated federal felony offenses."

Fines don't work, Copeland observed; the collection rate is a mere 6 percent, largely because fines are imposed at the end of the criminal justice process, by which time most criminals have dissipated their assets or placed them beyond reach. By contrast, civil or asset forfeiture enables the government to freeze assets or seize them at the start rather than at the end of the legal process. Copeland believes, too, that as agents and prosecutors become better trained, the number of unjust forfeiture cases and innocent victims, few to begin with, diminish and the entire forfeiture process becomes fairer.[51]

Contrary to Copeland, however, forfeiture has not been a success. On June 22, 1993, he bragged to the House Committee on Government Operations that since 1985 the Justice Department had transferred over $1.2 billion in federal forfeiture proceeds to more than three thousand state and local law enforcement agencies, had added $540 million in forfeiture proceeds to federal prison construction, and had reinvested over $400 million in federal prosecutorial and investigative efforts.[52] That's a *cumulative* total of less than $2.5 billion from 1985 to 1993. Add an additional $2 billion for state and local forfeitures—a figure that is grossly excessive, and assume a cumulative total of $4.5 billion. What part is that of the profits of organized crime? No one would guess that drug trafficking is less than $100 billion a year, not cumulatively but every year. As long ago as 1987 the Subcommittee on Crime of the House Committee on the Judiciary estimated it was a $130 billion business.[53] Assume current profits of $100 billion from drug trafficking and forget all other profits of crime. Forget the many billions from illegal gambling that organized crime makes annually. Forget the profits of organized crime from infiltrating legitimate business. Forget the government's estimate that money laundering activities range from $100 billion to $300 billion annually. Forget the mindboggling profits from white-collar crime, which forfeiture supposedly threatens.[54] Compare the exaggerated *cumulative* forfeiture total mentioned above to just drug trafficking in a single year. The cumulative total of $4.5 billion in forfeitures turns out to be scant, an unimpressive amount, and, if prorated for the annual forfeiture take, is not more than a small percentage of overhead costs or the cost of engaging in the drug business, a wee fraction of the total drug trafficking take. Thus, even if one ignores the moral issue of law enforcement agencies looting from innocent people, the forfeiture program has not been successful, and it has been administered abusively. The program is necessary if only because no criminal should profit from his crime. But reforms of the laws governing forfeiture are long overdue, as is some restraint in their operation against people who are not even accused of crime, let alone convicted of it.

One reform that victims of forfeiture laws would like to see is the abolition of rewards for informers. Representative John Conyers of Michigan, past chairman of the House Government Operations Committee, has scathingly criticized the Department of Justice's practice of rewarding informers who "make cases" by tipping off federal agents about drug trafficking. Informers can get as much as 25 percent of the value of assets that are forfeited as a result of tips. Informing has become big business for which the annual Department of Justice budget provides between $20 to $25 million annually, derived from forfeiture proceeds. About two dozen informers made between $100,000 and $250,000 in 1991. At least eight informers exceeded the quarter-million dollar figure, one receiving as much as $780,000, another $591,000 in 1991. Almost anyone may be an informer—the ticket agent at an airlines counter or some sleazy underworld figure who is a regular snitch. A Hell's Angel who was a confessed drug user earned at least $250,000 from assets forfeited as a result of his information—one-fourth the total of $1 million that he received from the FBI in the late eighties.[55]

A professional thief who spent twenty-eight years in prisons wrote from first-hand knowledge about informers for the *New York Times*. He called them the "new bounty hunters" who testify against associates and also "set up drug deals." They sell drugs and then help bust their customers in order to share their property and money. The government calls that a "reverse sting." A DEA informant "has more power than an agent can ever dream of," wrote the thief. DEA snitches "under the tutelage of cynical agents lied, cheated and did whatever was necessary to make the cases and the rewards."[56]

Cary Copeland has argued that rewarding informers is good business. The Department of Justice pays no more than 25 percent to informers for the properties confiscated thanks to their tips. If informers received $30 million, he observed, that means that the department had netted $120 million in forfeited moneys, thanks to the informers.[57]

Copeland is right, but there is an additional price to be paid because of informers. Their misinformation in civil forfeiture cases can result in forfeitures. People have lost homes, businesses, and farms because informants have wrongly declared that they are involved in criminal activity. Since the individuals are not criminally prosecuted—it is only their assets that law enforcement wants—the misinformation of the informant is not tested in court. Innocent owners sometimes get their properties back; there is an innocent owners defense that can be made, as a subsequent chapter explains, but years may elapse, the properties may deteriorate, and legal costs are expensive.

Moreover, misinformation may be costly in other ways, as the case of Don Carlson reveals. He was a vice president of a Fortune 500 corporation in San Diego. DEA and Customs agents acting on a bad tip assaulted his suburban home late one night in search of drugs, hoping to obtain a forfeiture of his assets. They observed him return home, light up his garage, enter the house, and shut off all lights in the house when he went to bed. What they saw should have revealed that they had the wrong address, that the house was not vacant, and that no drugs were stored in the garage, contrary to the informant's tip. Nevertheless, according to Carlson, they stormed his home and smashed open the door, screaming obscenities, without identifying themselves as law enforcement officers.

Carlson, believing that robbers were coming at him, tried to dial 911 and fired his revolver toward the front door; the officers shot him three times. He spent six weeks in intensive care and suffered permanent circulatory loss and nerve damage, resulting in the seriously impaired use of an arm and a leg and also a paralyzed diaphragm. Needless to add, Carlson was innocent and no drugs were found in his home. The government did not apologize to him, compensate him for the damages, or pay the $350,000 for his medical bills, which will continue throughout his life. The informant, however, was indicted for supplying misinformation that was the basis of a faulty search warrant.[58] The use of informers and rewarding them from forfeiture funds is a continuing practice; as Copeland observed, it pays. It also victimizes.

Chapter Eight

Sharing Forfeiture Proceeds

After President George Bush handed a check for $1.5 million in forfeiture funds to officials in Lakewood, Colorado, for law enforcement purposes, the Lakewood police bought not only law enforcement items but also spent $1,235 on the chief's Christmas party, $208 on an aquarium, $2,100 on a buffet for policemen who worked on Labor Day, $720 on amusement park tickets, and $32,375 on banquets.[1]

Little Compton, Rhode Island, whose population of under 3,500 makes it the second smallest town in the smallest state, probably has the best police force—all seven—that money can buy. The town's share of $27 million seized from a local hashish smuggler came to over $4 million. The police chief had to be imaginative in finding ways to spend the money on law enforcement in a town that had no robberies in 1993, let alone murders or rapes. He rewarded his lieutenant, who was mainly responsible for the investigation, with a Pontiac Firebird and by funding his salary for a ten-year period, including health and retirement benefits, costing $720,000. He bought a $16,000 wood chipper for the maintenance department on the supposition that getting downed trees off the streets enabled the police to perform their duties more effectively. The same amount went for a computer, which could be used to monitor the police department's budget, and nearly as much for truck maintenance.

The town's drug awareness program benefited from $484 spent on teddy bears, and the whole town enjoyed the fireworks on the Fourth of July paid for by the police chief. Although he believed that the guidelines on spending the money were not very restrictive or clear, he understood that for a new building that would serve the fire department, as well as his own, he needed permission from the Department of Justice—and got it. That item was budgeted at nearly $1 million. Of course, he also outfitted his force with police necessities such as new weapons, bulletproof vests, cellular phones, video cameras, and heat-sensing devices to seek out hidden criminals.[2]

Lakewood and Little Compton received their money from the Department of Justice under the Comprehensive Forfeiture Act of 1984, which provided for "equitable sharing" of forfeiture proceeds. The act revolutionized forfeiture proceedings in the nation in several ways, among them equitable sharing. Under equitable sharing a community involved in a seizure of assets relating to a crime (almost any federal felony can result in forfeiture) receives part of the value of those assets, on condition that the money is spent only on law enforcement.

Representative John Conyers of the House Committee on Government Operations said, "However, no one monitors what that spending actually is. In fact, we now know that the basic rule of thumb for the Justice Department in providing spending guidance is whether it can pass two tests: (1) The Straight Face Test, which asks, Can you tell me this with a straight face? And (2) The *Washington Post* Test, which asks: If taken out of context and put on the front page of the *Washington Post*, will it still look good?"[3] The Lakewood and Little Compton experiences doubtlessly justify the sarcasm, but in fact they are aberrational. Such abuses are unusual if not rare.[4] On the other hand a 1992 study by the General Accounting Office showed that seven out of fifteen law enforcement agencies found federal guidance on how to spend forfeiture moneys "to be vague and confusing."[5]

Cary Copeland, when director of the Justice Department's Executive Office for Asset Forfeiture, in testimony offered in 1992 before a House committee, declared that the 1984 statute brought forfeiture into the twentieth century because it transformed the way the government handled revenues from forfeitures and fines. Until then all money and properties deriving from federal fines and forfeitures had to be deposited in the general treasury, and Congress, by appropriations, spent the money for purposes authorized by its enactments.

One of the innovations of 1984 was the creation of two funds, the Assets Forfeiture Fund of the Justice Department and the Customs Service Fund, now the Treasury Fund. Their existence permits the collection, administration, and distribution of federal forfeiture proceeds under centralized controls, and also allows all such proceeds to be reinvested in law enforcement. In addition the fund underwrites a variety of costs, including the costs of storing and maintaining forfeited assets. Sometimes, the government discovers that the real property it has confiscated has a mortgage that must be paid or that the business it has confiscated has bills to pay; the government must pay all such costs in order to prevent losses when selling the real estate or business. Until the Customs Service learned that properties must be cared for, the government neglected the seized vessels in the Miami River and lost tens of thousands of dollars while they deteriorated. The government could not sell them to recoup costs; moreover the scenic waterway, clogged with rotting ships, became an environmental menace and a floating junkyard.[6] The Assets Forfeiture Fund provides moneys to keep forfeited assets in good condition so that the government can realize a profit on their sale.[7]

The fund also enables all federal law enforcement agencies to share in the spoils. If the Immigration and Naturalization Service is responsible for a forfeiture, it benefits from a proportionate augmentation of its budget. The Justice Department may transfer forfeiture moneys to any federal agency to the extent of its involvement in a particular seizure and forfeiture. The department may also draw on the fund for the purpose of paying for the vessels, vehicles, and aircraft that law enforcement agencies use; they must be bought, maintained, and equipped for law enforcement purposes. Sometimes the Justice Department even provides a federal agency with a usable car or helicopter that was once the property of a federal felon, most likely a drug trafficker. The department's fund also pays rewards to informers, contributes to the costs of erecting new penitentiaries, and pays for any remissions and mitigations that have been authorized.

Equitable sharing of proceeds was another innovation of the Comprehensive Forfeiture Act, allowing the United States to divide with state and local law enforcement agencies the assets of the forfeiture fund. Nothing revolutionized forfeiture in this country as much as equitable sharing. Its impact has been enormous, because it provides an intense incentive for law enforcement agencies at the state and local levels to search for assets connected with crime and to seize them for forfeiture. The incentive is self-aggrandizement: what the police take they will likely get to keep for their departments under federal law. Under state law, which varies, they might not profit from cracking down on criminal activity that yields forfeitable assets or they might not profit as much. Under federal law, however, they are entitled to a kickback that now is 80 percent and until late 1989 was 90 percent.[8]

The Department of Justice may transfer to a state or local

147

law enforcement agency confiscated properties and moneys from the fund, subject to several considerations specified in the act of 1984. The share must be equitable in the sense that it bears a reasonable relationship to the degree of the participation by the state or local agency in the law enforcement operation that resulted in the confiscation, and the transfer should encourage further cooperation between the United States and the members of the federal system.

Fostering such cooperation is one of the three fundamental goals of the Justice Department's forfeiture program. The first is law enforcement: the punishment and deterrence of criminal activity by depriving criminals of property used or acquired through illegal conduct. Cooperation among law enforcement agencies through equitable sharing of forfeiture assets is the second goal; the third is producing revenue to finance law enforcement.

Another restriction on equitable sharing is that the Department of Justice shall not transfer any money unless it is to be used for law enforcement purposes; moreover, equitable sharing must increase rather than decrease the budget of the agency involved in the forfeiture. The actual amount to be transferred from the department fund to the state or local agency depends on the directness of that agency's participation in the forfeiture operation and on whether it originated the information leading to the seizure, provided indispensable assistance, and identified the assets for seizure. The approved uses of shared moneys include the purchase of vehicles, weapons, protective equipment, and equipment for investigative communications. They also include the payment of first-year salaries and overtime for law enforcement officers, expenses for training them, the use of reward money, and costs connected with building and operating prisons.

Even if the United States did not act jointly with state

or local law enforcement agencies in a particular operation resulting in confiscation, the locals may still benefit from cooperating with the feds by a process called "adoptive" forfeiture. Although the state or local agency was entirely responsible for a seizure, it might reap advantages by turning the case over to the United States to process the actual forfeiture. The United States, which has adopted the case, skims off a small percentage of the proceeds and returns the rest to the agency that made the seizure. The federal share in an adoption case was initially 10 percent but was increased to 20 percent if the property was judicially contested. The adoption case must involve seized property that is forfeitable under federal law and meets a certain minimum value. Real property, for example, must be worth at least $20,000, a vehicle at least $5,000.[9]

Why would a state or local law enforcement agency responsible for a seizure be willing to turn it over to the United States for adoption, resulting in the loss of a percentage of the entire amount? Greed. Giving a case up for adoption avoids the consequences of conducting the forfeiture under state law, which directs the disposition of the proceeds. In the District of Columbia, which Congress itself controls, forfeiture moneys go into a fund for drug abuse prevention, the rehabilitation of addicts, and public education. In a dozen states the amount of money that can be returned to law enforcement is expressly limited, ranging from only 10 percent in New Hampshire to 50 percent in Massachusetts. California allots 65 percent to the entities participating in the seizure but that allows a cut for prosecutors' offices. Law enforcement in every one of those dozen states would gain considerably more by turning cases over to the United States for adoption.

The laws of only seven states (Alaska, Delaware, Maine, Michigan, Montana, Ohio, and Texas) provide for all forfeiture moneys to be assigned to law enforcement. Only those seven states have laws that do not provoke their sheriffs and police to turn to the feds, yet even in those seven the particular police department making a seizure has no guarantee that it will get more than a proportionate share of the proceeds. However, if it turns the case over to the Justice Department for adoption, Justice takes only 15 to 20 percent (formerly, 10 percent) and all the rest goes to the particular department. In twenty states, whose laws govern the disposition of such moneys, no provision whatever is made for any moneys to go to law enforcement. The moneys are earmarked for other purposes or go into the general fund. Eleven states have no law on the subject, making insecure the chances that law enforcement, let alone the seizing agency, would get a share of forfeiture moneys. Thus in every state in the Union and the District of Columbia, state and local law enforcement agencies have a powerful incentive to request federal adoption of all cases in which those agencies had single-handedly made a seizure.[10] An Oklahoma prosecutor, who headed the National District Attorneys Association, complained that the adoption program diminished the forfeiture revenues of his department, because if the local police had let state law govern their seizures, his department would have been cut in for a share. The police, however, chose adoption to avoid sharing with the prosecutor.[11]

Not surprisingly, a Justice Department survey revealed that law enforcement recipients were nearly unanimous in the beliefs that the equitable sharing stimulated cooperation between federal and local officers and that their share of forfeiture moneys significantly aided their ability to fight crime. A North Carolina law enforcement official probably expressed a common opinion when he told a congressional committee, "Gentlemen, forfeiture sharing or equitable sharing is probably the best law Congress has ever passed, as it applies to State and local government to foster cooperation."[12]

Because of equitable sharing and adoption, which is a form of equitable sharing, the United States has deposited over $1 billion with state and local law enforcement agencies since the Comprehensive Forfeiture Act of 1984 went into effect. That act made possible stupendous increases in the amount that the United States confiscated in cash and saleable properties, a total of nearly $3 billion through 1992 and an additional reservoir of almost $2 billion in unsold physical assets.[13] Before 1984 federal forfeiture income was severely limited and the law enforcement agencies of state and local government received not one dollar from the United States. After the 1970 legislation, the United States could confiscate all conveyances used to facilitate drug crimes, all raw materials for the making of drugs, and anything used to produce or store them. In 1978 the Psychotropic Substances Act considerably expanded the assets forfeitable for drug offenses by adding all moneys and proceeds from drug crimes. As a result federal forfeiture income zoomed. Through 1978 only about $30 million had been forfeited under all federal statutes, criminal and civil. During the first year that the act of 1978 was effective, the value of DEA forfeitures increased twentyfold.[14]

Even so, before the act of 1984 became effective, said a Justice Department official in 1988, "we counted federal forfeitures in the tens of millions of dollars. Today . . . we count federal forfeitures in the hundreds of millions of dollars."[15] Forfeiture receipts have just about doubled every year from 1985, making the share of state and local law enforcement agencies increase explosively. Since 1990, they have received annually about 40 percent of the total deposits in the Asset Forfeiture Fund. That 40 percent is now almost $300 million a year.[16] About 3,500 police departments and 1,250 sheriff departments, especially those in large population centers, have benefited from equitable sharing and adoption. Prosecutors' offices have also profited, not just from federal funds but also from increased numbers of prosecutors. The number of successful forfeiture cases and the income they bring help determine the size of staffs. More money means more prosecutors, which in turn means more forfeiture cases, because prosecutors have quotas to fill and budget projections to satisfy.

Giving a stake in forfeiture moneys to police and prosecutors entails considerable risk of corrupting law enforcement's values as well as skewing policy. A senior official in the Customs Service remarked that if the police had "a guy with a ton of marijuana and no assets versus a guy with two joints and a Lear jet, I guarantee you they'll bust the guy with the Lear jet."[17] At the least the police becomes dominated by revenue enhancement that benefits them, diverting them from law enforcement for its own sake. Law enforcement becomes subordinated to making money for one's department. The interests of justice, which law enforcement is supposed to uphold, can erode. Money influences. It makes mercenary instincts prevail over other considerations. Thus, civil forfeiture overwhelmingly dominates criminal forfeiture: the criminal isn't prosecuted; his assets in the form of proceeds and instrumentalities are prosecuted, convicted, and forfeited. Also, the police become highwaymen, stripping people of their valuables, then allowing them to go on their way. A federal district court made the point too delicately, saying: "More and more courts are voicing frustration at what appears to be overreaching by the United States in the drug war, particularly in forfeiture cases where law enforcement agencies have a 'built-in' conflict of interest because they share in the product of seizure."[18]

152

Representative John Conyers called forfeiture a "cash cow" that distorted law enforcement's priorities. "We're getting cash off the streets instead of drugs," he said.[19] If the police had nothing to gain from forfeiture, they would more likely be fighting crime than looking for assets to confiscate in order to satisfy their profit motive.

Michael Zeldin, once the director of the Justice Department's Executive Office for Asset Forfeiture, declared in 1993 that "the desire to deposit money into the asset forfeiture fund became the reason for being of forfeiture, eclipsing in certain measure the desire to effect fair enforcement of the laws as a matter of pure law enforcement objectives."[20] He accused his successor, Cary Copeland, of managing the forfeiture office "with an eye toward maximizing moneys in the fund, rather than good law enforcement." Forfeiture "horror stories," he reported, were common after Copeland promised that if Congress would pay for more federal prosecutors (he got 175 of them), they "would be used to generate money through asset forfeiture. Their marching orders were, 'Forfeit, forfeit, forfeit. Get money, get money, get money.'"[21]

The reason for the emphasis on money was that the projected forfeiture revenues for the department usually exceeded actual revenues. Attorney General Richard L. Thornburgh notified all federal attorneys in 1990, "We must significantly increase production to reach our budget target. . . . Failure to achieve the $470 million projection would expose the Department's forfeiture program to criticism and undermine confidence in our budget projections."[22] A Justice Department law enforcement official wrote, "Increasingly, you're seeing supervisors of cases saying, 'Well, what can we seize?' when they're trying to decide what to investigate. . . . They're paying more attention to the revenues they can get . . . and it's skewing the cases they get involved in."[23] In a 1992 study by the General Accounting

Office on how state and local police use shared assets, the first item on a list of sixteen was "police officer salaries and overtime."[24] But in a 1994 Department of Justice *Guide to Equitable Sharing*, the payment of salaries for existing officers is declared to be "impermissible." Only new and temporary officers may receive their salaries from shared funds and all officers may receive overtime from them.[25] The war on crime and drug trafficking becomes distorted when its policies are shaped by the lure of forfeiture proceeds instead of the objective of curbing illegal activity.

The department's adoption policy not only circumvents state forfeiture laws but undermines them. For that reason adoption has been the subject of considerable criticism from state supporters. Representative William J. Hughes of Florida, for example, spoke of the police subverting state policy when they sought federal adoption.[26] Accordingly, Congress intended to curtail adoption sharply beginning October 1, 1989, by providing that the attorney general should be certain that "property is not transferred following utilization of an adopted seizure process to circumvent any requirement of State law that limits the disposition of property forfeited to State or local agencies."[27]

Not surprisingly, law enforcement, which exuberantly supported equitable distribution and adoption, vehemently opposed a change in Justice Department policy. The head of a state crime control department, who spoke for the National Criminal Justice Association, said that all the police executives he had talked to were "scared to death" that Congress would take away equitable forfeiture.[28] He had the audacity to state that if the attempt to curtail adoption policy went into effect, it would "discourage state and local law enforcement agencies from cooperating with federal enforcement officials in investigating and prosecuting cases involving drug violations."[29] The same officer complained that his state's law assigned all forfeiture moneys to education, and he warned of "devastating impact" on cooperative law enforcement if the state law became operative because of the abolition of adoption.

Somehow there is something shocking in the notion that unless the cops are rewarded with a financial bonus they will not do everything possible to suppress criminal activities—indeed that they will not cooperate against racketeers and drug traffickers. In 1970 when Congress enacted forfeiture legislation in connection with the RICO and CCE acts, the purpose of forfeiture was to throttle the economic basis of the criminals. It became an end in itself as a support of police budgets, connected to the threat that if the revenue did not go to the police, they lacked incentive to enforce the law against crime.

An exchange between a congressman and a federal attorney is revealing. The congressman observed that in the preceding year, 1987, California had received about $48 million in adoptive forfeiture funds out of a total of $117 million. He asked the federal attorney to explain "the extensive use of adoptive forfeiture" by California and why it should have qualified for almost half of the money. The federal attorney explained that under California law, the proceeds of forfeited property did not go back to law enforcement. "The money in California, as I understand it, goes to a mental health fund of some sort. Therefore, there are not as many incentives on the part of State and local law enforcement to use their own State procedures. So, what we have in California is an inordinate amount of cases that are being pursued through the adoptive forfeiture process." The congressman wanted to know if the attorney implied that abolition of adoption would result in less money being forfeited. The attorney said, "Yes sir, in California particularly." The congressman concluded, "What you are telling me basically is that the Federal Government is complicit with the law enforcement agencies in California in trying to in essence subvert the California State passed law." If the Justice Department did that in his state, the congressman added, he would be "furious." "The Federal Government is literally trying to subvert the State law" by preventing forfeiture funds, seized by state and local officers, from going to purposes designated by state law.[30]

Notwithstanding the congressman's outrage, the pressure on Congress from police officers around the nation and the International Association of Chiefs of Police was too much. Congress first postponed for two years the time that its legislation on adoptive forfeiture would go into effect and then quietly revoked the measure, leaving adoption in full force.[31] All the temptations for police departments to abuse the forfeiture program continue.

Cary Copeland, as director of the Department of Justice's forfeiture office, flatly asserted in 1993, "Abuses are not occurring in the federal forfeiture program," a statement published appropriately on April Fool's Day.[32] He added that the United States government could not be responsible for abuses by state and local law enforcement agencies. In fact, however, equitable sharing and adoption, which are federal programs, reward state and local abuses. It is true, though, that most of the abuses associated with forfeiture originate with state and local law enforcement agencies rather than federal officers. The United States condones those abuses by rewarding them, but its own act is getting cleaner. Generally speaking, federal officers, whether from FBI, DEA, Customs, the U.S. Marshals Service, Immigration and Naturalization, Treasury, or Justice Department prosecutors, are better trained and supervised and more law-abiding than their counterparts on the state and local level. Federal officials still make mistakes, but most of their flagrant abuses belong to the earlier years and have since been corrected, or, at least, steps have been taken to diminish their reoccurrence. A dozen drug deputies of the Los Angeles County Sheriff's Department were convicted in 1993 for routinely falsifying reports to show the existence of probable cause for seizures of cash and for stealing about $60 million.[33] No federal analogy exists.

Copeland eagerly pointed out that the federal program was improving in ways that made old abuses unlikely to recur. In testimony before Congress in 1992 he proudly asserted, "Federal law enforcement agents are the most carefully selected, highly educated, and well-trained in the world." Federal agencies that engaged in forfeiture were once ignorant and untrained, as the GAO study of 1981 had revealed, but by the close of the 1980s they possessed specialized seizure and forfeiture teams throughout the nation. The Justice Department's investigators and prosecutors benefited from similar specialized training. The department spent about $6 million annually to develop such personnel.[34]

An officer from the criminal division of the Justice Department testified in 1988 that the department had made "great progress" in training its personnel in the forfeiture matters, thanks to the availability of money from the assets forfeiture fund to pay for the teaching programs. The department sponsored biannual national conferences whose objectives were to enhance the expertise of United States Attorneys in forfeitures and related matters. Specialized manuals existed for agents and prosecutors.[35]

The Justice Department also hired private counsel for nonlitigable matters requiring special knowledge in corporate, real estate, banking, and securities law. Bankers too helped in matters involving money laundering. The FBI ran its own training programs in forfeiture for its agents.

157

Copeland in 1989 bragged about adding 175 new assistant U.S. Attorneys, plus support staff, all of whom would be trained as forfeiture specialists. The department was even developing video training materials.[36]

The U.S. Marshals Service, which administers the Assets Forfeiture Fund, has its own handbook on the management of seized assets and conducts training conferences concerning the management of real property and different kinds of businesses. The United States has confiscated fraternity houses at the University of Virginia, a ranch with Paso Fino horses, a Long Island pet cemetery that sold for $650,000, multimillion-dollar Miami Beach homes, and the world's largest card casino, in Bell Gardens, California, worth $100 million—and the marshals have managed all of these. They have also managed gas stations, banks, ranches, office buildings, apartment complexes, floral shops, recording studios, drug stores, marinas, foundries, and almost every sort of imaginable property. They have become expert and know how to pass on their experience.[37]

Copeland claimed in 1992 that the department's forfeiture program was based on two principles: to confiscate wealth that criminal activity used or produced, and "to protect innocent owners from unfair application of forfeiture laws." "In sum," he testified, "our asset forfeiture program is staffed with the most highly trained personnel in all of law enforcement."[38] Along the same lines, he testified a year later, in 1993, that among recently adopted policies was one aimed at expediting payments to innocent property holders whose property should be returned. Indigent parties who could not afford to post bond could file *in forma pauperis* petitions to get a waiver of the bond requirement in order to contest forfeitures. In words not characteristic of Copeland, he said the department was seeking to examine those pauper petitions "fairly" and to grant them where appropriate. Similarly the department has adopted a model national code of professional conduct for asset forfeiture, which Copeland described as "The Ten Commandments for Asset Forfeiture."[39]

The new code is intended for all law enforcement officers, including those in state and local departments who had made "questionable seizures." Such seizure jeopardized public confidence in forfeiture proceedings, Copeland remarked, and consequently the Justice Department meant to provide leadership for police officers everywhere. The first of the "Ten Commandments" of the new national code is: "Law enforcement is the principal objective of forfeiture. Potential revenue must not be allowed to jeopardize the effective investigation and prosecution of criminal offenses, officer safety, the integrity of ongoing investigations, or the due process rights of citizens." Some of the other commandments provide that the salary of prosecutors and law enforcement officers should not depend on forfeitures; whenever practicable, and always in cases involving real property, officers should seek to establish probable cause before a judicial officer; officers should rely on a manual on seizure and forfeiture; attention should be given to the claims of innocent owners; forfeiture proceeds should be kept in a separate fund and be accountable; seized property should be managed to protect its value; "seizing entities shall avoid any appearance of impropriety in the sale or acquisition of forfeited property."[40]

In his effort to show that the Justice Department was concerned with fairness and sought to avoid abuse, Copeland even informed the House committee that the department was aware of concerns about the probity of "drug dog alert on currency." New "state-of-the-art equipment" was being acquired to permit a scientific backup test to dog alerts in currency seizures. No one asked him what difference such a test could make if most currency in circulation did in fact show drug traces. Apart from the meaningless practice of dog alerts on drugs, no doubt can exist that at the federal level abuses in the administration of the forfeiture program have diminished. Federal officials have become more sensitized to the issue of abuse and the potential unfairness toward innocent owners. But the unfairness inherent in the system remains: so long as innocence is an irrelevant consideration to the question of whether property is guilty, injustices will continue.

Chapter Nine

The Innocent Owner's Defense

The worst feature of forfeiture, both civil and criminal, is its failure to provide adequately for the rights of innocent people. Civil forfeiture is inherently hostile to the innocent because the owner's innocence simply does not matter. Not he but his property is the target of the legal proceeding. On the mere showing of probable cause, which can be established with circumstantial evidence, hearsay ("in whole or in part"), or an anonymous informant's tip,[1] the owner or claimant of the property must show by a preponderance of evidence that the property is "innocent" in the sense that it is not booty, or a means of committing a crime, or an asset acquired with criminal proceeds.[2] The burden of proof shifts to the owner or claimant as soon as the government discharges its relatively simple obligation to show probable cause. Shifting the burden of proof turns upside down the presumption of innocence. The property is presumed guilty until the owner can show that it is innocent.

Thus, in the major Supreme Court case involving civil forfeiture, the Supreme Court upheld the forfeiture of a vessel that had been leased to someone who smoked a marijuana cigarette on board without the knowledge of the owner of the vessel. The owner had merely rented the vessel to the smoker, but the owner's innocence is not a defense. The Court expressed the harsh belief that the loss of the vessel would teach the owner to exercise greater caution before renting it. But the Court did not state what the owner might or should have done to exercise such caution. The Court made much of the fact that the owner could not plead that the vessel had been taken without his knowledge or consent; he must therefore show that he had taken all reasonably prudent steps to prevent illegal substances from being used aboard the vessel. Only then might the outcome have been different, but the nature of those prudent steps remains a mystery.[3]

The case is important, though, not just for the holding that due process does not require a hearing before the owner of the vessel loses it to forfeiture. It is important too because the Court, by obiter dicta, suggested standards, tough standards, that offered some protection to the innocent. If the property had been used "without his privity or consent" and if he was not only "uninvolved in and unaware of the wrongful activity, but also that he had done all that reasonably could be expected to prevent the proscribed use of his property," he could get it back.[4]

The overwhelming majority of the nearly two hundred civil forfeiture statutes of the United States contain no innocent owner defense. In cases arising under those statutes, the Supreme Court's severe standards apply. Innocent owners must show that they have done everything reasonably expected to prevent the misuse of their property. In the most important and most frequently enforced civil forfeiture statutes, involving conveyances, proceeds, and real property, Congress has provided an innocent owner defense that is more liberal than the Court's. Congress requires proof that the owner neither knew nor agreed to the illegal use; it does not demand proof that all reasonable steps were taken to prevent the illegal use of the property. But even Congress's requirement is burdensome. In civil forfeiture the innocent owner is always greatly disadvantaged.

162

So too, others who are third parties are disadvantaged; they may have a stake in the property as well as the owner who seeks to prove his innocence. Those third parties whose interests may be injured when the government takes property by forfeiture include co-owners, bona fide purchasers, lien holders, secured creditors, garnishees, and assignees. Initially the only innocent owner defense available to anyone in a civil forfeiture case was proof that the illegally used or acquired property had been stolen. If, however, it had been lawfully borrowed or loaned and then became involved in a crime, the owner's innocence and ignorance did not matter; the property was forfeited.[5] Then in 1978 Congress liberalized the Court's standards by allowing a party to plead that the illegal act had occurred "without the knowledge or consent" of the owner.[6] Under the congressional rule the innocent owner had no obligation to prove that he took all reasonable steps to prevent the illegal use of his property.

If the owner did not know of the illegal activity engaged in by another person using his property or did not consent to it, his property would not be forfeited. Courts divided, however, on the question of whether the innocent owner had the obligation of proving both a lack of knowledge and a lack of consent or just one of the two. The act of Congress uses "or," meaning one or the other, but some federal courts require a showing of both. They reject the innocent owner defense even if it reveals that although the individual knew of the illegal activity, he refused to consent to it.[7] In other federal courts a person who knows of the illegal use of his property may avoid forfeiture if he can prove that he did not consent.[8]

The federal courts do not agree or clarify what they want of claimants. The question is, what constitutes an adequate innocent owner defense? Some courts even add to the congressional standard the one suggested by the Supreme

Court, requiring that, in addition to the owner's proof that he did not know of or consent to the illegal activity, he took all reasonable steps to prevent it.[9] Those courts believe that the only way to prove that the owner did not consent is for him to demonstrate that he took all reasonable steps to prevent the illegal activity. What those steps are seems to vary from case to case, but several federal courts agree that "the claimant must demonstrate both that it lacked actual knowledge and that it did everything reasonably possible to ascertain whether the property is subject to forfeiture."[10] The Fifth Circuit Court of Appeals prefers to decide each case on the basis of its facts without applying a fixed standard to them. That court said that the Supreme Court had merely advanced a nonbinding suggestion that did not aid "in determining whether a statute that does provide such a defense requires the owner to lack actual knowledge only or also lack knowledge that could have been acquired by nonnegligent conduct."[11]

The federal courts simply have not clearly or uniformly explained the innocent owner defense, and Congress has not intervened to settle the matter. Whatever that defense is, it was not satisfactorily advanced by the woman who knew that her son had a criminal record for drug dealing but permitted him to keep the car keys. She forfeited the car because he used it to facilitate a drug transaction. Another owner lost his car because the friend whom he allowed to use it had a criminal record known to him, making irrelevant the fact that the owner did not even know and could do nothing about the fact that another person borrowed it from his friend to consummate a drug deal. Although the car was taken without the owner's knowledge or consent, the user did not steal it and returned it after using it. Only if the car had been stolen would the owner's innocence have mattered.[12] On the other hand, the innocent owner defense

164

prevailed over the government in the case of a woman who allowed her ex-husband to drive her car to show it to a prospective buyer, and the ex-husband used the car to carry an illegal drug that he intended to sell.[13]

In 1988, Congress amended the innocent owner defense in conveyance cases involving drug trafficking. In addition to showing a lack of knowledge or consent concerning the infraction, the individual claiming innocent ownership must also show that it had been committed without his "willful blindness."[14] Congress did not want anyone closing his eyes to a violation. That is, the innocence of the party relying on the innocent owner's defense must be clear. In one case showing willful blindness, a woman tried to preserve her interest in her home by relying on the rule that neither a husband nor a wife can alienate the other's interest in jointly held property. She claimed not to know of her husband's involvement with drug dealing. Yet he kept substantial amounts of cocaine in their house and sold cocaine from the premises over a four-year period. The court concluded that she either knew of her husband's guilt or deliberately blinded herself to it.[15]

As part of the 1988 statute, Congress provided that anyone using very small quantities of drugs for personal use or growing a little marijuana for personal use should not be victimized by forfeiture. The public had become outraged by the so-called zero-tolerance policy of the Reagan administration. The DEA had been seizing valuable assets on finding infinitesimal amounts of controlled substances. Thus, home and farms had been civilly forfeited because the owners had grown a few marijuana plants for their private consumption, without any involvement in trafficking, and expensive yachts had been forfeited because federal agents had discovered 1/100 of an ounce of marijuana in one case and 1/28 of an ounce in another.[16] By its 1988 legislation,

Congress governed the maximum amount of each kind of drug that might be personally used without forfeiture, so that the innocent owner defense in such cases depends in part on the amount involved.

In a criminal forfeiture case innocence is a complete defense for the defendant. But others may have a stake in the property as well: third parties who stand to lose because of forfeiture in the event of a conviction. As in a civil case, the third parties include lien holders, bona fide purchasers, co-owners, and the like. Their interests in the property may be sacrificed in a criminal forfeiture case as well as a civil one. According to the 1970 legislation establishing criminal forfeiture, the government had the obligation of disposing of the forfeited property in a commercially feasible manner, "making due provision for the rights of innocent persons." Neither the RICO nor CCE acts of 1970 indicated how to make that provision, and Congress failed to remedy that situation until the Comprehensive Forfeiture Act of 1984.[17]

By that act Congress belatedly amended the 1970 acts by providing for an ancillary hearing to protect third-party interests, after a guilty verdict. Interested third parties have thirty days, from the government's publication of its intent to dispose of the property, to petition for a judicial hearing to preserve their interests in the property. No jury trial is possible. The party may prove a legal interest in the property prior to the commission of the crime that led to the prosecution and forfeiture, or he may prove a superior interest to that of the defendant. If, however, he obtained his interest following the commission of the crime, he must prove that he is a "bona fide purchaser for value" of the contested property and has no reason to believe that it was forfeitable.[18] The third parties are in the same position as a claimant in a civil forfeiture case, in the sense that the burden of proof is wholly upon them to show their legal interest by a preponderance of evidence—a standard usually used only in civil cases.

Ever since the Comprehensive Forfeiture Act of 1984, the relation-back doctrine has applied in criminal as well as civil cases.[19] That means, according to the government, that it takes title to the property at the instant it is used or acquired illegally or is bought with illegal proceeds. However, the government must perfect its title by winning its suit to have a court forfeit the property; theoretically the defendant lost his title when he committed the crime. That means that he had no legal right to sell or assign it and that anyone who acquired it, even if utterly unknowing of its involvement in crime, could not have taken title. If the third party can prove that he obtained his interest in the property *before* its illegal use or acquisition, he can prove his innocence. But if the third party's interest dates from any moment *after* the commission of the crime, it belongs to the government if it wins court approval. The third party cannot acquire what was not the first owner's to sell following its acquisition by the government. The period between the moment of the crime and judicial forfeiture is a hazy one as to legal ownership.[20]

The act of 1984 that made the relation-back doctrine applicable in criminal cases omitted an innocent owner defense. That defense operates in civil cases involving the relation-back doctrine. However, in criminal cases a third party who is innocent or any innocent owner is not entirely without legal claim and may get a hearing, because some courts have mitigated the harshness of the relation-back doctrine. As the manual for DEA agents says, "There have always been judges and juries that refuse to follow the law. Unable to accept the harshness of forfeiting a non-negligent person's property . . . they have defied or 'bent' the law to prevent forfeitures."[21] However, for the most part the lack of a clear innocent owner defense operates to permit forfeiture of property belonging to a completely innocent person.

For example, the relation-back doctrine defeated the innocent owners' claim in an interesting inheritance case. A man who was a drug smuggler left a multimillion-dollar estate to his four daughters in Jamaica. The court acknowledged that they were uninvolved in their father's crimes, but because the government had obtained the forfeiture of the properties as drug proceeds, the subsequent bequest to the heirs was devoid of legality. In this instance the innocent owner defense protected only the interests of those who had a legal stake in the property before the relation-back doctrine went into operation.[22] The court refused to allow the heirs to profit from their father's crimes, and they did not come within the language of the statute protecting bona fide purchasers.

In cases of lien holders whose claim to assets predate their seizure, judicial opinion differs. A controversy exists over whether the innocent lien holder should receive benefits only before the commission of the act that triggers the relation-back doctrine, or whether he can also benefit from that moment to the actual seizure of the property; the seizure may come much later. In one case, the federal court would not ignore the principle that the relation-back doctrine entitled the government to the property at the moment of its illegal use, yet the court allowed the lien holder to receive interest payments from the time of the illegal act to the time of the seizure.[23]

In another case the lien holder's stake in the asset preceded not only the seizure but the illegal activity, giving him a clear innocent owner's defense that obliged the government to pay him interest until it returned all the principal. The government, having become entitled to the property by forfeiture, had the same obligations as the original mortgagor whom it superseded.[24] If property is subject to forfeiture, the innocent lien holder may not have a right to foreclose on a delinquent mortgagee. The federal courts differ on this issue, some holding for the government and against the lender of the mortgage despite his innocence with respect to the criminal conduct that provoked government forfeiture.[25]

In the most notorious case involving lien holders, Mr. and Mrs. Carl Sheldon of Moraga, California, the government lost in the long run after having inflicted considerable damage. The Sheldons sold their home and, taking back a deed of trust on it from the buyer, became the mortgage holder on the house. Several years later the buyer was convicted of a crime, and the United States obtained the house by criminal forfeiture, despite the Sheldon's prior claim. The Sheldons were unable to collect mortgage payments and could not foreclose on the government. They fought the government and eventually, as innocent lien holders, got the house back only to discover that the government had allowed the house to deteriorate so badly that repairs cost more than the sale price. The Sheldons then claimed that they were entitled to collect the costs for what in effect had been a government taking in violation of the Fifth Amendment's guarantee that no property can be taken but for just compensation. The government rightly contended that a forfeiture should be distinguished from a taking, but because it had prevented an innocent lien holder from foreclosing on the mortgage and had so badly neglected the property, the court required the government to compensate the Sheldons. However, if the government had obtained the property in a civil forfeiture case, rather than a criminal one, the court said it would have decided the other way.[26] Accordingly, the victory for innocent ownership was distinctly limited; moreover, if the government had not neglected the property, it would have been wholly exempt from the just compensation clause of the Fifth Amendment.

In a criminal case, the relation-back doctrine is only part of the innocent owner's problem, because he is not a party to the prosecution and cannot petition for a hearing until after the prosecution has been concluded and a jury has returned a special verdict awarding forfeiture to the government. The government, which has seized the property, has five years before deciding whether to prosecute. Even if the prosecution is more timely, under the best of circumstances, cases wend their way through the system slowly. The property can be mismanaged or uncared for during that time, with the result that it may deteriorate and its value diminish. If the purchaser of a building is a drug dealer, the building's seller, who may have depended on the mortgage payments, might find that should the government confiscate the building, he or she cannot sell it, cannot rent it, and may have lost it altogether.

Moreover, the judgment of forfeiture in a criminal case is based on a jury's determination that the defendant is guilty and that beyond all reasonable doubt the property was somehow involved in the crime. Because "beyond all reasonable doubt" is the highest burden of proof, the burden on the co-owner or bona fide purchaser to establish his own innocence seems worse than if he had merely to counter the government's showing of probable cause. Indeed, since the government would not likely have taken the property if it had not belonged to the defendant, in effect the third party confronts the handicap of having to show that despite a lawful judgment and despite the evidence that he could not rebut at the trial, he rightfully owns the contested property. Technically it is possible to do so, because Congress has provided that the government's title is rebuttable.[27]

In a 1987 case, a man acting as a front for a drug trafficker bought a Miami condominium for $200,000. The money came from drug proceeds in the branch of a crooked bank, the Bank of Credit and Commerce International, in the Cayman Islands. The front man subsequently borrowed $38,000 from a different bank, using the condo as collateral. After the government confiscated the condo as the product of drug proceeds, the bank that lent the $38,000 sought to get its money back. The government contested the suit, but the bank's claim of innocence won. The federal district court reasoned that the bank had properly determined that the front man was the owner of record and had no reason to believe that he had purchased the condo with drug moneys. The bank had made an appraisal on the condo before agreeing to the loan. It knew the customer, with whom it had been doing business for eighteen years; he had made substantial deposits in the past and had repaid an earlier loan. The bank's conduct in the case fit a pattern of standard banking business.[28]

By contrast, in a somewhat similar case decided three years later, the government won because the bank could not prove innocent ownership; it had not used appropriate banking practices. A kingpin drug dealer purchased a house through a front corporation, refurbished it at a cost of $350,000, and moved in. The house was worth $1.2 million. When he learned that the IRS was making inquiries about him, he decided to sell the house, but in order to protect his equity in it, he borrowed $800,000 on it from Republic National Bank. The bank complied with his request to transfer the loan to a Swiss account. Although the bank asserted that it had no actual knowledge that the kingpin's money came from drugs, the court was not satisfied with the bank's innocent owner defense. The bank had done nothing to determine the purpose of the loan, had not conducted a title search of the property that served as collateral for the loan,

171

did not know anything about the corporate front, did not inquire how the loan would be repaid, and had complied with the request to transfer the loan moneys to the Swiss bank account. All this, showing a departure from good business practices, suggested that guilty knowledge might be attributed to the bank.[29]

Another case showed even harsher judicial requirements for proof of innocence. Upon his arrest, a drug dealer who had sold cocaine from his home sought a bail bond hearing before a federal magistrate, who fixed the amount at $50,000. Present at the hearing was a representative from a bonding company, which lent the defendant the $50,000 for his bond, in return for a promissory note from him and a mortgage on his home as security. The magistrate ruled that the accused had an equity in his home worth $50,000, enough to make flight unlikely. The bonding company, of course, put up the money after the commission of the crime; that was the nature of its business with accused parties. Six months later but before the criminal trial, the government instituted civil forfeiture proceedings against the defendant's home, because it had been the site of cocaine dealing. The 1984 act of Congress allows the forfeiture of real property used to facilitate a crime.[30]

Then the defendant disappeared, forfeiting his bond. The bonding company then sought to get back its $50,000 by enforcing its claim on the home. The federal district court ruled against the company, reasoning that it should have known that the house was subject to forfeiture. Accordingly, the government not only retained the $50,000 bond but also got the house, and the bonding company, which had relied on the magistrate's findings, lost both.[31] However, the company could not have claimed an innocent owner's defense because it had not secured its interest in the home before the relation-back doctrine went into operation, and the charges against the defendant had informed the company that its client may have been guilty. The company, in effect, "forfeited" the bond money as an innocent bystander rather than as an innocent owner. No way existed for it to prove that it had taken all reasonable precautions to prevent the illegal use of the house. Yet the company itself was innocent and had not been in collusion with the defendant. The case also makes bond more difficult to obtain from the criminally accused who stands to forfeit property. It also reveals once more that innocence is irrelevant in a forfeiture case.

Congress has not acted but the Supreme Court in a 1993 case has somewhat clarified matters concerning the innocent owner defense and the relation-back doctrine. The basic murkiness of those matters may account for the fact that the case produced no majority opinion. The Court divided so badly that a four-member plurality governed, because its conclusion attracted the concurrence of two other justices who disagreed on everything else, while three other justices dissented out of concern for entirely different matters.[32]

In this case the government sought the forfeiture of the home of a woman who had bought it with a $240,000 gift from her lover, who had made the money trafficking in drugs. The government alleged that the woman never lawfully owned the property, because its ownership had reverted to the government at the moment of the trafficker's crimes; the house, having been bought with drug proceeds, belonged to the government. The woman, who swore that she had no knowledge of the tainted origins of the money, claimed the innocent owner's defense.

Justice John Paul Stevens, for the Court plurality, repudiated the government's arguments. It had relied on the relation-back doctrine, which, by the 1984 act of Congress, had provided that "all right, title, and interest in property . . .

shall vest in the United States upon commission of the act giving rise to forfeiture under this section." But the Court found that a 1978 act, authorizing forfeiture of proceeds from unlawful drugs, took precedence, and the 1978 act explicitly protected innocent owners who could prove that they neither had knowledge or consent of the unlawful use of their property. In effect the Court did what Congress should have done: amend the 1984 act dealing with real property to include the innocent owner's defense.[33]

The government tried to ward off such a ruling by arguing that the innocent owner's defense applied only to bona fide purchasers for value, but the Court properly saw no justification for limiting the innocent owner's defense to such purchasers. The government's argument would have had the effect of eliminating the innocent owner's defense for all others. It was also a shaky argument because the provision for bona fide purchasers derived from the 1984 statute, enacted two years after the owner bought the home. Therefore the government relied heavily on the relation-back doctrine of the common law.

Justice Stevens remarked that the common law doctrine "applied the fiction that property used in violation of law was itself the wrongdoer that must be held to account for the harm it had caused." Thus, the offending property became the defendant, and under the relation-back doctrine, "a decree of forfeiture had the effect of vesting title to the offending res [thing] in the Government as of the date of its offending conduct." But the vesting of the title was "not self-executing."[34]

With precedents going back to the time of Chief Justice John Marshall, Stevens proved his point. Marshall in 1806 had said, "Nothing vests in the government until some legal step shall be taken for the assertion of its right."[35] If the government wins a forfeiture judgment, Stevens asserted, the vesting of its title relates back to the time the property became forfeitable, but until the government has won that judgment, "someone else owns the property." The government had argued, however, that any proceeds traceable to an illegal drug transaction cannot become another individual's private property, but the Court shot down that proposition, too. The statute, it noted, made an exception for property innocently owned; the government cannot profit from the relation-back doctrine until a judgment of forfeiture following an opportunity for the presentation of the innocent owner defense.

Justice Antonin Scalia made the point attractively. The government, he said, thought that the relation-back doctrine commenced at the time of the commission of the offense. The government found the name of the doctrine to be "something of a misnomer," because its ownership went back to the moment of the illegal act. "But the name of the doctrine is not wrong," Scalia observed; "the government's understanding of it is wrong. It is a *retroactive* vesting of that title only upon entry of the judicial order of forfeiture or condemnation."[36] Scalia separately concurred on the basis of a technically different interpretation of the statute. And the three dissenters, who had altogether different fish to fry, said nothing in disagreement with the plurality's views on the relation-back doctrine or the innocent owner's defense.

The Court did not decide the question of whether the woman who invoked the innocent owner defense had successfully proved her point; that was left for a lower court to decide. The Court simply noted that she had "assumed the burden of convincing the trier of fact that she had no knowledge" of the illegal source of the moneys with which she had bought the house. The Court did not cope, either, with a problem mentioned in friend-of-the-court briefs on how extensively the government might trace property back to proceeds derived from a drug transaction. If, for example, the woman who bought the house involved in this case had sold it and with the moneys bought another, could it too be said to be traceable to drug proceeds? At what point did the link in the chain become free of such traceability? The Court gladly left the question for some future case that might actually raise it.

Its decision in this case was significant for stunting the government's exaggerated notions based on the relation-back doctrine as well as for invigorating the innocent owner defense. The Court had ruled that if the owner did not know that dirty money had bought her property, the lack of such knowledge, alone, was sufficient to establish the innocent owner defense. If she did not know of the money's source, she could not have agreed with the misuse that produced it; there was no question whether her property, the house and land, had been misused. Therefore, nothing was settled on the unraised question whether the innocent owner must also prove that she had done everything reasonably expected to prevent the misuse of her property. The case has not settled the conflicts that set federal courts against each other. Nor has the case weakened the relation-back doctrine. It weakened, rather, only the government's extreme view of that doctrine.

Chapter Ten

Constitutional Issues

Forfeiture proceedings have provoked many constitutional challenges. Objections based on freedom of the press have been raised to dispute forfeiture of obscene materials. The ban on unreasonable seizures of the Fourth Amendment seems especially pertinent to forfeiture cases. Forfeitures also implicate the Fifth Amendment's due process, self-incrimination, and double jeopardy clauses. The Sixth Amendment's right to be represented by counsel comes into play when forfeiture, civil or criminal, confiscates an attorney's fees, and the same amendment's provisions on speedy trial, confrontation of witnesses, and compulsory process seem to be at risk in a civil forfeiture's probable cause proceeding. The Seventh Amendment guarantees a civil trial in cases involving $20 or more, while the Eighth protects against cruel and unusual punishments as well as against excessive fines. Both the Seventh and Eighth Amendments have a strong relevance to *in rem* proceedings that confiscate properties summarily or on the basis of merely probable cause.

Prosecutions of obscenity have long been controversial, because of the special constitutional status of freedom of expression. Moreover, obscenity defies a clear definition, though most of us, like Justice Potter Stewart, know it when we see it. It is not just sexually explicit material, although that is what "pornography" refers to. Obscenity is a legal term that refers to materials provoking prurient interest. A work is obscene, according to the Supreme Court, if "the average person, applying contemporary community standards," finds it prurient; it depicts sexual conduct "in a patently offensive way"; and taken as a whole "it lacks serious literary, artistic, political or scientific value."[1] That definition obviously has inherent vagueness, but the point is that if a work is obscene, the First Amendment does not constitutionally protect it. The criminal laws of the United States and of the states make it punishable. In 1984, on evidence that organized crime made money from dealing in obscenity, Congress amended RICO to include the obscenity business.[2]

In the first federal prosecution, a jury found the defendants guilty of distributing $105.30 worth of obscene materials in interstate commerce. RICO allows the forfeiture, by a special verdict of a jury, of "any interest . . . acquired or maintained" through racketeering, or "any interest" giving the felon "any kind of source of influence over" the illegal enterprise, or "any" property derived from proceeds obtained from racketeering. The judge required the jury to find a substantial connection between the illegal activity and the proceeds, before returning a guilty verdict. The jury forfeited three hardcore bookstores and eight videotape clubs, assets worth over $1 million, to which the judge added a three-year prison sentence and a $75,000 fine.[3] The case raised the question of whether the wholesale seizure and forfeiture of the bookstores and the videotape clubs, on the basis of a $105.30 worth of obscene materials, extended to materials not found to be obscene. And the forfeiture of over $1 million in assets for a crime worth $105.30 raised the question of whether the disproportionate penalty violated constitutional guarantees against excessive punishment.

The federal district court that tried the case ruled, in 1987, that contrary to the defendants' argument that RICO chilled First Amendment freedoms, no proof existed to show that book dealers would be deterred from dealing in non-obscene erotic literature. Nor did the draconian RICO forfeiture deter dealers from selling "protected speech at the margin." The court based its propositions on the fact that federal obscenity statutes had already passed constitutional muster. RICO was designed to chill obscenity, which is unprotected expression. The First Amendment does not shield illegal activity. The judge offered no proof for his assertions, nor could he have had any, because there was no knowing whether dealers of erotic literature, which was constitutionally protected, censored themselves to avoid trouble by refusing to stock questionable books.

The court declined to engage in a proportionality analysis under the Eighth Amendment. But it emphasized that seizure of materials that might be constitutionally protected was valid "where there is proper proof that they were acquired or maintained with the ill-gotten gains from racketeering activity, including dealing in obscenity."[4] In a subsequent opinion, the court added that although the $105.30 worth of materials were obscene, testimony that it proved that defendants' chief business was selling obscene material could not be admitted in evidence. The court explained that no presumption of obscenity could be made consonant with the First Amendment.[5] In the abstract, that provided some protection to the other materials, but the judge subordinated that protection to the fact that racketeering proceeds bottomed the acquisition of all non-obscene materials. That was an extremely weak basis for justifying their forfeiture. RICO should not be superior to the First Amendment.

The Supreme Court did not decide a comparable case until 1993, although in 1989, in a case involving a state

RICO act that prescribed forfeiture for obscenity, the Court held that the mere existence of probable cause is not sufficient to justify taking books and films out of circulation; there must first be a proper determination that they are obscene and therefore unprotected by the First Amendment.[6] The 1993 case, *Alexander v. United States*, was much like the district court one of 1987. The defendant, who owned thirteen pornographic stores and theaters, was convicted on multiple obscenity and RICO counts. The convictions were based on four magazines and three videotapes. In addition to six years in prison and a fine of $100,000, the defendant forfeited his entire pornographic empire—all books, materials, stores, and theaters, as well as $9 million in cash acquired from his sales.[7] The Supreme Court sustained the constitutionality of the RICO forfeitures, although it remanded the cases to the court below for an Eighth Amendment determination of whether the punishment was excessive.

Chief Justice William Rehnquist's opinion for a 5–4 majority is a disaster to anyone who cares about freedom of expression. In Ray Bradbury's *Fahrenheit 451* the firemen burn books, all of which are outlawed. In *Alexander v. United States* the government destroyed books, not just dirty books but the owner's entire stock, approximately 100,000 books including for the most part books not found to be obscene—indeed, including books found by a jury not to be obscene. RICO allows an entire business to be forfeited if it is the product of racketeering or conducted by racketeering methods. In effect, if dirty money stocks an adult bookstore with the likes of D. H. Lawrence, John Updike, and Philip Roth, as well as sheer porno, all the books can be burned by the government. In *Alexander*, the chief justice informs us in a footnote that the brief for the United States conceded that because it did not wish to "go into the business of selling pornographic materials—regardless of whether they were legally obscene—the Government decided that it would be better to destroy the forfeited expressive materials than sell them to members of the public."[8]

"Regardless of whether they were legally obscene"! If they were not legally obscene they should be constitutionally protected. The question of whether they should be sold to the public arose, incidentally, because forfeited properties, unless consisting of contraband or something dangerous to the public, are usually sold for the cash the government can get for them. Destroying confiscated drugs makes sense; destroying expressive books not found to be obscene emulates Bradbury's firemen. Among Rehnquist's stunning thoughts is the incorrect contention that "the First Amendment does not prohibit . . . forfeiture of expressive materials as punishment for criminal conduct."[9] Until this case, that was a function of the amendment.

Rehnquist ruled that this was not a case involving prior restraint. In such cases, he declared, the government either required permission in advance of publication or prohibited publication; the government had "restrained materials suspected of being obscene without a prior judicial determination that they were in fact so." That did not happen in this case.[10] However, Justice Anthony M. Kennedy, in an angry dissent, insisted that it had happened in this case. But the majority contended that the case showed no prior restraint because the law did not forbid Alexander "from engaging in any expressive behavior in the future." Here, said Rehnquist, "the assets in question were not ordered forfeited because they were believed to be obscene, but because they were directly related to petitioner's past racketeering violations." RICO requires a "pattern" of violation, consisting of two or more violations: thus, Rehnquist referred to the past.

But the question he did not discuss was whether RICO could constitutionally forfeit non-obscene books. The statute, Rehnquist merely said, "is oblivious to the expressive or nonexpressive nature of the assets forfeited."[11]

That should have been the reason the statute was unconstitutionally applied to Alexander's entire inventory of books. Rehnquist declared, however, without reasoned judgment, that RICO does not criminalize protected speech. He meant that in a literal sense; it criminalizes, rather, obscene works and works connected to racketeering; those were the reasons the Court assigned to the destruction of all the books. As for the supposed chilling effect on First Amendment freedoms, Rehnquist thought that it derived legitimately from criminal sanctions; prison should scare criminals.

Kennedy expressed shock because the Court's opinion allowed the government to destroy an entire book and film business "for a single past speech offense," and he added: "Until now I had thought one could browse through any book or film store in the United States without fear that the proprietor had chosen each item to avoid risk to the whole inventory and indeed to the business itself." RICO's forfeiture provisions, he argued, are different from ordinary fines and prison sentences, because its stated purpose is to destroy the offending enterprise. As construed by the majority, he believed, any bookstore could be forfeited as punishment for obscenity. The First Amendment demanded sensitive, not draconian, interpretation. Two or more obscenity convictions within a ten-year period, under RICO, now meant forfeiture not only of unlawful items and the proceeds from their sale but the "entire interest involved in the RICO violations and any assets affording the defendant a source of influence over the enterprise."[12]

The decision in this case was especially disappointing because on the same day the Court held that some reasonable relationship should exist between the gravity of the offense and the forfeiture of property.[13] Moreover, protected materials should not be destroyed because of some taint from an owner who sold obscene works. We can only hope that Ruth Bader Ginsburg's succession to the seat of Byron White, who voted with Rehnquist, will result in a 5–4 majority the other way in future cases—assuming that Stephen Breyer votes, as Harry Blackmun did, with Kennedy. Until then the First Amendment has become subordinate to the needs of forfeiture.

In *Boyd v. United States* the Supreme Court in 1886 held that although an *in rem* proceeding is civil in nature, forfeiture has a quasi-criminal character because it is punitive as well as remedial. Accordingly, the protections of the Fourth Amendment and the clause of the Fifth banning compulsory self-incrimination extend to a claimant protesting civil forfeiture. The *Boyd* Court declared itself "clearly of opinion that proceedings instituted for the purpose of declaring the forfeiture of a man's property by reason of offences committed by him, though they may be civil in form, are in their nature criminal."[14]

The Court reaffirmed this ruling in 1965 respecting the Fourth Amendment in a case from Pennsylvania. In the course of a supposedly illegal search, police seized evidence discovered in the trunk of a car and sought its forfeiture in an *in rem* proceeding. The defendant, invoking the exclusionary rule, objected to the admission of the evidence on grounds that it had been illegally seized. The state supreme court held that the exclusionary rule derived from criminal law and did not apply to civil forfeiture cases. The Supreme Court, reversing the state, unanimously applied the rule of *Boyd*: the Fourth Amendment operates in civil forfeiture cases because of their punitive character.[15]

On the other hand the Fourth Amendment operates weakly in civil forfeiture cases. The only teeth in the amendment consists of the Court's exclusionary rule, which lacks incisors. The rule is that any evidence seized in violation of the Fourth Amendment must be excluded from a criminal prosecution. In a literal sense, then, the rule should have no application in a civil suit, but the Court, having invented the rule to make the Fourth Amendment meaningful, meant it to apply to civil forfeitures because they are quasi-criminal. The purpose of the exclusionary rule is to deter police misconduct that breaches the amendment, or, as the Court said, "to compel respect for the constitutional guaranty in the only effectively available way— by removing the incentive to disregard it."[16]

The problem, however, is that if convictions are not the objective of the police, the rule cannot deter them. Without a prosecution there is no proceeding from which to exclude the illegally obtained evidence. If the objective of law enforcement officers is to confiscate property, because they have a stake in augmenting their department's revenues, the exclusionary rule is impotent. It cannot deter civil forfeitures, especially when the financial incentive for the law enforcement agency to violate the Fourth Amendment is so powerful. Forfeiture has become an end in itself, an alternative to prosecution.

To be sure, if the police relied on illegally seized evidence to establish probable cause before a magistrate, he would throw out the case. But probable cause is easy enough to establish with a tip, circumstantial evidence, hearsay, or valid evidence even if discovered after the illegal seizure.[17] As one court said, "Any evidence which is the product of an illegal search or seizure must be excluded at trial, but . . . forfeiture may proceed if the Government can satisfy the requirements for forfeiture with untainted evidence."[18] An illegal seizure does not bar forfeiture. Justice Oliver Wendell Holmes, for the Supreme Court, declared that if the seizure is illegal, "the owner of the property suffers nothing that he would not have suffered if the seizure had been authorized."[19] What is needed is a governing doctrine that the Court will not adopt, namely that any violation of the Fourth Amendment results in a cancellation of the forfeiture and the return of the property. Short of that, in civil forfeiture cases, the exclusionary rule is an object of contempt to law enforcement officers.[20]

So is the warrant requirement of the Fourth Amendment. Several exceptions to the warrant requirement had long existed, such as search and seizure incident to arrest, or with consent, or in exigent circumstances. A forfeiture exception has also developed, partly because an *in rem* proceeding deemphasizes an owner's rights. Thus, an auto dealer may lose a car that a buyer has used in a drug deal, even though the buyer made only a $100 deposit on the purchase.[21] An officer may seize property without a warrant whenever he believes that he has probable cause that it is forfeitable. The Fourth Amendment is supposed to apply to one's "effects" as well as one's house, papers, and person. However, Congress has failed to refer to warrants in most forfeiture statutes, and courts afford property very few privacy expectations. The theory seems to be that if the property is forfeitable, the government does not need a warrant to take what it already owns. Once the property is associated with crime, whether as a means to it, a product of it, or an acquisition from it, title to it reverts to the government under the relation-back doctrine; therefore, an officer may seize it regardless of whether there are proceedings against the guilty owner or claimant. In effect the association with crime taints the property so that it no longer warrants the protection of the law.[22]

However, law enforcement authorities cannot be utterly cavalier about the warrant requirement. In one case, where the police had seized a car eleven months after it had been involved in a cocaine sale, the federal court ruled that although exigent circumstances can justify warrantless searches, a search and seizure should occur at the time of the event triggering the forfeiture.[23] But, if a car is legitimately in custody, a warrantless inventory search may be made to protect the owner's property as well as protect officers against any subsequent charge of theft from it; they may seize any contraband during an inventory search, even if belatedly made, and introduce that evidence in a subsequent prosecution.[24] In sum, although the Fourth Amendment extends to forfeiture cases, federal courts have made its protections a sham.

In 1974 the Court reaffirmed *Boyd*'s Fifth Amendment principle: the self-incrimination clause extends to civil forfeiture cases. The government, having arrested a man who failed to report his gambling activities as required by an act of Congress, confiscated the cash on his person. He objected on Fifth Amendment grounds and the government contended that in civil forfeiture cases the self-incrimination clause was irrelevant. The Supreme Court disagreed, saying that when "the forfeiture statutes are viewed in their entirety, it is manifest that they are intended to impose a penalty only upon those who are significantly involved in a criminal enterprise. It follows . . . that the Fifth Amendment's privilege may be properly invoked in those proceedings."[25]

The law governing double jeopardy, however, is quite different. In the key case, the government sought the forfeiture of a batch of emeralds that had been imported in violation of customs procedures. First, however, the government sought to convict the importer for smuggling, but his trial

186

ended in an acquittal. When forfeiture proceedings were instituted against him, he claimed that he was being exposed to double jeopardy in violation of the provision in the Fifth Amendment that says no person shall "be subject for the same offence to be twice put in jeopardy." That means he cannot be tried twice for the same offense by the same jurisdiction, nor can he be punished twice. Although the government had the obligation of proving an intent to defraud in order to win the case, the Court in 1972 held that the forfeiture in this instance, under customs law, was civil in nature, especially because it was intended to enforce tariff regulations by preventing forbidden merchandise to circulate freely. Its purpose, according to the Court, was remedial, not criminal. The ban against double jeopardy was not violated if the government sought both a criminal and a civil sanction for the same act. The clause banned an attempt to punish twice criminally for the same act, not criminally once and civilly once. Accordingly the Court sustained the forfeiture of the emeralds.[26] Its opinion entirely ignored its previous findings that civil forfeiture was quasi-criminal in nature, enough so to justify the protections against compulsory self-incrimination and unreasonable search and seizure.[27]

In a 1984 double jeopardy case the Court reconfirmed that in a civil forfeiture proceeding, the protection against double jeopardy does not exist.[28] The government prosecuted a man who sold weapons without a license; the jury, believing that federal agents had entrapped him, returned a verdict of not guilty. The government then instituted an *in rem* action for forfeiture of the weapons. Again the Court chose its precedents very selectively, ignoring those in which it had regarded civil forfeiture as quasi-criminal. Seeing only a remedial civil sanction in the *in rem* proceeding, the Court ruled that the double jeopardy clause was not applicable because Congress had intended the civil forfeiture to be essentially remedial and not a punishment; the Court agreed that keeping weapons out of the hands of unlicensed dealers was remedial rather than punitive.

In a more realistic opinion of 1989 the Court acknowledged that a civil proceeding may advance punitive as well as remedial goals. It endorsed the principle that if the sanctions in a particular case served the goals of punishment, a defendant who had already been punished in a criminal case may not be subjected to a civil sanction that additionally punishes him. In the case before the Court the individual, a manager of a medical service company, had been convicted of filing false Medicare claims that netted him $585 in reimbursements. After receiving a prison sentence and a fine of $5,000, the government sued him civilly for false claims, and he became liable to a civil penalty of $2,000 on each of his false claims, so that he owed more than $130,000. The Court regarded that amount as bearing no relation to the government's loss and costs; rather it was an extra punishment, exposing him to double jeopardy.[29] The principle of the case, which involved a fine rather than a forfeiture, applies foursquare to forfeitures. Indeed, in 1993 the Court held that a civil forfeiture is tantamount to a fine and therefore is protected against being excessive by the Eighth Amendment's ban on excessive fines.[30] Even so, the law is that forfeitures being civil sanctions are not punishments entitling their victims to seek the protection of the double jeopardy clause.

Nevertheless, the 1993 holding that civil forfeiture constitutes a punishment opened the way for lower federal courts to draw the conclusion that a punishment via civil forfeiture when added to a punishment after conviction for a crime constitutes a double punishment in violation of the double jeopardy clause. The constitutional principle is that no offense can be punished criminally more than once.[31] In late 1994 the United States Court of Appeals for the Ninth Circuit extended that principle to civil forfeiture cases in which the government had also convicted the offender criminally. The court held that to take a person's property in an *in rem* proceeding, civilly, after he had been sentenced to prison in an *in personam* proceeding, denied him the Fifth Amendment's protection against double jeopardy.[32]

As a result of this ruling two drug dealers, serving life sentences for having run a huge methamphetamine ring, were entitled to receive back from the government criminal proceeds that had been forfeited in the civil case, including Jaguars, Porsches, planes, and helicopters in addition to $405,000 in cash. Allowing felons to benefit from their crimes makes for ridiculous law that will not likely stand the Supreme Court's scrutiny. The Ninth Circuit's ruling conflicts with rulings in similar cases by several other federal circuit courts—the Fifth, Tenth, and Eleventh—as well as by the Supreme Court that both civil and criminal proceedings do not constitute double jeopardy. The problem, however, is that if civil forfeiture is a criminal punishment, logic is on the side of the Ninth Circuit. On the other hand, strict logic would regard a punishment of both fine and imprisonment as double punishment in violation of the double jeopardy clause, but it is not. Why, then, should forfeiture and imprisonment be double jeopardy? The forfeiture of narcotics proceeds does not have to be seen as criminal punishment; it is, rather, merely depriving a narcotics felon of assets that were never rightly his.

The Ninth Circuit did not, however, rule that the criminal proceeds belong to the felon, only that if the government chooses to prosecute him criminally, it cannot also proceed against his ill-gotten gains by civil forfeiture. Criminal forfeiture remains a way for the government to repossess the assets it would have preferred to seize civilly. In a criminal forfeiture case, of course, the indictment must stipulate the assets subject to forfeiture; if the jury returns a guilty verdict plus a special verdict for forfeiture, the government obtains those assets. But by stipulating those assets in the indictment, the government in effect puts the accused person on notice that his properties are subject to forfeiture. Unless the government can obtain a restraining order at the time of the indictment, the accused will have an opportunity to conceal the assets or sell them unless substitute assets can be seized. In any case, the need for a restraining order poses numerous problems for the government. Some courts are stingy with ex parte injunctions in criminal cases when guilt has not been proved. Moreover, the government's chances of obtaining a conviction are reduced, because the accused has the benefits of all constitutional rights.

The Ninth Circuit would force the government to choose between civil forfeiture or criminal proceedings but not both. As a practical matter, the Ninth Circuit's decision limits civil forfeiture to cases in which criminal convictions might seem difficult. Cases on the double jeopardy clause are sure to arise before the Supreme Court; it has not settled double jeopardy law in forfeiture cases. In all likelihood it will rule that seizing criminal proceeds is not necessarily a punishment or not merely a punishment; it is also a permissible remedial objective. If the Court does not rule this way, Congress is likely to enact a measure to that effect, authorizing federal courts to proceed civilly in forfeiture cases in order to remedy the situation in which a federal felon profits from his crime.

In 1993, the Supreme Court, which had had difficulty seeing that civil forfeiture can constitute punishment as well as a remedy, sensibly decided a Fifth Amendment due process case. The case was *United States v. James Good.* Good was a petty drug dealer who was caught, pleaded guilty, and was sentenced to a year in jail. Four and a half years later, the United States filed an *in rem* action seeking forfeiture of his home and land. On a showing of probable cause before a federal magistrate, the United States seized the property without prior notice to Good and without an adversary hearing. He responded that the seizure deprived him of property without due process of law and, additionally, was void because it was untimely. The Supreme Court sustained his due process argument against the contention by the United States that probable cause under the Fourth Amendment rendered unnecessary the observance of due process in a civil forfeiture case.[33]

Justice Anthony Kennedy for the Court restricted his opinion to real property cases: the due process clause requires notice and a hearing before the government can seize real property in an *in rem* proceeding. In the leading civil forfeiture case, involving Pearson Yacht Company in 1974, the Court had ruled that the government could seize the yacht without prior notice and hearing, because it could be moved out of jurisdiction and get away. However, real property can neither be moved nor concealed. Seizure of Good's property deprived him of valuable ownership rights, contrary to the guarantee of due process.

Justice Clarence Thomas, from the Court's right wing, expressed considerable unease about forfeitures of real property in a separate opinion. He thought that the act of 1984 authorizing forfeiture of real property was "so broad that it differs not only in degree, but in kind, from its historical antecedents." Thomas then questioned whether the scope of the act could be supported by the "central theory behind *in rem* forfeiture, the fiction 'that the thing is primarily considered the offender.'" His point was that under the act, huge tracts of land as well as improvements on it, having "no connection with crime other than being the location where a drug transaction occurred," are subject to forfeiture. Thomas found difficulty in seeing how "such real property is necessarily in any sense 'guilty' of an offense." He believed that current practice appears "far removed from the legal fiction upon which the civil forfeiture doctrine is based," making necessary that in some appropriate case that the Court should "reevaluate our generally deferential approach to legislative judgments in this area of civil forfeiture."[34] That statement may presage the Court's far more active stance in forfeiture cases in the future.

Fair procedures should not be confined to the innocent. Drug dealers like Good are entitled to their constitutional rights. Recognition of the government's argument would have meant that innocent owners would be unable to show that a violation involving their property had occurred without their knowledge or consent. The government had no obligation in a probable-cause hearing to offer any evidence on the question of innocent ownership, yet Congress had established an innocent owner's defense in cases involving forfeiture of real property. No pressing need justified the government's seizure without notice and hearing. Justice Kennedy acknowledged, however, that in old precedents, the government had permitted the seizure of real property, but he distinguished away those precedents: they involved the government's collection of debts or taxes. Here the sanctity of the home was involved. On the lesser question, whether the four-and-a-half-year lapse of time between the offense and the seizure was too long, the Court ruled that the statute of limitations gave the government a five-year period.

Four justices dissented. Chief Justice Rehnquist, who regarded the majority opinion as "ill-considered," "disruptive," and "unprecedented," supported the government's position. He addressed the probable cause issue. Justice Sandra Day O'Connor spoke to the due process issue. She viewed the majority's opinion as conflicting with a century of the Court's case law, which had not upheld the requirements of notice and a hearing in cases involving forfeiture of real property. Her position was that all the process that is due is provided at the mandatory forfeiture hearing, which follows seizure. The Fifth Amendment, she accurately observed, protects against deprivation of property, any property, personal as well as real property. The Court's rule for just real property lacked justification, in her opinion. She did not explain why precedents that the majority distinguished away should have been followed or why allowing a pre-seizure hearing was unreasonable.

Notice and hearing cannot come too early, especially where one's home is concerned. In any event, the Court's due process position hardly handicaps the government in its civil forfeiture cases. The minority view in favor of only a post-seizure hearing has the flavor of the White Queen's "punish first and then get on with the trial" doctrine in *Through the Looking Glass*. The majority minimized the chance that the government will seize the property of innocent owners. Any restraint on government error is beneficial.

The Second Circuit Court of Appeals has expressed its alarm at the widespread denial of due process of law, saying: "We continue to be enormously troubled by the government's increasing and virtually unchecked use of the civil forfeiture statutes and the disregard of due process that is buried in those statutes."[35] That sums up the matter perfectly.

Due process of law should also require a decision against shifting the burden of proof to the claimant once the government has satisfied the lowest possible standard of proof: a showing of probable cause in a civil forfeiture proceeding. Shifting the burden of proof and requiring the claimant to prove innocence utterly reverses the presumption of innocence. The Supreme Court has never decided a case that deals with shifting the burden of proof, but several federal courts of appeal have deferred to Congress's civil forfeiture acts by holding that shifting the burden does not violate due process of law.[36] The only justification for such decisions is the personification fiction that makes the property the defendant, stripping it of constitutional rights. Property cannot prove its innocence, although its claimant might. The claimant or owner has been denied due process by having to do so by a preponderance of evidence. The government should have to prove the guilt of the property by the same standard, rather than merely by probable cause. In realty, of course, it is the property *owner* who is presumed guilty.[37]

The Supreme Court has not been open-minded in Sixth Amendment cases. That amendment states in part, "in all criminal prosecutions the accused . . . shall have the assistance of counsel." At the time the Bill of Rights was adopted, the right to counsel meant no more than the right to be represented by counsel of one's choice at one's own expense.[38] By judicial interpretation, however, the right to counsel has enormously swelled in meaning, because the entire adversary system of criminal justice as well as the meaningful enforcement of all other rights depend on the right to counsel. Accordingly, denial of the right to counsel, denial even of the right to the effective assistance of counsel, is a denial of due process of law or of fundamental fairness. That is the reason that the Supreme Court's pair of 1989 decisions on the right to counsel in criminal forfeiture cases were so disappointing. The Court held that forfeiture of assets with which to appoint counsel of one's choice did not violate the Fifth Amendment's due process clause or the Sixth Amendment's right-to-counsel clause.[39]

In one case the defendant was charged with violation of both the RICO and CCE acts for having directed a large-scale heroin distribution enterprise by racketeering methods. As soon as he was indicted, the government obtained a restraining order freezing his assets pending trial. Unable to retain an attorney of his choice, he was represented by a court-appointed lawyer. He claimed that the restraining order infringed the right to counsel and due process of law. In the companion case, a man charged with directing a massive drug trafficking operation in violation of CCE was restrained from transferring any of his assets. Nevertheless, he retained a law firm for $25,000. Subsequently he entered a plea agreeing to forfeit his assets. The law firm, seeking adjudication of its third-party interests, sued the government, arguing that an attorney's fees are exempt from forfeiture.

The right to the effective assistance of counsel profoundly affects the odds of whether an accused person will escape the penitentiary and the forfeiture of his assets. At stake is whether justice will be done in his case, a matter that is of crucial interest to society as well as to him. Criminal forfeiture cases are extraordinarily complex and time-consuming. They require a special expertise on the part of counsel on both sides. The prosecutors receive highly technical training to qualify them for such cases. If a person is denied counsel of his choice and his assets are frozen, he becomes a client of an appointed counsel, likely someone who is from a public defender's office. Public defenders tend to be young, inexperienced lawyers or second-rate older ones, who are adept at assembly-line justice. They or even publicly appointed private counsel may not be wholly independent of the government that pays their salaries. And no matter what their commitment to their positions and to their clients, they are ill-equipped to defend anyone charged with RICO or CCE violations. Such cases require defense counsel with a level of experience and know-how they simply do not have; they probably do not even have the time to devote to a long, drawn-out, technical proceeding.[40]

Our whole system of criminal justice, based on the adversary principle, is geared to a fair determination of guilt or innocence. When the prosecutorial forces of organized society are marshaled against a man accused of crime, "Abandon all hope, ye who enter here" best describes his chances if he is bereft of the effective assistance of counsel. Even the innocent suspect not yet formally accused is in a high-risk situation if he faces police and prosecution without a capable lawyer. The man who is championed by such counsel retains the chance of ensuring that his powerful adversaries, who act for the government, will behave according to the rules of a dangerous game. Shortcuts and errors that derive from overzealousness, mistaken judgments, prejudice, and legal improprieties have shamefully stained our system of criminal justice. Trial judges also commit blunders that sacrifice individual rights, subvert the rule of evidence, or mistakenly apply the law. No small part of defense counsel's task is to police the agencies of law enforcement by holding them accountable to the law. Overburdened in their work and ready to believe the worst, they too often stray into the paths of lawlessness or error against the defendant.

A guilty man needs and is entitled to a lawyer of his choice if he can afford one, and he should not even be permitted to plead guilty without one. No layman has the experience and knowledge required to plea-bargain with the prosecutor's office. Plea bargaining refers to the off-the-record, out-of-court negotiations between prosecution and defense for a mutually beneficial trade: the defendant waives all of his rights to trial by jury, the right not to incriminate himself by pleading guilty, and the right to cross-examine witnesses against him; he pleads guilty in exchange for a more lenient sentence for reduced charges. The prosecutor avoids the many problems inherent in a trial, saves the public a lot of time and money, and disposes of the case with another conviction notched on his record. Only a knowledgeable criminal lawyer can impanel a jury, assess the probable case against his client, know the admissibility of the evidence against him, figure the likelihood of conviction, and be familiar with the court's sentencing practices.

Most cases do not even come to trial, because they are settled with a guilty plea. The most crucial decision that a defendant can make with the advice of counsel is how to plead at his arraignment. A decision to plead guilty depends heavily upon the deal that his counsel can make with the prosecutor. The expertise of defense counsel is indispensable to the guilty, as well as the innocent, and is the best safety factor built into the adversary system to guarantee that justice will be done.

In a criminal forfeiture case, when the government obtains a restraining order freezing the defendant's assets, he cannot afford to retain counsel of choice. Even in the absence of a restraining order, if the jury finds him guilty and agrees to the forfeiture of assets specified in the indictment, wiping him out, he cannot pay counsel. Any money he has paid to counsel must also be forfeited. The relation-back doctrine, making the forfeiture relate back to the time of the first commission of the crime, vests the right to the property in the government at that early date. Any money paid to a lawyer becomes part of the assets forfeitable from the moment of the commission of the crime.

A lawyer will not take a case knowing that his fees are

forfeitable unless he wins an acquittal. Even then, if a pretrial injunction has frozen his client's assets, congressional enactment has placed the lawyer in the position of a third party: the statute requires him to show that he was reasonably without cause to know that the assets with which he will be paid were subject to forfeiture. The lawyer cannot show that. And he cannot take a case if his fees are contingent upon winning an acquittal. That would be unprofessional conduct, a violation of the bar association's code of ethics, because a defense attorney in a criminal case cannot serve on a contingency basis and cannot be in a position in which his advice to his client affects his own financial interest. Nor would he be able to serve his client by having him make honest and full disclosures. A forfeitable fee makes an ineffective attorney.

The upshot is that experienced counsel will not take criminal forfeiture cases, depriving not just the client but the criminal justice system of the services of the most effective counsel. Moreover, no constitutional right to counsel exists before indictment. The assistance of counsel can be effective only if he is available when needed. He is needed from the time that a criminal investigation begins to focus on a suspect; he is needed at the grand jury stage of a case; but if he is appointed, he enters the case after the indictment.

Indeed, the criminal forfeiture laws make everyone who provides services to the criminal liable to lose any money they receive from him or any money owed to them by him, even for medical attention and food as well as legal services. The relation-back doctrine followed by a conviction in a RICO or CCE prosecution beggars the defendant. That, as a matter of fact, was the objective of those statutes: to wipe out the economic basis of the racketeer's or drug trafficker's operation.

Justice Byron White, for a 5–4 majority of the Supreme Court, made a sound observation: "A defendant has no Sixth Amendment right to spend another person's money for services rendered by an attorney, even if those funds are the only way that that defendant will be able to retain the attorney of his choice. A robbery suspect, for example, has no Sixth Amendment right to use funds he has stolen from a bank to retain an attorney to defend him if he is apprehended."[41] White, the reader should notice, has already convicted the defendant in the criminal forfeiture case and in the robbery case. White also assumed that the defendant used someone else's money. The presumption of innocence is a common victim in civil forfeiture cases, but in criminal forfeiture cases the standard of proof-beyond-reasonable-doubt is supposed to prevail. White gave the impression that the purpose of a prosecution was to convict suspects, not determine whether they are innocent or guilty. He also assumed that the money for retaining counsel of choice derived from criminal proceeds, a fact that the government had an obligation of proving at the trial.

White balanced the government's interest in the defendant's assets against constitutional rights derived from the Fifth and Sixth Amendments, and found the government's interest to be superior. The relation-back doctrine was constitutional; under it, the government's property rights, obtained from the time of the commission of the crime, must prevail; it "overrides any Sixth Amendment interest in permitting criminals to use assets adjudged forfeitable to pay for their defense." To believe otherwise meant that the defendant not only could spend assets on attorneys but also on "exercises of the right to speak, practice one's religion, or travel."[42] As for the defendant's right to due process, the Court pronounced it "unavailing." White's opinion in the companion case, dealing mainly with statutory interpretation, merely reaffirmed the constitutional findings of the first one.

The four dissenting justices, speaking through Justice Harry Blackmun, emphasized the "devastating consequences of attorney's fee forfeiture for the integrity of our adversarial system of justice." Blackmun criticized the majority for finding the right to counsel of choice "so insubstantial that it can be outweighed by a legal fiction"—the relation-back doctrine. The right to counsel of choice assured "some modicum of equality between the Government and those it chooses to prosecute." Taking away that right by taking away assets to pay for counsel results in private counsel being "unwilling to continue, or to take on, the defense," imperiling the criminal justice system's adversarial character and stretching "already scarce resources of a public defender's office . . . to the limit." Counsel is tempted to encourage guilty pleas. As the forfeiture mechanism expanded to more and more categories of federal crime and was copied by the states, anyone accused of a crime that generates economic gain will be unable to find experienced private counsel. "In short, attorney's-fee forfeiture substantially undermines every interest served by the Sixth Amendment right to chosen counsel."[43]

The Seventh Amendment supposedly guarantees a common law trial by jury in all civil suits involving more than $20. The government has highly technical ways of getting around that in civil forfeiture proceedings. It seizes property in accord with the Federal Rules of Civil Procedure Supplemental Rules for Admiralty Rule C. That means that the court which approves of probable cause is sitting as if it were an admiralty court, and such a court operates without juries. Or, the government may proceed under the act of Congress authorizing the Department of Justice to show probable cause to a magistrate that the property in question is subject to civil forfeiture. Either way, the government finesses the Seventh Amendment. There seem to be no cases challenging the government on Seventh Amendment grounds.[44]

The Eighth Amendment's ban on ex post facto laws protects criminal forfeiture defendants and can operate on behalf of victims of civil forfeiture. The Seventh Circuit ruled that the ex post facto clause prevents a state from forfeiting obscene material under an act of 1989, because the state used forfeiture as an additional punishment for people who have already been convicted of obscenity before 1989.[45] In effect the state applied its statute retroactively, and the statute, according to the court, evinced a criminal purpose of supplementing existing sanctions.

A decision to the effect that the ban on ex post facto laws applies to civil forfeitures was made when the government sought to obtain forfeiture of a real estate lot under a 1978 act, which authorized forfeiture of all proceeds derived from drug sales. The problem was that the transaction involving the real estate occurred in 1976, making subsequent forfeiture a violation of the ex post facto clause. The decision was possible only because the district court considered forfeiture to be punitive.[46]

In 1993, however, the Supreme Court unanimously made a startling and unprecedented decision in an Eighth Amendment case, ruling that the ban on excessive fines applies to *in rem* civil forfeiture proceedings.[47] The case was *Austin v. United States*, decided the same day as the reprehensible decision in *Alexander v. United States*, allowing the forfeiture and destruction of thousands of non-obscene books owned by a RICO violator. Austin was a petty cocaine dealer who had been sentenced by a state court to seven years in prison. The United States then sought the civil forfeiture of Austin's home and auto body shop. He protested, contending that the excessive fines clause of the Eighth Amendment applied to *in rem* civil forfeiture proceedings; the government argued that it applied only in criminal cases.

Justice Harry Blackmun for the Court found nothing in the history of the clause limiting it to criminal cases. The purpose of the clause was to limit the government's power to punish, which it could do civilly as well as criminally. Reviewing civil forfeiture cases, Blackmun concluded that forfeiture was always regarded, at least in part, as a punishment. That seems somewhat surprising, given all the previous emphasis by the Court, from the earliest nineteenth-century cases, on the fact that civil forfeiture targeted guilty property, not its owners. It seems surprising, too, given the previous emphasis on the remedial and regulatory character of civil forfeitures, rather than on their punitive character. Indeed, because they were not punitive, the Court had justified the denial of constitutional protections in civil forfeiture cases.

The precedents seemed to be on the government's side until the Court ruled otherwise. It refused to formulate a test for determining whether a particular forfeiture is "excessive" and returned the case to the court below to consider that matter. The Court was unanimous on the major issue that the Eighth Amendment, not being limited to criminal cases, comprehended civil forfeitures, which were tantamount to fines, thereby qualifying for inclusion in the excessive fines clause. Four justices, concurring separately, refused to endorse Blackmun's reconstruction of the past but otherwise agreed with the majority.

Blackmun's opinion in *Austin* could revolutionize court decisions on the question of whether severe punishments in forfeiture cases violate the Eighth Amendment's protection against either cruel and unusual punishment or impose punishments that are grossly disproportionate to the offense. Such punishments are everyday stuff in forfeiture cases. A person who used his home phone to arrange for a drug deal lost his home to forfeiture, though he never had drugs in the house and did not use it to make a sale.[48] A boat was lost to forfeiture because marijuana residue was found in a concealed compartment.[49] A Porsche was forfeited after a DEA agent found less than one-fourth of a gram of marijuana in it.[50]

Still more extreme cases occur when an entire enterprise is forfeited. The government took all the assets of a beauty college whose owner made false claims for the tuition costs of veterans.[51] In another case a man bribed a government official to gain the award of contracts amounting to less than $500,000, and the government demanded all the stock he had honestly purchased ten years previously, valued at $8.5 million, plus his pension, his salary over a five-year period, and still more. The court found technical reasons to refuse the forfeiture of the stock but forfeited all else.[52] Excessive punishments that are disproportionate to the crime are common, as the obscene books case illustrates.

Even worse are the even more common cases where the punishment is inflicted on innocent people, sometimes wiping out their businesses, as in the instance of Billy Munnerlyn, who lost his air charter business and incurred huge fees after the government confiscated his Lear Jet because he had unknowingly transported a passenger carrying drug moneys.[53] Michael Sandsness is another innocent person whose business was destroyed by the government. He owned gardening supply stores in Eugene and Portland, Oregon, and among the merchandise that he sold were halide grow lights. They could be used to grow African daisies indoors, to get tomatoes started early, or even to get marijuana to prosper in a basement. Sandsness was not responsible for the uses to which his merchandise was put by customers, although the government thought otherwise. The DEA found marijuana growing under halide lights sold by Sandsness. Without mentioning marijuana, agents questioned an employee of his as if they intended to do something sneaky with halide grow lights, which they bought. The DEA then raided Sandsness's stores, seized his inventory and his bank accounts, and warned his landlord that unless he evicted Sandsness, the DEA would seize the entire building. Sandsness was evicted. He sold his business in order to pay creditors and was bankrupted.[54]

A final illustration of excessive punishment is *United States v. Busher*, a 1987 Ninth Circuit case in which the government sought forfeiture of a defendant's valuable real estate plus his interest in a company that obtained three defense contracts illegally. That interest was worth $3 million, nearly ten times the value of the illegal contracts. The Ninth Circuit agreed that an excessive RICO forfeiture could violate the Eighth Amendment. Yet it declared that if the jury determined that the property had been illegally acquired, "it must find forfeitable the defendant's entire interest in that property." Forfeiture, the court said, is not unconstitutional because "it exceeds the harm to the victims or the benefit to the defendant." RICO was intended to be punitive. The Eighth Amendment "prohibits only those forfeitures that, in the light of all the relevant circumstances, are *grossly* disproportionate to the offense committed."[55] On remand the district court reaffirmed its prior order forfeiting all of Busher's stock and real estate.[56]

The Supreme Court's *Austin* decision may eventually end such severe punishments on Eighth Amendment grounds. That's a step in the right direction; there should be some rational relationship between the gravity of an offense and its penalty. All in all, to say, as one prominent defense attorney has remarked, that the war on drugs has become a "war on the Constitution," is an exaggeration but one that makes a good point.[57] The more recent decisions, excepting the one approving the forfeiture and destruction of non-obscene books, have tended to uphold constitutional rights. The Court, however, has a long way to go before it adequately remedies scores of years of having failed to sustain those rights. The real culprit, however, is Congress, to whose judgment the Court frequently defers.

Chapter Eleven

Reforms Ahead

Congress should reform the forfeiture laws. Even if these laws satisfactorily attained their objectives, reform should still have a high legislative priority as a simple matter of fairness. But failure clings to them in several notable ways. Consider the haul from forfeiture laws. Even if the *cumulative* sum of forfeitures amounted to $5 billion, an inflated figure, it is a trickle compared to the torrential profits made *annually*, not cumulatively, by organized crime and white-collar crime: $5 billion compared with several hundred billion. Compare the cumulative sum of forfeitures to just the annual federal budget for drug programs, which amounts to at least $10 billion a year, or, if the National Institute for Drug Abuse in 1992 was correct, $20 billion.[1] Consider too the cost of providing special medical care to "crack" babies, the offspring of cocaine-addicted mothers; that amounts to $2.5 billion *annually*, a figure worth comparing to the $2.5 billion for the *cumulative* value of forfeited properties from enforcement of federal laws from 1985 to 1992.[2] That cumulative value from 1985 to 1994 comes to less than $5 billion, which does not even amount to 5 percent of the annual profits from drug trafficking and much less than 5 percent of the annual profits from white-collar crime. The "take" from forfeiture signals failure, not success. Therefore, in the context of the entire situation, financial losses would not be significant if the "take" were to be eroded by a radical reform such as abolition of civil forfeiture. The protection of property and personal rights might well be worth the cost.

The shortcomings of the forfeiture laws become still more evident when we recall that the backers of the 1970 federal legislation, which imposed criminal forfeiture for so many different crimes, repeatedly insisted that it would take the profit out of crime, eradicate the criminal infiltration of legitimate businesses and labor organizations, and put an end to criminal tactics in business and trade unions. Clearly, those objectives have not materialized. A scholar who studied all cases brought under RICO concluded that "RICO has been a nearly total failure as a weapon against the kind of activity that led Congress to enact it."[3] Very few RICO indictments involved the charge that the accused used the proceeds of a pattern of racketeering activity to acquire an interest in an enterprise, or managed it by racketeering; and, in those few cases the result usually was an acquittal or, if a conviction, a reversal on appeal.

On the other hand there were many cases involving fraud and other crimes committed by legitimate businessmen, whose businesses had not been infiltrated. "Thus, the provisions of RICO most explicitly directed against infiltration of legitimate entities by organized crime have proven all but totally useless in dealing with the particular harm at which they were aimed."[4] When criminals take over a business, they tend to use it as a front for their illegitimate activities, rather than as a means of driving out competition by criminal means.

The cases under RICO brought against Mafia-types have not been numerous but they have resulted in significant triumphs. Anthony (Fat Tony) Salerno, a Mafia boss, was convicted of racketeering charges, including corruption in the concrete industry. Imprisoned for life, he and his associates lost "tens of millions of dollars" from forfeitures of their interests in the concrete industry.[5] RICO prosecutions against Mafia chieftains have been common; RICO forfeiture cases against them have not. One involved Mafia control of New York City's carpenter union through the Genovese crime family. At the time of that case in 1990, the *New York Times* reported that it was the fourteenth such suit under RICO.[6] Another major RICO forfeiture case resulted in the confiscation of the known properties of John Gotti, a Mafia figure serving a life sentence.[7] RICO's forfeiture victories against criminal types have been infrequent but significant, especially compared with cases involving Mafia infiltration in legitimate businesses. RICO convictions have helped bust the mob, though few convictions have been attended by forfeitures. Successful attacks on wholly criminal enterprises and criminal activities were not anticipated by RICO's legislative proponents.

In trade unions, criminal takeovers of legitimate unions have been far more frequent and successful than takeovers of legitimate businesses, and have resulted in labor racketeering and corruption. RICO has been more successful in the labor field than in driving out criminal infiltration of legitimate business. RICO has also resulted in significant prosecutions of white-collar crime, mostly in cases involving ordinary business frauds. "By far the greater number of RICO indictments in the white collar area had no connection whatever to organized crime."[8] RICO's legislative proponents did not expect that it would be more successful against fraudulent businessmen than against Mafia-types infiltrating business. Nor did they anticipate RICO's successes against white-collar criminals such as Michael Milken and Charles Keating, involving forfeitures of cash in enormous amounts.

An interesting aspect of such cases is that the forfeitures, however enormous, did not pose a deterrent effect. The prospect of losing money does not deter a Milken or a Keating. Imprisonment does. To such men, imprisonment is an overwhelming, crushing punishment whose deterrent effect is beyond exaggeration. As a matter of fact, even major mobsters are deterred by imprisonment, not loss of assets, contrary to the assumptions of the congressmen who supported the criminal forfeiture statutes of 1970. RICO has been so effective not because of its forfeiture provisions but because its reach is so extended and it inflicts severe prison penalties. RICO put Salerno and Gotti in prison for life, and only subsequently produced forfeitures of their properties. Organized crime has been deterred not by forfeiture but by imprisonment, notwithstanding all the congressional speeches to the contrary.

Even though successes such as the enormous forfeitures in the Milken and Keating cases are not common, a critic of forfeiture laws would be irrational to advocate their abolition. Both civil and criminal forfeiture are penalties for criminal involvement, and no criminal should be able to profit from crime. No one urged revision of the criminal forfeiture laws, presumably because they are cribbed and cabined by constitutional constraints. Civil forfeiture laws, by contrast, have been targeted for drastic criticism by would-be reformers. Civil forfeiture laws can be traced back to the First Congress, are numerous, cover disparate topics, and have been far more productive than their criminal analogues, yet have attracted the severest criticism. The press and criminal defense lawyers have led advocates of reform, but among them have been financial and commercial institutions that have suffered in cases involving mortgages, liens, and loans. The *Orlando Sentinel* won a Pulitzer Prize for its hostile series on civil forfeiture, and the influential six-part series in the *Pittsburgh Press* was written by two

Pulitzer Prize–winning reporters. The *Christian Science Monitor* also published an unsympathetic series on forfeiture. Newspapers across the nation have run damaging stories and editorials on forfeiture, as has CBS's popular program "60 Minutes" and such influential voices as the *New York Times* and the *Miami Herald*.

The National Association of Criminal Defense Lawyers has led advocates of legislative reform. Among the defense lawyers is David B. Smith, once a founder of the Department of Justice civil forfeiture program. Smith, who reversed course on the subject, is probably the nation's foremost authority on forfeiture.[9] The leaders of the criminal defense bar also include Nancy Hollander, former president of the National Association of Criminal Defense Lawyers (NACDL), and her successor, John Henry Hingson, who has pronounced forfeiture "government thievery." E. E. Edwards III, who championed Willie Jones and like Hollander and Smith has testified before Congress in favor of reform, is co-chair of the association's Forfeiture Abuse Task Force.[10]

On June 15, 1993, Republican congressman Henry Hyde of Illinois introduced the Civil Asset Forfeiture Reform Act of 1993. Republican senator James M. Jeffords of Vermont introduced the same bill in the Senate. Hyde, a noted conservative who champions property rights and tough measures on crime, was flanked by Hollander and by Nadine Strossen, president of the American Civil Liberties Union. The *Washington Post*, editorializing on "Mr. Hyde's Good Cause," observed that he did not often have such allies. He issued "A Briefing Paper" on the subject of civil forfeiture that made national news, explaining its history and operation, government income from it, and the reasons for the reform act. The *Chicago Tribune* pronounced the Hyde bill "an asset to justice." The presumption of innocence, according to the editorial, is one of "the most vital and treasured tenets of United States criminal law. It is the popular embodiment of the all-important 'due process' right assured in our Constitution," but has been "twisted inside-out in the increasingly abused civil laws governing the forfeiture of assets."[11]

Hyde declared that under civil forfeiture, "the standard is guilty unless proved innocent." On the basis of the government's showing of probable cause, which is the lowest standard of proof, the burden of proof immediately shifts to the owner or claimant of the property to show by a preponderance of evidence that the property was not involved in a crime. The property's owner may be entirely innocent of the crime or may even have been acquitted after having been charged; but his innocence does not matter, and in the overwhelming majority of cases of civil forfeiture, the people who lose their property are never accused of crime. The Hyde bill would modify this situation by fixing upon the government the burden of proof. Moreover, the standard of proof would be more than probable cause, more even than a preponderance of evidence but less than proof beyond reasonable doubt. It would be proof by clear and convincing evidence. That would minimize the government's use of circumstantial evidence, hearsay, and innuendo. It would place the burden of proof where it ought to be and necessitate on the government's part a showing of the connection between the crime and the property it seeks to have declared forfeited.[12] Law enforcement's response was well stated by Sheriff Johnny Mack Brown of Greenville, South Carolina, the president of the National Sheriffs Association, who declared, "Shifting the burden of proof to the government would be shifting things in favor of the criminals in this country."[13]

The Hyde bill would also provide for the appointment of

counsel for indigents. Under present law a person who is financially unable to obtain private representation has no right to appointed counsel in civil forfeiture cases, a fact that helps account for the paucity of challenges to forfeiture from innocent victims. The Department of Justice's Assets Forfeiture Fund would underwrite the cost of counsel, with the amount per case fixed at the maximum for appointed counsel in federal felony cases ($3,500 for trial; $2,500 for appeal).

Another provision of Hyde's bill would eliminate the discrepancy among the various federal courts on the innocent owner's defense. Some courts require a showing that the owner had no knowledge of the property's use in a crime *and*, additionally, did not consent to such use, while others also require a showing that the owner used reasonable precautions to prevent the illegal use. Hyde's bill would standardize the innocent owner's defense and make it easier by requiring that the owner demonstrate "either" that he did not know of "or" consent to the illegal use.

Present law requires that an owner must post a bond of 10 percent of the value of the seized property but not less than $250 nor more than $5,000 in order to contest its forfeiture in court, and he has only a ten-day period, from the date of publication of the notice of seizure, in which to file a claim. Hyde's bill would extend that period to sixty days, a far more realistic period, and would eliminate the posting of the cost bond. If the government initiates a forfeiture proceeding against some property, its owner ought not have to put up cash to help cover the government's cost of litigation or of maintaining the property until a court decides its fate.

Hyde's bill would also eliminate the exemption now enjoyed by the government against damage claims resulting from losses or injury to the property while in the government's custody, pending judicial disposition. Finally the bill would permit a court, on a showing of "substantial hard-ship" by the property's owner, to require its return pending final judicial disposition.

The Hyde bill, despite all the praise heaped upon it, is a modest proposal that scarcely goes far enough in reform-ing the civil forfeiture laws. A liberal Democrat, Congress-man John Conyers of Michigan, who until 1995 chaired the House Subcommittee on Government Operations, intro-duced a far more sweeping bill, the Asset Forfeiture Justice Act. Having presided over two investigations into the opera-tions of the civil forfeiture laws, he had heard testimony from the leading criminal defense attorneys, such as David Smith, Nancy Hollander, and E. E. Edwards; he made their ideas his policies.

Excepting cases involving unpaid duties and smuggled items, the Conyers bill in effect abolished civil forfeiture by providing that proceedings for the forfeiture of property "shall be conducted only upon conviction of the owner of such property for the crime upon which the forfeiture is based." If the bill were to be passed, the government could no longer prosecute property by *in rem* proceedings. The personification fiction would become obsolete: property could no longer be held guilty. The government could not win forfeiture of property belonging to innocent owners or owners who had been tried and acquitted. Another provi-sion of the Conyers bill required *in personam* proceedings even against vessels, which since time immemorial have been subject to *in rem* proceedings.[14]

Other radical provisions of the bill transformed the pre-vailing equitable sharing and adoptive forfeiture policies. Conyers said, when chairing a forfeiture investigation: "We found a pattern and practice of abuse by state and local law enforcement that is fostered by a federal program with built-in financial incentive that cannot help but impact law enforcement priorities." Conyers meant to abolish those built-in incentives. He continued: "A law designed to give cops the right to confiscate and keep the luxury possessions of major drug dealers mostly ensnares the modest homes, cars and hard-earned cash of ordinary, law-abiding people. This was not the way it was supposed to work."[15] If the Conyers bill were passed, it would no longer work that way.

The bill provides that forfeiture proceeds currently returnable to the state or local law enforcement agencies under the equitable sharing program would hereafter be returned to state treasuries "for disposition according to State law." Moreover, at least 50 percent of the federal share of forfeitures would be available for "community-based crime-control programs," including private nonprofit ones, and for "drug education, prevention, and treatment." The amounts for these objectives would be determined by state law, "with priority given to the communities in which the assets involved are seized." Nothing would go to the law enforcement agencies that made the seizures except as provided by state law. To further insure that objective, another provision transformed adoptive forfeiture by banning the return of any funds that might be used to circumvent state laws governing the disposal and use of forfeiture proceeds.

An objection by the head of the National Sheriffs Association against the Hyde bill is better suited against the Conyers bill. Sheriff Brown objected, "Whose side is he on—the drug dealers' side or ours? For the first time in 27 years, we have the upper hand against drug dealers. To lose asset forfeiture is to lose the most effective tool law enforcement has ever had."[16] Sheriff Brown did not speak to the issue of how equitable sharing and adoptive forfeiture taint law enforcement and skew its policies.

Another drastic break with past procedure in the Conyers bill is the proposed abolition of the relation-back doctrine, by which title to property involved in crime or acquired with criminal proceeds is putatively vested in the government at the moment of the occurrence of the crime. The end of the relation-back doctrine would mean that bona fide owners of such property and legitimate lien holders would not be disadvantaged in a subsequent legal proceeding for its possession. The government's legal title would vest only after winning a special verdict of forfeiture in court or, in some cases, in an administrative proceeding, and such a verdict could be had only after a criminal conviction of the property owner. Without a verdict in its favor, the government would have no right to contested property.

One clause of the bill would have the effect of overturning the Supreme Court's decisions that made attorneys' fees forfeitable. The Conyers bill exempts from forfeiture "any property which has been paid or pledged as bona fide attorneys' fees." That would reinvigorate the Sixth Amendment right to counsel of choice at the expense of allowing crooked proceeds to pay the cost. Whether a robber should be able to use his loot to buy a lawyer is debatable, but one's counsel of choice is the best guarantor of due process rights. In opposition, Terrence Farley, director of the National Drug Prosecution Center, declared, "What you're going to have is every dope dealer in the world getting a free lawyer." That remark, misdirected against the Hyde bill, makes more sense as an objection to the Conyers bill.[17] A less controversial protection of Sixth Amendment rights would provide for court-appointed counsel for indigents in forfeiture cases, as in the Hyde bill.

Conyers seeks, too, to prevent houses from being seized and forfeited simply because of a phone call being made or received to facilitate a drug crime. Similarly he seeks to protect land from confiscation simply because a bit of it has been used to grow marijuana. These objectives would be met by restricting the kinds of property subject to forfeiture after conviction: controlled substances; raw materials, equipment, and supplies to produce them; containers for them; conveyances used to transport or conceal them; records of any sort concerning them; drug paraphernalia; and real property "used primarily" to violate the law if the owner knew or consented. To further insure that the property confiscated will directly relate to the crime, the Conyers bill includes a provision of proportionality: the value of the property forfeited may not exceed the gain derived from the offense or the loss caused by it. That would end the excessive punishments that are so common under the current forfeiture laws.

The Conyers bill, like Hyde's, would also shift the burden of proof to the government by requiring it to establish by clear and convincing evidence that the property is subject to forfeiture. Both bills would eliminate the cost bond and extend from ten to sixty the number of days a person has to file a claim for the property. That would lessen the chances that a claimant's property will be lost simply because he failed to meet a summary deadline for filing. The Conyers bill also eliminates the government's discretion as to the time it seeks forfeiture after it has made a seizure. Delays, often unnecessary and arbitrary, have occasioned hardships to innocent owners who have been deprived of their property without a hearing, sometimes resulting in neglect and deterioration of the property's value. The Conyers bill aims to end the government's failure to act; it seeks to prevent cases from languishing by giving the claimant his day in court as speedily as possible. It fixes a sixty-day period after a seizure for the government to serve notice that it plans to institute forfeiture proceedings. Forfeiture would be barred if the government fails to meet the deadline for giving notice. Currently no statutory requirement exists obligating the government within any time limit to provide notice of a seizure and intention to forfeit.

A related provision of the Conyers bill, like Hyde's, opens the government to suit for damages to the property while in government custody. The Conyers bill also requires the return "forthwith" of any property that has been seized if the government loses a forfeiture suit or has not initiated forfeiture proceedings within a year from the time of the seizure. In addition to the return of the property, the government would be obligated to pay interest on any cash or negotiable documents that it had held in the interim. Conyers also seeks to limit to $250,000 the annual amount paid to an informer and to obligate the attorney general to publish information annually concerning awards to informers.

The Conyers bill is an ideal one but a politically inexpedient one. Its chances of enactment are as unlikely as snow in the tropics. But Congress in mid-1993 was in a sympathetic mood to reform civil forfeiture in some way, if a compromise measure could be agreed upon. Texas congressman Jack Brooks, then chairman of the House Judiciary Committee, which would hear and report any bills on the subject of forfeiture, had signaled his willingness to hear witnesses on behalf of both bills.

That prospect energized the Clinton administration into a decision that it should be leading and moderating the way. Attorney General Janet Reno wrote Brooks a letter informing him that she was instructing the Department of Justice to review civil forfeiture for the purpose of recommending changes in policies and procedures. "The Department's goal," she wrote, "is to maintain and strengthen, if necessary, this important and effective law enforcement tool while at the same time improving current procedures to insure fairness and due process to all innocent property holders." Members of her staff, she reported, had already met with representatives of the bar associations and prominent members of the criminal defense bar, and would be meeting with federal, state, and local law enforcement officials. Reno calculated that in about seventy-five days she would be able to present to Congress an administration bill that would "deprive criminal wrongdoers of their ill-gotten gains through procedures which fully protect the lawful property interests of innocent owners." Accordingly, she requested Brooks to hold off his committee's consideration of any forfeiture legislation until Justice completed its study and developed its own "legislative package" striking "the correct balance to achieve the goal of tough, effective and fair law enforcement."[18]

Justice's proposals were framed mainly by Irwin Nathan, the principal associate deputy attorney general, and Stefan Cassella of the Criminal Division's Asset Forfeiture Office. The proposals took twice as much time to develop than Reno had estimated, but they were remarkably detailed and comprehensive. A copy of the Justice Department bill runs seventy-one pages, accompanied by a departmental "analysis" of fifty-two single-spaced pages. Michael Zeldin, the head of the Asset Forfeiture Office from 1988–90 and a reasonable man compared to his successor, Cary Copeland, said the Justice Department's bill "came a long way from the Bush administration's 'no compromise' stand on asset forfeiture." Zeldin believes the department's bill to be "a good-faith attempt to forge a middle ground between defense desires and prosecution desires." According to Zeldin the administration's proposals "made it easier for claimants to get into court and easier to prevail on the merits of their claims," which explains why "the government wants certain things for itself—expanding its tools of forfeiture."

By contrast, David B. Smith, now a member of the defense bar's task force on asset forfeiture but formerly one of the founders of the Justice Department's asset forfeiture program, savaged its bill. "If I had to choose between taking the Justice bill hook, line, and sinker and having no change in the current law," he said, "I'd rather have no change in the law." According to Smith, the bill "is overwhelmingly a prosecutor's wish list."[19] The evidence shows that Smith, not Zeldin, is right. In fact, the department's bill is extraordinarily reactionary. It takes away more than it offers. Cheryl Anthony Epps, the legislative director of the NACDL, nicely made the point: the department's "procedural reform" proposals, she said, "resemble legal legerdemain—now you see it, now you don't."[20]

The department's bill begins with a major reform: the government should bear the burden of proof in a civil forfeiture case. Unlike the Hyde and Conyers bills, Justice dilutes the proposition by proposing a standard of preponderance of evidence rather than clear and convincing evidence. If the Conyers proposal to abolish civil forfeiture ever succeeded, then the standard would be proof beyond a reasonable doubt. In light of the Supreme Court's *Austin* decision of 1993, realistically acknowledging that civil forfeiture imposes a criminal penalty, proof by a preponderance of evidence is inadequate.[21] Proof by a preponderance of evidence in a civil forfeiture case is better than a mere showing of probable cause, but it reflects a grudging way to propose this particular reform; still, it is quite liberal compared to most of the rest of the bill.[22]

Buried in the bill is a provision that radically alters the standard of proof for criminal forfeiture: "the party bearing the burden of proof shall be required to prove the matter at issue by a preponderance of the evidence."[23] That would substantially reduce the government's burden from the need for proof beyond reasonable doubt to the much lower standard, making the burden of proof for criminal forfeiture the same as it would be in civil forfeiture cases, if the Justice Department's recommendations became law. The provision is probably unconstitutional as a violation of due process of law, which requires proof beyond reasonable doubt in criminal cases.[24] However, five circuit courts have held that the standard of proof for criminal forfeiture in criminal prosecutions involving drugs is merely a preponderance of evidence. This is the basis of the department's recommendation, but those circuit courts, which are out of synchronization with others, probably misconstrued the act of Congress governing criminal drug prosecutions. In any case not even those five circuits have applied the lower burden of proof in any other criminal forfeiture cases. Congress should not only reject lowering the standard of proof in criminal forfeiture cases; it should amend the drug statute whose ambiguous wording allowed the five circuits to water down the normal burden of proof beyond reasonable doubt in criminal cases.

The Justice Department bill contains a provision sought by the defense bar, fixing a sixty-day period from time of seizure to the date that notice must be given to claimants that the government plans to seek forfeiture of the property. That is also a recommendation of the Hyde and Conyers bills, but they do not mute it by exempting the U.S. Customs Service and by allowing the government to seek forfeiture at a later date, after having returned the property following expiration of the sixty-day period. In fact, current policy of the Department of Justice, according to a departmental directive effective March 1, 1993, requires the return of the property and the termination of the forfeiture proceeding. The proposed bill alters that directive and permits a sort of double jeopardy until the statute of limitations expires five years after the commission of the crime that put the property into jeopardy.

The next section of the bill again takes as much as it gives. First it gives a thirty-day period (not sixty as in the Hyde and Conyers bills) for a claimant to file a claim and then it continues the cost bond, which both other bills would abolish. Continuation of the bond, except in cases involving indigents, shows a curmudgeonly attitude on the part of the department. Abandoning the bond would have cost little yet would have made a symbolic concession to both Hyde and Conyers. Instead, the Justice Department seems deliberately provocative and hard by insisting that people must pay for the privilege of contesting forfeiture. The exemption of paupers from the bond is something but is of no value to people of modest means who must post the bond in cash and find a lawyer within thirty days.

Nowhere in the bill is legal legerdemain more abundantly clear than in the provision on the innocent owner defense. Although the most frequently enforced civil forfeiture acts contain the defense, requiring proof that the owner neither knew of nor consented to his property's illegal use, most civil forfeiture acts do not contain such an offense. The Justice Department's bill has the virtue of establishing an innocent owner's defense for all civil forfeiture statutes and of fixing one standard for all. But it is not the standard of proof that the person neither knew of nor consented to the illegal use of his property. There are cases in which the person knew of the illegal use but did not consent to it, a fact that makes still more onerous the standard of proving that he did not know of *and* did not consent to its illegal use. The Justice Department bill requires still more by fixing the most onerous standard of all: proof that one "did everything that reasonably could be expected" to prevent or terminate the illegal use of the property. That standard provides the least possible protection to an innocent owner, and the Justice Department's bill would make it apply even to the currently existing statutes that permit proof of a lack of knowledge *or* consent.

How a person can prove that he took *all* reasonable precautions against the illegal use is unclear, and the standard itself is impractical and unjust. It allows a prosecutor to determine whether the owner made an adequate investigation or took sufficient precautions. In the case of an owner's acquisition of the property after the acts giving rise to the forfeiture had occurred, he would have to demonstrate that he was not only a bona fide purchaser but had no reasonable cause to believe, at the time of the purchase, that the property was subject to forfeiture. That is justifiable. The bill adds that if the government established the illegal use of the property, the bona fide purchaser must also show that he did all that could be expected to end the illegal use. The requirements imposed on the innocent owner at the time of the illegal use are much less reasonable than those imposed on the subsequent bona fide purchaser.

An outrageous provision in the Justice Department's bill would allow for an adverse inference to be drawn if a claimant asserted his Fifth Amendment right to refuse answer on grounds of self-incrimination. This provision is clearly unconstitutional as a burden on the exercise of a constitutional right.[25] To assume that the exercise of this or any other right, such as representation by counsel or trial by jury, implies guilt is to emasculate the right. The fact that the guilty benefit from the right, as they do from all other rights as well, is no reason to assume that one who exercises it has condemned himself. The very purpose of the right is to prevent involuntary self-condemnation. It is a right that applies to all proceedings, civil as well as criminal, including forfeiture proceedings and pretrial proceedings. The Justice Department bill, however, would penalize its use in forfeiture and pretrial proceedings by assuming guilt with respect to the matter on which the right has been invoked. Invoking it in a civil forfeiture proceeding is essential to preserving an opportunity to invoke the right in a criminal proceeding, which might well accompany or follow the civil one. Even in the absence of a criminal proceeding, burdening the right against compulsory self-incrimination violates the Fifth Amendment because, as the Supreme Court has held, a forfeiture proceeding imposes a criminal penalty.[26]

The Justice Department's bill allows government prosecutors to use grand jury information in civil forfeiture cases and allows them to acquire evidence in such cases by means normally used only in criminal cases. The grand jury should not be a means of the government's investigation in civil forfeiture cases. If it were, the government would be playing with a deck stacked in its favor. It could capitalize on grand jury rules of secrecy; it could have the advantage of using criminal methods to build its case without allowing the constitutional protections available in criminal cases; and it could hamper civil claimants from securing evidence in their own behalf. The government could, for example, use grand jury subpoenas to gather evidence for a civil forfeiture case, leaving the claimant to depend only on civil tactics. The bill provides that the government could take testimony under oath and "by subpoena, summon witnesses and require the production of any books, papers, correspondence, memoranda, or other records which the Attorney General [or any of his attorneys] deems relevant or material to the inquiry." "Any" records could include personal ones, the compulsory production of which violates the right against self-incrimination.[27] The sections in the bill authorizing grand jury information and civil investigative demands are, like many others in the bill, contrary to Janet Reno's promise to propose procedures that "insure fairness and due process."[28]

Another provision in the bill allows federal prosecutors to

obtain disclosure of tax returns for use in investigations leading to civil forfeiture proceedings. Currently, the right to use such information applies only in criminal cases. The bill would also expand civil as well as criminal forfeitures to cover the proceeds of every federal offense on the statute books, including misdemeanors as well as all felonies. These are among the very many expansions of government power in this bill, which is supposed to be a response to reformist impulses. Sections 201 through 211 constitute Title II of the bill, which is called "Expansion of Substantive Forfeiture."

One of the criminal forfeiture provisions deals, lethally, with the right to be represented by counsel of choice, under the heading "Assets Needed to Pay Attorney's Fees." It starts as if it will benefit the defendant by providing him with a hearing at which he can show by a preponderance of evidence that he has insufficient assets, other than the property at issue, to retain counsel. However, even if he meets that burden of proof, he does not get to keep the assets to pay for the attorney. If the government can merely show "the existence of probable cause to believe that the restrained property is likely to be forfeited upon the conviction of the defendant," the probable cause established by an indictment "shall be determinative." Only if the government fails to meet its probable cause burden may a court permit the defendant to use the asset to retain counsel.[29]

In another section, the Justice Department bill would extend its present authority to impose pretrial restraints. Property that constitutes substitute assets is not now subject to injunction. Injunctions freezing property subject to forfeiture help prevent its transfer or concealment, but if the criminal manages to outsmart the government by preventing it from seizing criminal assets, the substitution of other assets for those used in a crime or deriving from a

224

crime is a necessary means of insuring that the criminal does not profit. However, Congress has not authorized the injunctive power to be used to preserve the availability of substitute assets before trial. The Department of Justice alleges that "until recently the courts were unanimous in their view that the restraining order provision applied both to property directly traceable to the offense and to property forfeitable as substitute assets." It turns out that "courts were unanimous" is a generalization based only on decisions by the Second and Fourth Circuit Courts and by two district courts.[30] The NACDL is only a bit more careful with the facts, alleging that the Justice Department gave "no explanation for why it needs to freeze wholly legitimate assets prior to trial," and that "a majority of the federal appellate courts" have held that the government "may *not* seize or restrain substitute assets." The government may, but not before trial according to a "majority" of the federal appellate courts—which turns out to be just three courts (the Third, Fifth, and Ninth Circuits), as opposed to the two that the Justice Department found to be a unanimous voice "until recently." The defense lawyers have a good point in arguing that the hardship on defendants from pretrial restraint of substitute assets would extend, too, to many third parties who "depend upon or have vested rights in the legitimate property" that the department proposal would restrain.[31]

Of the fifty-one sections in the Justice Department bill, the section on pretrial restraint of assets is one of the many that expand government power or load the dice in favor of government interests. The short way to assess the bill is to describe it, as David B. Smith said, as a "prosecutor's wish list." It is unfair and will violate due process rights, if it is passed. Its chances of being enacted are considerably greater than that of the Conyers bill but far less than the chances of the Hyde bill. The latter now has the bipartisan support of scores of congressmen, and probably is a compromise package that will muster the most votes. The coalition that backs reform will combat the Justice Department bill as the Pearl Harbor of their aspirations. Banks, mortgage companies, and other proponents of property rights will surely lobby against many provisions of the department's bill that diminish their interests as third parties, innocent owners, or lien holders, while civil libertarians and the criminal defense bar will just as surely mount a campaign for constitutional rights.

Congressman Hyde holds the balance of power. The November 1994 elections, which produced Republican majorities in both houses of Congress, resulted in Hyde's becoming chairman of the House Judiciary Committee. Although he would never have conceded anything on the need to shift the burden of proof from victim to government, some observers believed that, before the elections, Hyde might have been more willing to compromise with the Department of Justice than with the radicals who support the Conyers bill; Hyde's legislative counsel implied as much when saying, "Other than the burden-of-proof issue, everything is negotiable. If you lock Mr. Hyde and the Justice Department in a room for a few days, I'm sure they'll come up with something mutually agreeable."[32] But Hyde has described civil forfeiture as an Alice-in-Wonderland phenomenon that beheads first and then gets on with the trial or, still worse, as a Kafka-like condition that convicts and penalizes without a trial or even an accusation.[33] That is an intolerable condition, and Hyde, who has also shown that he is willing to associate himself with the ACLU and the NACDL on this issue, is not likely to be the patsy of a Department of Justice responsible to Janet Reno and Bill Clinton. Nor is John Conyers a nonentity who can be ignored.

Real if modest reform is likely. Law enforcement hawks

like Sheriff Johnny Mack Brown will probably hold onto equitable sharing and adoptive forfeiture but will have to pay a price for a victory that pits conservatives against state laws. Any bill that survives Congress will probably be so nuanced that every interest will gain something and none will be utterly defeated. Hyde's bill stands the best chance of adoption, given his new prominence and power. On the other hand, some Republican leaders have promised to support a variety of constitutional amendments that the Judiciary Committee might have to consider. If amendments are introduced to authorize school prayer, balanced budgets, terms limits, and a line-item presidential veto, Hyde's committee won't get around to the subject of forfeiture for a long time.

Notes

Chapter 1

1. "U.S. Eases Rule on Drug Linked Ship Seizures," *Los Angeles Times*, May 21, 1988, sec. 2, p. 3.

2. John Dillin, "Law Would Rein In Agents," *Christian Science Monitor*, June 17, 1993, p. 2; ibid., September 28, 1993, p. 10; Hyde, "Civil Asset Forfeiture: A Briefing Paper," p. 2.

3. Jeff Brazil and Steve Berry, "Deputies Take $19,000 and Leave a Woman in Despair," *Orlando Sentinel*, June 14, 1992; John Dillin, "Tracking More Than Just Speed," *Christian Science Monitor*, October 4, 1993, p. 8.

4. Andrew Schneider and Mary Pat Flaherty, *Presumed Guilty: The Law's Victims in the War on Drugs*, series of articles reprinted from the *Pittsburgh Press*, August 11–16, 1991, p. 22.

5. Ibid., p. 15, from story entitled "Drugs Contaminate Nearly All the Money in America."

6. Ibid., p. 12, from story entitled "Drug Agents More Likely to Stop Minorities," including the quotation. *Jones v. U.S. Drug Enforcement Agency*, LEXIS 5409, April 23, 1993. See also Jones's testimony, *Department of Justice Asset Forfeiture Program* (Hearing before the Legislation and National Security Subcommittee of the House Committee on Government Operations), pp. 10–15, 68–71. Jones's lawyer was E. E. "Bo" Edwards.

7. John Dillin, "Seized Assets Are a Bitter Harvest," *Christian Science Monitor*, October 5, 1993, p. 6.

8. *Department of Justice Asset Forfeiture Program*, pp. 16–45, 173–251, which includes the Sheldons' testimony and documents on their case. "Couple Wins Forfeiture Case against Feds," *Christian Science Monitor*, October 18, 1993, p. 4.

9. Schneider and Flaherty, *Presumed Guilty*, pp. 31–32; Hyde, "Civil

Asset Forfeiture: A Briefing Paper," pp. 2–3; and Miniter, "Property Seizures on Trial," p. 33.

10. Schneider and Flaherty, *Presumed Guilty*, p. 7.

11. Ibid., pp. 9–10.

12. Bradbury, "Report on the Death of Donald Scott," quotation at p. 51. John Dillin, "Citizens Caught in the Cross-Fire," *Christian Science Monitor*, October 1, 1993, pp. 6–7.

13. 250 F. Supp. 183, 185 (1966).

14. 250 F. Supp. 410 (D.C.N.D. Tex.), rev'd sub nom. *King v. United States*, 364 F. 2d 235, 236 (5th Cir. 1966).

15. *J. W. Goldsmith, Jr.–Grant Co. v. United States*, 354 U.S. 505, 510–11 (1921). I deal with Blackstone's views below, this chapter.

16. *United States v. United States Coin and Currency*, 401 U.S. 715, 719–20 (1971).

17. Quoted in Hyde, "Prosecution and Punishment of Animals," p. 697.

18. Evans, *Criminal Prosecution*, p. 9.

19. Ibid., pp. 188–89; Holmes, *Common Law*, pp. 19–35.

20. Appendix X of Evans, *Criminal Prosecution*, pp. 265–86, contains a chronological list of 191 cases involving the capital punishment of animals, from 824 to 1906.

21. Holdsworth, *History of English Law*, 2:47.

22. Bracton, *De Legibus et Consuetudinibus Angliae*, 2:284; Stephen, *History of the Criminal Law of England*, 3:77; Holmes, *Common Law*, p. 21.

23. Blackstone, *Commentaries on the Laws of England*, 4:380–88.

24. Hale, *Pleas of the Crown*, pp. 419–21, 477.

25. The New York case is described in Morris, *Studies*, p. 229. The remaining examples of deodand in this paragraph come from Karraker, "Deodands," pp. 712–17.

26. Morris, *Studies*, pp. 220–30, reported American cases on deodand and also misreported as deodand cases those in which surviving relatives received the forfeiture. The deodand cases that I refer to in this paragraph are accurately described by Morris, whose primary sources I checked.

27. Karraker, "Deodands," pp. 716–17.

28. Blackstone, *Commentaries on the Laws of England*, 1:301–2.

29. Holmes, *Common Law*, p. 5.

30. *Baker v. Bolton*, 1 Campb. 493 (1808).

31. Levy, *Chief Justice Shaw*, pp. 155–58.

32. Finkelstein, "Goring Ox," pp. 171–74, an invaluable article. Lord Campbell's Act, 9 & 10 Vict. ch. 93 (1846).

33. Finkelstein, "Goring Ox," p. 171, for the quotation from Lord Campbell.

34. Quoted in Holdsworth, *History of English Law*, 2:477.

Chapter 2

1. Cauble's case is reported in *United States v. Ruppel*, 666 F. 2d 261 (5th Cir. 1982), *United States v. Cauble*, 706 F. 2d 1322 (5th Cir. 1983), and Lauter, "U.S. Seizure of Assets Accelerates." On Milken, see *New York Times*, April 25, 1990, p. A1; on the bank, see *New York Times*, December 20, 1992, p. A1.

2. Cheh, "Constitutional Limits"; Clark, "Civil and Criminal Penalties and Forfeitures."

3. Pollock and Maitland, *History of English Law*, 2:461–80; Holdsworth, *History of English Law*, 3:67–69.

4. Blackstone, *Commentaries on the Laws of England*, 4:97.

5. Stubbs, *Constitutional History of England*, 1:90, 96, 101–3; Pollock and Maitland, *History of English Law*, 2:598–603; Van Caenegem, *Royal Writs in England*, 77:16–17.

6. Lea, *Superstition and Force*, pp. 22–99; Moriarty, *Oaths in Ecclesiastical Courts*, pp. 12–22.

7. On trial by battle, see Lea, *Superstition and Force*, pp. 101–247; on escheats, year and a day, and treason, see Pollock and Maitland, *History of English Law*, 2:461–70; McKechnie, *Magna Carta*, pp. 337–39.

8. On Henry II, see Stenton, "England. Henry II," pp. 554–91.

9. *Washington Post*, February 26, 1994, p. A1.

10. McKechnie, *Magna Carta*, p. 380; Thayer, *Preliminary Treatise*, pp. 41–60; Pollock and Maitland, *History of English Law*, 1:137–42; Holdsworth, *History of English Law*, 1:312–13; and Haskins, *Norman Institutions*, pp. 196–238.

11. Kiralfy, *Potter's Historical Introduction*, pp. 347, 350; Plucknett, *Concise History of the Common Law*, pp. 101–6, 455–58. On outlawry, see Keane, *Outlaws of England*.

12. Van Caenegem, *Royal Writs*, 77:55–56, 82–96, 260–335; Pollock and Maitland, *History of English Law*, 1:145–49, 2:644–49; Holds-

worth, *History of English Law*, 1:324–25; Thayer, *Preliminary Treatise*, pp. 81–86.,

13. Chapter 32 of Magna Carta; McKechnie, *Magna Carta*, pp. 337–38.

14. Holdsworth, *History of English Law*, 3:70 (quotation), 8:307–22. Chapter 2 of Hurst, *Law of Treason*, is a splendid survey of "English Sources of the Law of Treason"; see pp. 14–67.

15. Blackstone, *Commentaries on the Laws of England*, 1:299.

16. Ibid., 1:302–3.

17. Ibid., 4:382.

18. Ibid., 4:18; Stephen, *History of the Criminal Law*, 2:274–71; Holdsworth, *History of English Law*, 2:449–50, 3:287–93.

19. Blackstone, *Commentaries on the Laws of England*, 1:388.

20. Ibid., 1:381, 385, 387.

21. On the relation-back doctrine, see Holdsworth, *History of English Law*, 3:69–70; Jankowski, "Tempering the Relation-Back Doctrine"; Zeldin and Weiner, "Innocent Third Parties and Their Rights"; 21 U.S.C. sec. 853(c). The 1814 decision was in *United States v. 1960 Bags of Coffee*, 12 U.S. 398, 405 (1814).

22. Holdsworth, *History of English Law*, 1:326–27; Thayer, *Preliminary Treatise*, p. 71; Pollock and Maitland, *History of English Law*, 2:650.

23. Pollock and Maitland, *History of English Law*, 2:619; Thayer, *Preliminary Treatise*, pp. 74–80; for the quotation, Plucknett, *Concise History of the Common Law*, p. 126.

24. Starkey, *The Devil in Massachusetts*, pp. 209–11.

25. Stephen, *History of Criminal Law*, 1:298–300; Thayer, *Preliminary Treatise*, pp. 75–80.

26. Holdsworth, *History of English Law*, 3:70, 72.

27. Massachusetts Body of Liberties, in Perry, *Sources of Our Liberties*, p. 149, para. 10; Trumbull and Hoadley, *Public Records of the Colony of Connecticut*, 1:536–37; Bartlett, *Records of the Colony of Rhode Island*, 1:162.

28. Goebel and Naughton, *Law Enforcement in Colonial New York*, p. 716.

29. *Respublica v. Doan*, 1 Dallas 86 (1784).

30. Browne, *Archives of Maryland*, 1:17, 19, 158.

31. Scott, *Criminal Law in Colonial Virginia*, pp. 107–10.

32. Hurst, *Law of Treason*, pp. 85–89.

33. Ibid., pp. 68–125; Chapin, *American Law of Treason*, pp. 73–80.

34. Act of April 20, 1790, 1 St. 117, ch. 9, sec. 24, codified 18 U.S.C. sec. 3563.

35. Kent, *Commentaries on American Law*, 2:385–86, and for the quotation, 4:427.

Chapter 3

1. An *in personam* proceeding may also fix the civil liability of an individual. All criminal cases are *in personam* but not all *in personam* cases are criminal.

2. Holmes, *Common Law*, p. 26. On the development of the English court of admiralty, see Robertson, *Admiralty and Federalism*, pp. 35–64.

3. Gilmore and Black, *Law of Admiralty*, pp. 20–24, 28–33, 39–40.

4. Harper, *English Navigation Laws*, pp. 387–414, is a digest of the laws; and Barrow, *Trade and Empire*, pp. 1–17.

5. Dickerson, *Navigation Acts*, pp. 10–11, 31–44; Harper, *English Navigation Laws*, pp. 89–90, 111–14; Robertson, *Admiralty and Federalism*, p. 294.

6. Holdsworth, *History of English Law*, 1:559–61; Blackstone, *Commentaries on the Laws of England*, 3:262; Harper, *English Navigation Laws*, pp. 109–23.

7. Ubbelohde, *Vice Admiralty Courts*, pp. 5–22; the quotation is from the *Pennsylvania Journal*, October 19, 1769, in Dickerson, *Navigation Acts*, p. 230; Lovejoy, "Rights Imply Equality"; Robertson, *Admiralty and Federalism*, pp. 70–94; Wroth, "Massachusetts Vice Admiralty Court."

8. Holmes, *Common Law*, pp. 27, 29–30.

9. Ubbelohde, *Vice Admiralty Courts*, pp. 12–19, and Harper, *English Navigation Laws*, pp. 53–57, 111–14, 183–84.

10. *Mitchell* qui tam *v. Torup*, Parker 227, 233 (1776), 145 Eng. Rep. 764, 766.

11. Casto, "Origins of Federal Admiralty Jurisdiction," pp. 122–23, 126–28, on state admiralty courts; see also Robertson, *Admiralty and Federalism*, pp. 96–103.

12. *Phile* qui tam *v. The Ship* Anna, 1 Dallas 187–208 (1787).

13. *Calero-Toledo v. Pearson Yacht Leasing Co.*, 416 U.S. 663 (1974).

14. Act of July 31, 1789, 1st Cong., 1st sess., chap. 5, secs. 5, 12, and 36, 1 Stat. 29, 36–37, 39, 43, 47. See also Act of August 4, 1790, 1st Cong., 2d sess., chap. 34, secs. 13, 22, 27, 28, 31, and 67, 1 Stat. 138, 157,

161, 163–65, 176; Act of March 22, 1794, 3d Cong., 1st sess., chap. 11, sec. 1, 1 Stat. 347; Act of March 2, 1807, 7th Cong., 2d sess., chap. 22, sec. 2, 2 Stat. 426. On forfeiture for piracy and slavetrading, see Waples, *Treatise on Proceedings in Rem*, pp. 215–27, 259–60.

15. Act of March 2, 1799, sec. 6; see John Dean Goss, *History of Tariff Administration*, p. 29.

16. Judiciary Act of 1789, chap. 9, 1 Stat. 77, quoted in Robertson, *Admiralty and Federalism*, p. 18.

17. David Sewall to Caleb Strong, March 28, 1789, quoted in Casto, "Origins of Federal Admiralty Jurisdiction," p. 156.

18. Doyle, *Crime and Forfeiture*, appendix, pp. 45–49, listing federal forfeiture statutes.

19. *United States v. La Vengeance*, 3 Dallas 297 (1796).

20. *United States v. The Schooner Betsy and Charlotte and Her Cargo*, 4 Cranch 443 (1808).

21. *United States v. The Palmyra*, 25 U.S. 1, 14–15 (1827).

22. *United States v. Brig Malek Adhel*, 43 U.S. 210, 233–34 (1844), citing *United States v. Schooner Little Charles*, 1 Brock. Rep. 347, 354 (1818).

23. The forfeiture act of the Confederate Congress is reprinted in McPherson, *Political History of the United States*, pp. 203–4.

24. *Armitz Brown v. United States*, 8 Cranch 110 (1814).

25. Quoted in Randall, *Constitutional Problems under Lincoln*, pp. 69–70. Emphasis added.

26. Prize Cases, 67 U.S. 635, 670 (1863).

27. *Miller v. United States*, 78 U.S. 268, 307 (1871).

28. Quoted in McPherson, *Battle Cry of Freedom*, p. 500.

29. U.S. Stat. at Large, XII, 589, reprinted in McPherson, *Political History of the United States*, pp. 196–97, 201.

30. *Congressional Globe*, 37th Cong., 2d sess. (1862), 1574, 1809, 2921, 2960, and App. 202, 267, 304.

31. Ibid., 1574, for Henderson; ibid., 2921, for Browning. For "hocus pocus," see remarks of Sen. Jacob Collamer of Vermont, ibid., 1809.

32. Ibid., 2294, remarks of Rep. J. W. Wallace; ibid., App. 167, remarks of Rep. E. Babbitt. See also 2294.

33. Lincoln's message of July 17, 1862, and the joint resolution are reprinted in *The Collected Works of Abraham Lincoln*, ed. Roy P. Basler, 8 vols. (New Brunswick: Rutgers University Press, 1953), 5:328–31; both are also reprinted in McPherson, *Political History of the United States*, pp. 197–98, 202–3. Emphasis added.

34. *Page, exr. of Samuel Miller, v. United States*, 78 U.S. 268 (1871). Justice D. Davis dissented from the disposition of the case but agreed with the majority on the constitutional issues. The Court also decided two companion cases: *McVeigh v. United States*, 78 U.S. 259 (1871), and *Tyler v. Defrees*, 78 U.S. 331 (1871).

35. Ibid., 322, 323.

36. Maxeiner, "Bane of American Forfeiture Law," pp. 768, 779–80 (n. 73), listing criminal forfeiture cases. The list does not prove his point that there were many, at least not in the nineteenth century.

37. *Dobbins v. United States*, 96 U.S. 395, 401, 404 (1878).

38. *Coffey v. United States*, 116 U.S. 436, 438, 440 (1886).

39. *Origet v. United States*, 125 U.S. 240 (1888).

40. Brandeis in *Olmstead v. United States*, 277 U.S. 438, 474 (1928).

41. *Boyd v. United States*, 116 U.S. 616, 634–35 (1886).

42. The Court subsequently repudiated much of its Boyd holding on the self-incrimination issue. See *Fisher v. United States*, 425 U.S. 391, 405–8 (1976).

43. *United States v. Zucker*, 161 U.S. 475 (1896).

44. *J. W. Goldsmith, Jr.–Grant Co. v. United States*, 254 U.S. 505, 509, 510, 511 (1921).

Chapter 4

1. See Edelhertz, *Nature, Impact, and Prosecution*, p. 3, defining white-collar crime as illegal acts committed by nonviolent means and by concealment and guile to obtain money or property or to avoid losing either. The $200 billion estimate is from Conyers, "Corporate and White-Collar Crime," pp. 287–88.

2. RICO is Pub. Law No. 91-452, codified at 18 U.S.C. sections 1961–68. The Continuing Criminal Enterprise Act is Pub. Law No. 91-513, codified at 21 U.S.C. sec. 848.

3. *Organized Crime Control* (Hearings before Subcommittee No. 5 of the House Committee on the Judiciary), on S. 30 and Related Proposals, Serial No. 27, 158. Hereafter cited as *Organized Crime Control* (Hearings).

4. "Message of the President of the United States Relative to the Fight Against Organized Crime, April 23, 1969, to the Congress," in *Measures Relating to Organized Crime* (Hearings), pp. 1069, 445. Hereafter cited as *Measures Relating to Organized Crime*.

5. *Organized Crime Control* (Hearings), p. 78.

6. *Congressional Record* 116 (January 21, 1970): 595.

7. Ibid., p. 597.

8. According to Sen. Joseph D. Tydings, March 3, 19, 1969, in *Measures Relating to Organized Crime*, p. 158.

9. Senate Reports, 91st Cong., 1st sess., Dec. 18, 1969; *Organized Crime Control Act of 1969*, Calender No. 612, Report No. 91-617, p. 76. Senate Reports hereafter cited as Sen. Rep.

10. Ibid., pp. 76, 78.

11. Sen. Rep. 76–77, citing Sen. Rep. No. 307, Special Comm. to Investigate Commerce, U.S. Sen., 82d Cong., 1st sess., 170–81 (1951). See also Sen. Rep. No. 141, 82d Cong., 1st sess., 1951.

12. Sen. Rep. No. 1784, 87th Cong., 2d sess., 1962, and Sen. Rep. No. 621, 86th Cong., 2d sess., 1960.

13. President's Commission on Law Enforcement and Administration of Justice, *Challenge of Crime*, p. 187.

14. Ibid., pp. 208–9, quotation at p. 209.

15. S. 30, in *Measures Relating to Organized Crime*, pp. 4–29.

16. *Congressional Record* 115 (1969): 9567.

17. *Measures Relating to Organized Crime*, pp. 107–13, 116, testimony of March 18, 1969.

18. S. 1861, *Corrupt Organizations Act of 1969*, in ibid., pp. 61–82. Sec. 1962 defined "prohibited racketeering activities" and sec. 1963 the criminal penalties, including forfeiture. The quotation is at p. 67.

19. Nixon's message to Congress, April 23, 1969, in *Measures Relating to Organized Crime*, pp. 448–50.

20. Ibid., Deputy Attorney General to McClellan, August 11, 1969, pp. 406–7.

21. *United States v. Mann*, 26 F. Cas. 1153, 1155 (C.C.D.N.H. 1812). 14 Stat. 179, Act of July 18, 1866. "Strictly penal" is in *Stockwell v. United States*, 80 U.S. 531, 551 (1871), and "denounces a forfeiture" in *United States v. Claflin*, 97 U.S. 546, 553 (1878).

22. Kleindienst to McClellan, August 11, 1969, *Measures Relating to Organized Crime*, pp. 409.

23. Ibid., pp. 456, 472.

24. Senate Committee on the Judiciary, *Report on Organized Crime Control Act of 1969*, Sen. Rep. No. 617, 91st Cong., 1st sess., 1969, 76. The House Report on RICO, No. 1549, 91st Cong., 2d sess., 1970, 57, said the same thing.

25. *Organized Crime Control Act of 1969*, Sen. Rep. No. 91-671, 76–80, 160.

26. *Congressional Record* 116 (January 21–23, 1970): 591, 592, 602, 603. Several senators who mentioned the criminal penalties provision failed to mention forfeiture.

27. Ibid., p. 972. The sole nay was Lee Metcalf of Montana, who did not speak.

28. *Organized Crime Control* (Hearings), p. 106.

29. Ibid., p. 107.

30. Ibid., p. 171; see also pp. 519 and 687 for other references to forfeiture, equally general and brief.

31. The city bar's analysis of RICO extends for almost fifty pages, of which Title IX received over four; ibid., pp. 327–31. The spokesman for the city bar offered oral testimony that also ignored the subject of forfeiture; ibid., pp. 369–70, for the Q. and A. on Title IX.

32. Ibid., pp. 401–3.

33. House Report No. 1549, 91st Cong., 2d sess. (1970), 57. House Reports hereafter cited as H. Rep.

34. *Department of Justice Asset Forfeiture Program* (Hearing before the Legislation and National Security Subcommittee of the House Committee on Government Operations), pp. 45–56 (case of Harlan Vander Zee discussed below, beginning of Chap. 7).

35. Ibid., pp. 187–88.

36. The House debate is in *Congressional Record* 116 (October 1970): 35,191–217 and 35,287–364.

37. *Asset Forfeiture: A Seldom Used Tool*, p. 40.

38. Useful articles on RICO include Tarlow, "RICO: The New Darling"; Blakey and Gettings, "Racketeer Influenced and Corrupt Organizations"; Bradley, "Racketeers, Congress, and the Courts"; Weiner, "Crime Must Not Pay"; Reed and Gill, "RICO Forfeitures."

39. Pub. Law No. 91-452, 84 Stat. 922 (1970), codified at 18 U.S.C. secs. 1961–68.

40. McClellan, "Organized Crime Act," pp. 143, 144.

41. Blakey, "Foreword: Symposium on Law," pp. 880; National Organization for Women Inc., 114 S.Ct. 798 (1993). The environmentalist issue is based on my personal conjecture.

42. *Comprehensive Drug Abuse Prevention and Control Act of 1970*, H. Rep. No. 91-1444 (pt. 1), 5, 50, 82. 21 U.S.C. sect. 848.

43. *Congressional Record* 116 (January 26, 1970): 1181–83.

44. Pianin, "Criminal Forfeiture," is a good introduction to the CCE Act.

45. Pub. Law No. 91-513, sec. 511 (1970); 84 Stat. 123–6, codified as 21 U.S.C. sec. 881.

46. 21 U.S.C. sec. 881(a)(6).

47. The quotation is from Myers and Brzostowski, *Drug Agents' Guide*, p. 6. The second edition of this guide, 1987, carried a similar statement, pp. 3–4. The government study is the GAO report (*Asset Forfeiture: A Seldom Used Tool*) cited in n. 37 above, p. 9.

Chapter 5

1. *Calero-Toledo v. Pearson Yacht Leasing Co.*, 416 U.S. 663 (1974). The case arose in Puerto Rico, which the Supreme Court treated as if it were a state for Fourteenth Amendment purposes.

2. Ibid., 691.

3. Ibid., 683 and 688.

4. Ibid., 689.

5. *Boyd v. United States*, 116 U.S. 616, 633–34 (1886); *One 1958 Plymouth Sedan v. Pennsylvania*, 380 U.S. 693, 700 (1965); *United States v. United States Coin and Currency*, 401 U.S. 715, 721–22 (1971).

6. 416 U.S. 663, 687 (1974).

7. 427 U.S. 297 (1976).

8. *Schad v. Borough of Mt. Ephraim*, 452 U.S. 61 (1981); see also *Young v. America Mini Theatres, Inc.*, 427 U.S. 50, 62 (1976).

9. *New Orleans v. Dukes*, 427 U.S. at 303.

10. *Morey v. Doud*, 354 U.S. 457 (1957).

11. Gellhorn, "Abuses of Occupational Licensing," p. 6, n. 2.

12. See further Leonard W. Levy, "Property as a Human Right," *Constitutional Commentary* 5 (1988): 169–84, reprinted in Levy, *Seasoned Judgments*, pp. 13–30.

13. *United States v. Marubini America Corp.*, 611 F. 2d 763 (9th Cir. 1980); *United States v. Thevis*, 474 F. Supp. 134 (M.D. Ga., 1979).

14. *United States v. Thevis*, 474 F. Supp. 134, 142.

15. *United States v. Martino*, 648 F. 2d (5th Cir. 1981).

16. *United States v. Turkette*, 632 F. 2d 396 (1980). *United States v. Errico*, 635 F. 2d 152 (2d Cir. 1980) held the opposite, as had *United States v. Cappetto*, 502 F. 2d 1351 (7th Cir. 1974), where the court held that enterprise meant both legitimate and illegitimate organizations.

17. *United States v. Martino*, 648 F. 2d (5th Cir. 1981).

18. *United States v. Turkette*, 452 U.S. 576 (1981).

19. *United States v. Martino*, 681 F. 2d 952 (5th Cir. 1982), overruling the 1981 decision cited above, n. 17.

20. *Russello v. United States*, 464 U.S. 16, 26, 28 (1983).

21. *Forfeiture of Narcotics Proceeds* (Hearings before the Subcommittee on Criminal Justice of the Senate Committee of the Judiciary), 1–7.

22. *Asset Forfeiture: A Seldom Used Tool*, p. i.

23. Ibid., pp. 9–15.

24. Ibid., pp. ii, 10, 12–13.

25. *Forfeiture of Narcotics Proceeds*, pp. 19, 51–60. *United States v. Meinster*, 488 F. Supp. 1342 (S.D. Fla. 1980) and 664 F. 2d. (5th Cir. 1981).

26. Ibid.

27. *United States v. Mandel*, 408 F. Supp. 679 (D.Md. 1976); see also *United States v. Scalzitti*, 408 F. Supp. 1014 (N.D. Pa. 1975), *United States v. Long*, 654 F. 2d 911, 915 (3d Cir. 1981);, *United States v. Veon*, 538 F. Supp. 237 (E.D. Cal. 1982), *United States v. Crozier*, 674 F. 2d 1293 (9th Cir. 1982), *United States v. Spilotro*, 680 F. 2d 612 (9th Cir. 1982), *United States v. Beckham*, 562 F. Supp. 486 (E.D. Mich. 1983).

28. *Comprehensive Crime Control Act of 1983*, Sen. Rep. No. 98-225, 193–96.

29. *United States v. Mandel*, 408 F. Supp. 679 (D. Md. 1976). Cf., *United States v. Bello*, 470 F. Supp. 723, 724 (S.D. Cal. 1979), where the court said that the Mandel opinion "emasculates" restraining orders.

30. See *United States v. Mannino*, 79 Cr. 744 (S.D.N.Y. 1980), and *United States v. Marubini America Corp.*, 611 F. 2d 763 (9th Cir. 1980).

31. Kurisky, "Civil Forfeiture of Assets." See also Wisotsky, *Breaking the Impasse*. These figures on the drug traffic are estimates, which vary from source to source. I drew on *Asset Forfeiture: A Seldom Used Tool*, p. 1, and Kurisky, "Civil Forfeiture of Assets," p. 240.

32. *Asset Forfeiture: A Seldom Used Tool*, p. i.

33. Ibid., pp. 16–24.

34. Appendix VI, Dept. of Justice letter, March 19, 1981, to GAO, ibid., pp. 58–75.

Chapter 6

1. On probable cause, see La Fave, *Search and Seizure*, 1:436–99.

2. Myers and Brzostowski, *Drug Agents' Guide* (rev. ed., 1987), pp. 15–19.

3. Ibid., pp. 208–15.

4. Ibid., p. 206. Judicial forfeiture is discussed in ibid., pp. 193–207.

5. Ibid., p. 159. On the relation-back doctrine, see above, Chap. 2, nn. 20–21, and related text.

6. Myers and Brzostowski, *Drug Agents' Guide* (rev. ed., 1987), pp. 242, 271, 277–78; *Comprehensive Crime Control Act of 1983*, Sen. Rep. No. 98-225, pp. 193–95, is a good comparison of the workings of civil and criminal forfeitures. Hereafter cited as *Crime Control Act of 1983* (Report).

7. *Forfeiture in Drug Cases* (Hearings on H.R. 2646, H.R. 4110, and H.R. 5371 before the Subcommittee on Crime of the House Committee on the Judiciary).

8. Ibid., p. 156, statement of Deputy Associate Attorney General Jeffrey Harris.

9. Ibid., p. 157.

10. Ibid., pp. 200–212. Taylor wrote "Forfeiture under 18 U.S.C. Sect. 1963—RICO's Most Powerful Weapon," *American Criminal Law Review* 17 (1980): 379, and "Problem of Proportionality in RICO Forfeiture," *Notre Dame Law Review* 65 (1990): 885–95.

11. Testimony of Irvin B. Nathan, in *Forfeiture in Drug Cases*, pp. 218–37, citing *United States v. Turkette*, 101 S.Ct. 2524 (1981).

12. *Comprehensive Criminal Forfeiture Act of 1982*, Sen. Rep. No. 97-520, p. 3.

13. Ibid., p. 4.

14. On the relation-back doctrine, see above, Chap. 2, nn. 20–21, and related text. The Supreme Court initially upheld the relation-back doctrine in civil forfeiture cases in *United States v. 1960 Bags of Coffee*, 12 U.S. 398, 405 (1814).

15. See *Comprehensive Criminal Forfeiture Act of 1982*, Sen. Rep. No. 97-520, pp. 6–21, for a section-by-section analysis of the proposed bill.

16. *Weekly Compilation of Presidential Documents* 19:478 (January 14, 1983); Reagan said that although the "provisions on forfeiture of criminal assets and profits fall short of what the Administration proposed, they are clearly desirable. Had they been presented to me as a separate measure, I would have been pleased to give my approval." See also *Crime Control Act of 1983* (Report), p. 192.

17. *Comprehensive Crime Control Act of 1983* (Hearings before the Subcommittee on Criminal Law of the Senate Committee on the Judiciary), pp. 803–4. Hereafter, *Crime Control Act of 1983* (Hearings).

18. Ibid., p. 811.

19. *Crime Control Act of 1983* (Report), p. 192.

20. Ibid., pp. 207–9.

21. Ibid., pp. 201–2.

22. Ibid., pp. 203–4.

23. *Calero-Toledo v. Pearson Yacht Co.*, 416 U.S. 663, 678 (1974).

24. *Crime Control Act of 1983* (Report), pp. 216–17, 219.

25. Ibid., p. 218.

26. *United States v. $321,470 U.S. Currency*, 874 F. 2d 298, 299 (5th Cir. 1989).

27. 799 F. 2d 1357 (9th Cir. 1986).

28. *Comprehensive Drug Penalty Act of 1984*, H. Rep. No. 98-845 (pt. 1). Hereafter cited as *Drug Penalty Act of 1984*.

29. *United States v. Marubini America Corp.*, 611 F. 2d. 763, 769 (1980), in which the court alluded to the shopkeeper in *United States v. Parness*, 503 D. 2d 430 (2d Cir. 1974).

30. *United States v. Huber*, 403 F. 2d 387, 397 (1979).

31. *Drug Penalty Act of 1984*, pp. 10–12.

32. Ibid., pp. 57–58.

33. *Anti-Drug Abuse Act of 1986*, Pub. L. No. 99-570, sec. 1153(a); Reed, "Criminal Forfeiture," is a good survey of the 1984 act.

Chapter 7

1. Statement of Harlan Vander Zee, former banker, San Antonio, in *Department of Justice Asset Forfeiture Program* (Hearing before the Legislation and National Security Subcommittee of the House Committee on Government Operations), pp. 45–68.

2. Ibid., p. 52.

3. Ibid.

4. Bush, "Impact of RICO Forfeiture," p. 996.

5. Quoted by Peter Cassidy, "Without Due Process," p. 34.

6. Rice, *Trafficking*, is a readable and thorough account.

7. *New York Times*, February 6, 1990, p. D24.

8. Ibid., December 20, 1991, p. A1; January 25, 1992, sec. 1, p. 1, and Business section.

9. *United States v. Regan*, 726 F. Supp. 447 (S.D.N.Y. 1989). The Princeton-Newport and Drexel Bunham Lambert cases are discussed in several articles in "Symposium on Law and the Continuing Enterprise: Perspectives on RICO," *Notre Dame Law Review* 65 (1990): 873–1073,

by William Taylor, Graeme W. Bush, Bruce David, Gordon Crovitz, and Joseph Bauerschmidt.

10. On Milken and Drexel Burnham, see *New York Times*, November 22, 1990, pp. A1 and D4. See also Bruck, *Predators' Ball*; Stein, *A License to Steal*.

11. *New York Times*, September 30, 1992, p. D15.

12. Ibid., April 24, 1992, p. B4; May 20, 1992, p. B1; May 27, 1992, p. B4.

13. Ibid., October 8, 1992, p. A34.

14. Ibid., October 2, 1992, p. B1; June 6, 1993, sec. 13B, pp. 1, 4.

15. Ibid., August 2, 1992, sec. 1, p. 37, and October 17, 1992, sec. 1, p. 31.

16. Ibid., August 2, 1992, sec. 1, p. 37.

17. Ibid.

18. Ibid.

19. Ibid., September 3, 1993, p. A17.

20. *Oregonian* (Portland), July 4, 1993, p. D1.

21. Andrew Schneider and Mary Pat Flaherty, *Presumed Guilty: The Law's Victims in the War on Drugs*, series of articles reprinted from the *Pittsburgh Press*, August 11–16, 1991, p. 3

22. Ibid., p. 4.

23. *USA Today*, May 18, 1992, pp. 1A, 7A.

24. *Oregonian*, June 20, 1990, p. D4.

25. Ibid., February 5, 1993, p. C11.

26. Ibid.

27. *Orlando Sentinel*, August 2, 1992, pp. A1, A21.

28. Ibid.

29. *Oregonian*, July 4, 1993, p. 7A.

30. Ibid., May 22, 1992, p. E7,

31. Ibid., February 5, 1993, p. C11.

32. Ibid.

33. Ibid.

34. Ibid.

35. *New York Times*, September 3, 1993, p. A17, quoting the San Jose newspaper.

36. *USA Today*, May 18, 1992, p. 1A.

37. *Review of Federal Asset Forfeiture Program* (Hearing before the Legislation and National Security Subcommittee of the House Committee on Government Operations), p. 35.

38. Ibid.

39. *San Francisco Chronicle*, December 29, 1993, sec. 1, p. 13.

40. *Federal Drug Forfeiture Activities* (Hearing before the Subcommittee on Crime of the House Committee on the Judiciary), p. 67.

41. *Orlando Sentinel*, June 14, 1992, pp. A1, 1–14, and August 2, 1992, p. A10.

42. Ibid., June 14, 1992, pp. A1, 1–14.

43. Ibid., June 15, 1992, p. A1.

44. Schneider and Flaherty, "Drugs Contaminate Nearly All the Money in America," in their *Presumed Guilty*, p. 15.

45. Ibid., pp. 5–6.

46. Ibid.

47. Ibid., continued from p. A1.

48. *Oregonian*, June 18, 1992, p. C1.

49. Ibid., March 25, 1992, p. B2, and *New York Times*, December 26, 1991, p. A20.

50. Cary H. Copeland, "Seizing Assets: Effective Anti-Crime Tool," *Chicago Tribune*, April 1, 1993.

51. For Copeland's testimony, see *Department of Justice Asset Forfeiture Program* (Hearing before the Legislation and National Security Subcommittee of the House Committee on Government Operations), pp. 78–100, and *Review of Federal Asset Forfeiture Program* (Hearing before the Legislation and National Security Subcommittee of the House Committee on Government Operations), pp. 73–82.

52. *Review of Federal Asset Forfeiture Program*, pp. 76–77.

53. *Forfeiture Portions of the Comprehensive Crime Bill and the Anti-Drug Abuse Act of 1986* (Hearing before the Subcommittee on Crime of the House Committee on the Judiciary), p. 1.

54. On money laundering, see *Federal Government's Response to Money Laundering* (Hearings before the House Committee on Banking, Finance, and Urban Affairs), pp. 1, 22. The figure for white-collar crime is supposed to be about $200 billion annually; see above, Chap. 4, n. 1.

55. *Review of Federal Asset Forfeiture*, pp. 382–83.

56. *New York Times*, April 17, 1993, pp. 1, 21.

57. *Review of Federal Asset Forfeiture*, p. 383.

58. Ibid., pp. 106–26.

Chapter 8

1. David Cauchon, "Are Seizures 'Legalized Theft'?" *USA Today*, May 18, 1992, p. 1A.

2. *Christian Science Monitor*, July 1, 1994, pp. 1, 4; *Review of Federal Asset Forfeiture Program* (Hearing before the Legislation and National Security Subcommittee of the House Committee on Government Operations), pp. 8, 18, 152–55.

3. *Review of Federal Asset Forfeiture Program*, p. 8.

4. *Asset Forfeiture: Improved Guidance*. See also testimony of Gene L. Dodaro, Associate Director, GAO, in *Federal Drug Forfeiture Activity* (Hearing before the Subcommittee on Crime of the House Committee on the Judiciary), pp. 23–26.

5. *Asset Forfeiture: Improved Guidance*, p. 2.

6. *Disposition of Seized Cash and Property* (Hearing before the Subcommittee on Federal Spending, Budget, and Accounting of the Senate Committee on Governmental Affairs), p. 1.

7. On the fund, see Troland, *Asset Forfeiture*, pp. 124–27, 136–38.

8. Ibid., pp. 128–35; and Executive Office for Asset Forfeiture, *Guide to Equitable Sharing* (1994 ed.), p. 8.

9. *Guide to Equitable Sharing* (1994 ed.), p. 4.

10. See *Federal Drug Forfeiture Activities* (Hearing before the Subcommittee on Crime of the House Committee on the Judiciary), pp. 210–14, for a summary of state laws on the subject.

11. *New York Times*, May 31, 1993, p. B1.

12. *Federal Drug Forfeiture Activities*, p. 15, testimony of Joseph W. Dean, head of North Carolina Department of Crime Control.

13. *New York Times*, February 19, 1993, p. A4, and May 31, 1993, sec. 1, p. 1.

14. *Asset Forfeiture: A Seldom Used Tool*, pp. 13, 59.

15. Testimony of Mark Richard, Deputy Assistant Attorney General, in *Disposition of Seized Cash and Property*, p. 9.

16. *National Drug Control Strategy*, February 1991, p. 74. The annual budgets give the value of assets received and useful information about forfeiture funds.

17. Quoted in *Oregonian*, February 8, 1993, p. B7.

18. *United States v. That Certain Real Property Located at 632–636 Ninth Ave., Calera, Ala.*, 798 F. Supp. 1540 (N.D. Ala., 1992).

19. Quoted in ibid.

20. Quoted in *New York Times*, May 31, 1993, sec. 1, p. 1.

21. Smith, *Prosecution and Defense*, 1:25, 26. On the 175 prosecutors, see below, text related to Chap. 8, n. 35.

22. *Oregonian*, July 4, 1993, p. D1.

23. Michael Isikoff, "Drug Raids Net Much Valuable Property—and Legal Uproar," *Washington Post*, April 1, 1991, p. A1.

24. *Asset Forfeiture: Improved Guidance*, p. 6.

25. *Guide to Equitable Sharing* (1994 ed.), p. 12.

26. *Congressional Record* 135 (October 4, 1990): 8861.

27. Quoted in Doyle, *Equitable Distribution and Adoptive Forfeiture*, p. 3, n. 4.

28. *Federal Drug Forfeiture Activities*, p. 16, testimony of Joseph W. Dean of North Carolina.

29. Ibid., p. 18. Dean's prepared statement is in ibid., pp. 18–28.

30. *Federal Drug Forfeiture Activity*, 94-995.

31. Doyle, *Equitable Distribution and Adoptive Forfeiture*, pp. 3–4, 9–10; *Congressional Record* 135 (October 4, 1990): 8860–63.

32. *Chicago Tribune*, April 1, 1993, op-ed.

33. *Los Angeles Times*, April 1, 1993, p. B1.

34. *Department of Justice Asset Forfeiture Program* (Hearing before the Legislation and National Security Subcommittee of the House Committee on Government Operations), pp. 87, 90.

35. *Federal Drug Forfeiture Activity*, testimony of Joe D. Whitley, Deputy Assistant Attorney General, March 4, 1988, pp. 75–82.

36. *Federal Drug Forfeiture Activities*, pp. 114–15.

37. Gallagher, *Management and Disposition of Seized Assets*, pp. 2–8; *New York Times*, September 8, 1991, p. A5, and May 29, 1993, sec. 1, p. 14.

38. *Department of Justice Asset Forfeiture Program*, p. 87.

39. *Review of Federal Asset Forfeiture Program*, pp. 70–71, 78–82.

40. Ibid., 83. The National Code of Professional Conduct for Asset Forfeiture is reprinted in *Guide to Equitable Sharing* (1994 ed.), p. 37. It also appeared in *The Police Chief* 16 (October 24, 1993): 39–40.

Chapter 9

1. *United States v. All Funds on Deposit or Any Accounts Maintained at Merrill Lynch*, 801 F. Supp. 984, 990 (E.D. N.Y. 1992). "The finding of probable cause may be based on hearsay evidence in whole or in part," Federal Rules of Civil Procedure, 41b.

2. *United States v. All Funds on Deposit in Any Accounts Maintained at Merrill Lynch*, 801 F. Supp. 984, 990 (1992).

3. *Calero-Toledo v. Pearson Yacht Leasing Co.*, 416 U.S. 663 (1974). See also Darmstadter and Mackoff, "Some Constitutional and Practical Considerations."

4. *Calero-Toledo v. Pearson Yacht Leasing Co.*, 416 U.S. 663 (1974) at 689–90. On this subject generally, see Goldsmith and Lenck, *Protection of Third-Party Rights*, Bureau of Justice Assistance pamphlet; Zeldin and Weiner, "Innocent Third Parties and Their Rights."

5. *Devito v. United States Department of Justice*, 520 F. Supp. 127 (E.D. Pa. 1981).

6. 21 U.S.C. sec. 881(a)(4,6,7).

7. *United States v. 6960 Miraflores Ave.*, 995 F. 2d 1558 (11th Cir. 1983); *United States v. One Parcel of Land Known As Lot 111-B*, 902 F. 2d 1443 (9th Cir. 1990); *United States v. One 1980 Bertram 58 Foot Motor Yacht*, 876 F. 2d 884 (11th Cir. 1989).

8. *United States v. 141 St. Corp.*, 911 F. 2d 870, 877–78 (2d Cir. 1990); *United States v. 6109 Grubb Rd.*, 886 F. 2d 618, 626 (3d Cir. 1989).

9. *United States v. One 1983 Homemade Vessel Named Barracuda*, 858 F. 2d 643, 647 (11th Cir. 1988); *United States v. One Cessna Model 210L Aircraft*, 890 F. 2d 77 (8th Cir. 1989); *United States v. One 1983 Pontiac Grand Prix*, 604 F. Supp. 8983 (E.D. Mich. 1983); *United States v. 11885 S.W. 46th St.*, 715 F. Supp. 355 (S.D. Fla. 1989).

10. *United States v. One Single Family Residence*, 683 F. Supp. 783, 788 (S.D. Fla. 1988); *United States v. 141st St. Corp.*, 911 F. 2d 870 (2d Cir. 1990); *United States v. One Parcel of Real Estate at 1012 Germantown Rd.*, 963 F. 2d 1496 (11th Cir. 1992).

11. *United States v. Premises Known as 2639 Meetinghouse Rd.*, 633 F. Supp. 979 (E.D. Pa. 1986).

12. *United States v. Mercedes Benz 380 SEL*, 604 F. Supp. 1307 (1984).

13. *United States v. One 1979 Datsun 280Z*, 720 F. 2d 543 (8th Cir. 1983).

14. Pub. L. 100-690, sec. 6075 (1988).

15. *United States v. 6109 Grubb Rd.*, 708 F. Supp. 698 (W.D. Pa. 1989).

16. Goldsmith and Linderman, "Asset Forfeiture and Third Party Rights," pp. 1272–73. See also Andrew Schneider and Mary Pat Flaherty, *Presumed Guilty: The Law's Victims in the War on Drugs*, series of articles reprinted from the *Pittsburgh Press*, August 11–16, 1991, pp. 28–30.

17. 21 U.S.C. sec. 853(f).

18. *Comprehensive Crime Control Act of 1983*, Sen. Rep. No. 98-225, pp. 208–9.

19. 21 U.S.C. sec. 881(h) (Supp.V 1987).

20. *United States v. A Parcel of Land, Buildings . . . Known as 92 Buena Vista Ave., Rumson, N.J.*, 113 S.Ct. 1126 (1993), discussed at the close of this chapter.

21. Myers and Brzostowski, *Drug Agents' Guide* (rev. ed., 1987), p. 33.

22. *United States v. Miscellaneous Jewelry*, 667 F. Supp. 232 (D. Md. 1987).

23. *United States v. One Piece of Real Estate Described In Part as 1314 Whitelock*, 571 F. Supp. 723 (W.D. Tex. 1983).

24. *In re Metmor Finances Inc.*, 819 F. 2d (4th Cir. 1987).

25. *United States v. 708–710 West 9th St.*, 715 F. Supp. 1323 (D.C. W. Pa. 1989); but see *United States v. Real Property Titled in Name of Shasin Ltd.*, 680 F. Supp. 332 (D. Hawaii 1987), for a contrary decision.

26. *Sheldon v. United States*, 19 Claims Ct. 247 (1990).

27. 21 U.S.C. sec. 853(d) (1988).

28. *United States v. A Fee Simple Parcel Situated in Bal Harbour*, 650 F. Supp. 1534 (E.D. La. 1987).

29. *United States v. One Single Family Residence Located at 6960 Miraflores Ave.*, 731 F. Supp. 1563 (S.D. Fla. 1990).

30. 21 U.S.C. sec. 881(a)(7).

31. *United States v. One Single Family Residence* ("Alvarez"), 683 F. Supp. 783 (S.D. Fla. 1988).

32. *United States v. A Parcel of Land*, 113 S.Ct. 1126 (1993).

33. Ibid., 1134.

34. Ibid., 1135.

35. *United States v. Grundy*, 3 Cranch 337, 350–51 (1806).

36. 113 S.Ct. 1126, 1138 (1993).

Chapter 10

1. *Miller v. California*, 413 U.S. 15, 20–21 (1973).

2. *Congressional Record* 130 (January 30, 1984): 5434; 18 U.S.C. secs. 1961–68.

3. Hayes, "Jury Wrestles with Pornography," is a good description of the trial.

4. *United States v. Pryba*, 674 F. Supp. 1504, 1518 (1987).

5. Ibid., 1518.

6. *Fort Wayne Books Inc. v. Indiana*, 489 U.S. 46 (1989).

7. *Alexander v. United States*, 113 S.Ct. 2766 (1993).

8. Ibid., 2770, n. 1.

9. Ibid., 2773.

10. Ibid., 2772.

11. Ibid.

12. Ibid., 2776.

13. *Austin v. United States*, 113 U.S. 2801 (1993), discussed below.

14. *Boyd v. United States*, 116 U.S. 616, 633–34; see above, Chap. 3, n. 41 and related text.

15. *One 1958 Plymouth Sedan v. Pennsylvania*, 380 U.S. 693 (1965).

16. *Elkins v. United States*, 364 U.S. 206, 217 (1960).

17. On the use of circumstantial evidence and hearsay, see *United States v. All Funds on Deposit in Any Accounts Maintained at Merrill Lynch*, 801 F. Supp. 984, 990 (E.D. N.Y., 1992); *United States v. One 56-Foot Yacht Named Tahuna*, 702 F. 2d 1276, 1283–84 (9th Cir. 1983).

18. *United States v. One 1977 Mercedes-Benz 450 SEL*, 708 F. 2d 444, 450 (9th Cir. 1983).

19. *Dodge v. United States*, 272 U.S. 530, 532 (1926).

20. See Nelson, "Should the Ranch Go Free?"

21. *United States v. One 1969 Plymouth Fury Automobile*, 509 F. 2d (5th Cir. 1975).

22. *United States v. One 1975 Pontiac Lemans*, 621 F. 2d 444, 450 (1st Cir. 1980); *United States v. Troiano*, 365 F. 2d 416, 418 (3d Cir. 1965). See generally Note, "The Forfeiture Exception to the Warrant Requirement: A Distinction Without a Difference," *Virginia Law Review* 67 (1981): 1035, and Herz, "Forfeiture Seizure," p. 960, and esp. pp. 967–68.

23. *United States v. Pappas*, 613 F. 2d 324 (1st Cir. 1979).

24. Ibid., 330–31.

25. *United States v. United States Coin and Currency*, 401 U.S. 719, 718 (1971).

26. *One Lot Emerald Cut Stones and One Ring v. United States*, 409 U.S. 232 (1972).

27. *Boyd v. United States* 116 U.S. 616, 634 (1886); *One 1958 Plymouth Sedan v. Pennsylvania*, 380 U.S. 693, 702 (1965); *United States v. United States Coin and Currency*, 401 U.S. 715, 716 (1971).

28. *United States v. One Assortment of 89 Firearms*, 465 U.S. 354 (1984).

29. *United States v. Irwin Halper*, 490 U.S. 435 (1989).

30. *Austin v. United States*, 113 S.Ct. 2801 (1993).

31. *North Carolina v. Pearce*, 395 U.S. 711 (1969).

32. *United States v. $405,089.23 U.S. Currency*, case involving Arlt and Wren, discussed in Mintz, "Inmates' Win," pp. 6–8.

33. *United States v. James Daniel Good Real Property*, 114 U.S. 492 (1993).

34. Ibid., 521–22.

35. *United States v. All Assets of Statewide Auto Parts, Inc.*, 971 F. 2d 896, 905 (2d Cir. 1992).

36. *United States v. $250,000 in U.S. Currency*, 808 F. 2d 895, 901 (1st Cir. 1987); *United States v. Santoro*, 866 F. 2d 1538 (4th Cir. 1989); *United States v. One 1970 Pontiac CTO*, 529 F. 2d 65, 66 (9th Cir. 1976); *Bramble v. Richardson*, 498 F. 2d 968, 970 (10th Cir. 1974).

37. See Petrou, "Due Process Implications"; Reed and Gill, "RICO Forfeitures"; Winn, "Seizures of Private Property."

38. Beaney, *Right to Counsel*, chap. 1.

39. *United States v. Monsanto*, 491 U.S. 600 (1989), and *Caplin & Drysdale v. United States*, 491 U.S. 617 (1989).

40. I found the following helpful for this discussion: testimony of William W. Taylor III, for the American Bar Association Criminal Justice Section's RICO Cases Committee, in *Forfeiture Portions of the Comprehensive Crime Bill and Anti-Drug Abuse Act of 1986* (Hearing before the Subcommittee on Crime of the House Committee on the Judiciary), pp. 89–99; testimony of Samuel J. Buffone, Vice Chairman, A.B.A. Criminal Justice Section's RICO Cases Committee, in *Federal Drug Forfeiture Activity* (Hearing before the Subcommittee on Crime of the House Committee on the Judiciary), pp. 119–39; Dettelbach, "Forfeiting the Right to Counsel"; and Schier, "Bill of Rights."

41. *Caplin & Drysdale v. United States*, 491 U.S. 617, 626 (1989).

42. Ibid., 628.

43. Ibid., 635–51.

44. Schecter, "Fear and Loathing," p. 1151, at pp. 1165–68.

45. *Sequoia Books Inc. v. Ingemunson*, 901 F. 2d 630 (7th Circuit, 1989).

46. *United States v. Lot No. 50 as Shown on the Map of Kingsbury*, 557 F. Supp. 72 (D. Nev. 1982).

47. *Austin v. United States*, 113 U.S. 2801 (1993).

48. *United States v. One Parcel of Real Estate Commonly Known as 916*

Douglas Ave., 906 F. 2d 490 (7th Cir. 1990).

49. *United States v. One 1982 28′ Int'l Vessel*, 741 F. 2d 1319 (11th Cir. 1984).

50. *United States v. One 1976 Porsche 911S*, 670 F. 2d 810 (9th Cir. 1979).

51. *United States v. Weatherspoon*, 581 F. 2d 595 (7th Cir. 1978).

52. *United States v. Horack*, 833 F. 2d 1235 (7th Cir. 1987).

53. See above, Chap. 1, n. 9, and related text.

54. Hyde, "Civil Asset Forfeiture: A Briefing Paper," p. 4.

55. *United States v. Busher*, 817 F. 2d 1409, 1414, 1415 (1987).

56. See generally Palm, "RICO Forfeitures and the Eighth Amendment"; Speta, "Narrowing the Scope of Civil Drug Forfeiture"; Bittle, "Punitive Damages and the Eighth Amendment."

57. *Review of Federal Asset Forfeiture Program* (Hearing before the Legislation and National Security Subcommittee of the House Committee on Government Operations), testimony of E. E. Edwards III, p. 258.

Chapter 11

1. *New York Times*, April 22, 1990, sec. 4, p. 6, and August 23, 1992, sec. 3, 13.

2. Ibid., April 22, 1990, sec. 4, p. 6.

3. Lynch, "RICO," pp. 661, 726.

4. Ibid., pp. 728–29.

5. *New York Times*, March 5, 1990, p. B1, and May 13, 1988, p. B1.

6. Ibid., September 7, 1990, p. B1.

7. Ibid., January 15, 1993, p. B3.

8. Lynch, "RICO," p. 750.

9. Smith, *Prosecution and Defense*.

10. *Review of Federal Asset Forfeiture Program* (Hearing before the Legislation and National Security Subcommittee of the House Committee on Government Operations), statement of Nancy Hollander; Hingson, as quoted in Dick Thomas, "The Strong Arm of the Law," *Oregonian*, July 4, 1993, p. D4.

11. Hyde, "Civil Asset Forfeiture: A Briefing Paper"; *Chicago Tribune*, June 20, 1993, editorial, sec. 4, p. 2; *Washington Post*, June 28, 1993, editorial, p. A18.

12. "A Bill to Reform Certain Statutes Regarding Civil Asset Forfeiture," H. Rep. No. 2417, 103d Cong., 1st sess., 1994.

13. Quoted in Klaidman, "Reshaping the Power to Seize," p. 1.

14. "Asset Forfeiture Justice Act," H. Rep. No. 3347, 103d Cong., 1st sess., 1994.

15. *Review of Federal Asset Forfeiture Program*, p. 9.

16. Quoted in Bendavid, "Asset Forfeiture," p. 20.

17. Ibid.

18. Janet Reno to Jack Brooks, October 18, 1993, reprinted in National Association of Criminal Defense Lawyers (NACDL), Forfeiture Abuse Task Force, publicity release dated May 2, 1994.

19. Klaidman, "Reshaping the Power to Seize," pp. 1, 22–23 for the quotations.

20. Epps, "DOJ Forfeiture Reform Proposal," p. 2. The *Washington Digest* is a publication of the criminal defense bar.

21. *Austin v. United States*, 113 S.Ct. 2801 (1993).

22. Sec. 1 of the Justice bill says it may be cited as "the Forfeiture Act of 1994."

23. Sec. 131, Standard of Proof for Criminal Forfeiture.

24. *In re Winship*, 397 U.S. 358 (1970).

25. *Griffin v. California*, 380 U.S. 609 (1965); *Garrity v. New Jersey*, 385 U.S. 493 (1967); *Spevack v. Klein*, 385 U.S. 511 (1967).

26. *Austin v. United States*, 113 S.Ct. 2801 (1993).

27. *Boyd v. United States*, 116 U.S. 616 (1886).

28. Sections 121 and 122. For Reno, see above, Chap. 11, n. 18, and related text.

29. Section 130(C).

30. *Section-by-Section Analysis of the Forfeiture Act of 1994*, sec. 136, p. 33.

31. NACDL Forfeiture Abuse Task Force, "Section-by-Section Analysis of the Department of Justice's Proposed Forfeiture Act of 1994," p. 16.

32. *Legal Times*, March 28, 1994, p. 23.

33. See the quotation from Hyde above, Chap. 7, n. 37, and related text.

Bibliography

Books

Barrow, Thomas C. *Trade and Empire: The British Customs Service in Colonial America, 1660–1775*. Cambridge: Harvard University Press, 1967.

Bartlett, John R., ed. *Records of the Colony of Rhode Island and Providence Plantation*. 10 vols. Providence, 1856–65.

Beaney, William M. *The Right to Counsel in American Courts*. Ann Arbor: University of Michigan Press, 1955.

Blackstone, Sir William. *Commentaries on the Laws of England*. 4 vols. London, 1765–69.

Bracton, [Henry]. *De Legibus et Consuetudinibus Angliae*. Edited by G. E. Woodbine. 6 vols. New Haven: Yale University Press, 1915–42.

Browne, William H., et al., eds. *Archives of Maryland*. 72 vols. Baltimore: Maryland Historical Society, 1883–1972.

Bruck, Connie. *The Predators' Ball: The Inside Story of Drexel Burnham and the Rise of the Junk Bond Raiders*. New York: Penguin Books, 1984.

Chapin, Bradley. *The American Law of Treason: Revolutionary and Early National Origins*. Seattle: University of Washington Press, 1964.

———. *Criminal Justice in Colonial America, 1606–1660*. Athens: University of Georgia Press, 1983.

Dickerson, Oliver. *The Navigation Acts and the American Revolution*. Philadelphia: University of Pennsylvania Press, 1951.

Edelhertz, Herbert. *The Nature, Impact, and Prosecution of White Collar Crime*. Lexington, Mass.: Lexington Books, 1970.

Evans, E. P. *The Criminal Prosecution and Capital Punishment of Animals*. London: William Heinemann Ltd., 1906.

Gilmore, Grant, and Charles Black. *The Law of Admiralty*. Mineola, N.Y.: Foundation Press, 1857.

Goebel, Julius Jr. *Felony and Misdemeanor: A Study in the History of Criminal Law*. New York: The Commonwealth Fund, 1937.

Bibliography

Goebel, Julius Jr., and T. Raymond Naughton. *Law Enforcement in Colonial New York: A Study in Criminal Procedure (1664–1776)*. New York: The Commonwealth Fund, 1944.

Goss, John Dean. *The History of Tariff Administration in the United States, from Colonial Times to the McKinley Administrative Bill*. New York: Columbia University Press, 1891.

Hale, Matthew. *Pleas of the Crown*. 1588. Reprint, edited by W. Stokes and E. Ingersoll. London, 1847.

Harper, Lawrence A. *The English Navigation Laws*. New York: Columbia University Press, 1964.

Haskins, Charles Homer. *Norman Institutions*. Cambridge: Harvard University Press, 1925.

Holdsworth, Sir William S. *A History of English Law*. 16 vols. Boston: Little, Brown, 1938–46.

Holmes, Oliver Wendell. *The Common Law*. Boston: Little, Brown, 1881.

Hurst, James Willard. *The Law of Treason in the United States: Collected Essays*. Westport, Conn.: Greenwood Publishing Co., 1971.

Keane, Morris. *The Outlaws of England*. Toronto: University of Toronto Press, 1961.

Kent, James. *Commentaries on American Law*. 4 vols. New York, 1830.

Kessler, Steven L. *Civil and Criminal Forfeiture: Federal and State Practice*. 3 vols. (looseleaf binding). Deerfield, Ill.: Clark, Boardman Callaghan, 1993–94.

Kiralfy, A. K. R. *Potter's Historical Introduction to English Law and Its Institutions*. 4th ed. London: Sweet and Maxwell, 1962.

Kornbluth, Jess. *Highly Confident: The True Story of the Crime and Punishment of Michael Milken*. New York: Morrow, 1994.

La Fave, Wayne R. *Search and Seizure: A Treatise on the Fourth Amendment*. 3 vols. St. Paul, Minn.: West Publishing Co., 1978.

Lea, Homer C. *Superstition and Force*. 3d ed. Philadelphia, 1878.

Lenck, William L. *See* Myers, Harry L., and Joseph Brzostowski, under "Government Documents."

Levy, Leonard W. *Chief Justice Shaw and the Law of the Commonwealth*. Cambridge: Harvard University Press, 1957.

———. *Seasoned Judgments: The American Constitution, Rights, and History*. New Brunswick, N.J.: Transaction Publishers, 1994.

McClintick, David. *Swordfish: A True Story of Ambition, Savagery, and Betrayal*. New York: Pantheon, 1994.

McKechnie, William Sharp. *Magna Carta: A Commentary on the Great Charter of King John*. New York: Burt Franklin, n.d. (reprint of Glasgow 2d ed. [1914]).

Bibliography

McPherson, Edward. *The Political History of the United States of America during the Great Rebellion, 1860–1865*. New York: Da Capo Press, 1972.

McPherson, James. *Battle Cry of Freedom: The Civil War Era*. New York: Oxford University Press, 1988.

Moriarty, Eugene James. *Oaths in Ecclesiastical Courts*. Washington, D.C.: Catholic University Press, 1937.

Morris, Richard B. *Studies in the History of American Law*. New York: Columbia University Press, 1939.

Perry, Richard L., ed. *Sources of Our Liberties: Documentary Origins of Individual Liberties in the United States Constitution*. New York: American Bar Foundation, 1959.

Plucknett, Theodore F. T. *A Concise History of the Common Law*. 5th ed. Boston: Little, Brown, 1956.

Pollock, Sir Frederick, and Frederic William Maitland. *A History of English Law before the Time of Edward I*. 2 vols. Boston: Little, Brown, 1895.

President's Commission on Law Enforcement and Administration of Justice. *The Challenge of Crime in a Free Society*. Washington, D.C.: Government Printing Office, 1967.

Randall, J. G. *Constitutional Problems under Lincoln*. Rev. ed. Urbana: University of Illinois Press, 1951.

Rice, Berkeley. *Trafficking: The Boom and Bust of the Air America Cocaine Ring*. New York: Charles Scribner's Sons, 1989.

Robertson, David W. *Admiralty and Federalism*. Mineola, N.Y.: Foundation Press, 1957.

Scott, Austin P. *Criminal Law in Colonial Virginia*. Chicago: University of Chicago Press, 1930.

Smith, David B. *Prosecution and Defense of Forfeiture Cases*. 2 vols. (looseleaf binding). New York: Matthew Bender, 1993.

Starkey, Marian L. *The Devil in Massachusetts*. New York: Alfred A. Knopf, 1950.

Stein, Benjamin J. *A License to Steal: The Untold Story of Michael Milken and the Conspiracy to Bilk the Nation*. New York: Simon and Schuster, 1994.

Stephen, Sir James Fitzjames. *A History of the Criminal Law of England*. 3 vols. London: Macmillan, 1883.

Stubbs, William. *The Constitutional History of England in Its Origin and Development*. 2d ed., 2 vols. Oxford: Clarendon Press, 1875.

Thayer, James Bradley. *Preliminary Treatise on Evidence at the Common Law*. Boston: Little, Brown, 1898.

Bibliography

Trumbull, J. Hammond, and Charles J. Hoadley, eds. *The Public Records of Connecticut*. 15 vols. Hartford, 1850–90.

Ubbelohde, Carl. *The Vice Admiralty Courts and the American Revolution*. Chapel Hill: University of North Carolina Press, 1960.

Van Caenegem, R. C. *Royal Writs in England from the Conquest to Glanvill*. London: Publications of the Selden Society, 1955.

Waples, Rufus. *A Treatise on Proceedings In Rem*. Chicago: Callaghan, 1882.

Wisotsky, Steven. *Breaking the Impasse in the War on Drugs*. New York: Greenwood Press, 1986.

Newspapers

Chicago Tribune
Christian Science Monitor
Los Angeles Times
New York Times
Oregonian (Portland)
Orlando Sentinel
Pittsburgh Press
San Francisco Chronicle
USA Today
Washington Post

Articles

Atkins, David P., and Adele V. Patterson. "Punishment or Compensation? New Constitutional Restrictions on Civil Forfeiture." *Bridgeport Law Review* 11 (1991): 371–81.

Baird, Bruce A. and Vinson, Carolyn P. "RICO Pretrial Restraints and Due Process: The Lessons of Princeton/Newport." *Notre Dame Law Review* 65 (1990): 1009–34.

Bendavid, Naftali. "Asset Forfeiture . . . Ripe for Reform." *Legal Times*, July 5, 1993, p. 20.

Bittle, Lyndon F. "Punitive Damages and the Eighth Amendment: An Analytical Framework for Determining Excessiveness." *California Law Review* 75 (1987): 1433–71.

Blakey, G. Robert. "Foreword: Symposium on Law and the Continuing Enterprise—Perspectives on RICO." *Notre Dame Law Review* 65 (1990): 873–84.

Blakey, G. Robert, and Brian Gettings. "Racketeer Influenced and Corrupt Organizations (RICO): Basic Concepts—Criminal and Civil Remedies." *Temple Law Quarterly* 53 (1980): 1009–48.

Bibliography

Bradbury, Michael D. "Report on the Death of Donald Scott." Office of the District Attorney, County of Ventura, California, 1993.

Bradley, Craig M. "Racketeers, Congress, and the Courts: An Analysis of RICO." *Iowa Law Review* 65 (1980): 837–97.

Brazil, Jeff, and Steve Berry. "Tainted Cash or Easy Money?" *Orlando Sentinel*, June 14–August 23, 1992.

Brew, John. "State and Federal Forfeiture of Property Involved in Drug Transactions." *Dickinson Law Review* 92 (1988): 461–81.

Brickey, Kathleen F. "RICO Forfeitures As Excessive Fines or Cruel and Unusual Punishments." *Villanova Law Review* 35 (1990): 905–27.

Bush, Graeme W. "The Impact of RICO Forfeiture on Legitimate Business." *Notre Dame Law Review* 65 (1990): 996–1008.

Canavan, Patricia M. "Civil Forfeiture of Real Property: The Government's Weapon Against Drug Traffickers Injures Innocent Owners." *Pace Law Review* 10 (1990): 485–517.

Cassidy, Peter. "Without Due Process: In the War on Drugs, You Don't Have to Be Guilty to Pay the Price." *The Progressive*, August 1993, 32–34.

Casto, William. R. "The Origins of Federal Admiralty Jurisdiction in an Age of Privateers, Smugglers, and Pirates." *American Journal of Legal History* 37 (1993): 122–43.

Cheh, Mary M. "Constitutional Limits on Using Civil Remedies to Achieve Criminal Law Objectives: Understanding and Transcending the Criminal-Civil Law Distinction." *Hastings Law Journal* 42 (1991): 1325–1413.

Clark, J. Morris. "Civil and Criminal Penalties and Forfeitures: A Framework for Constitutional Analysis." *Minnesota Law Review* 60 (1976): 379–500.

Coffey, Paul E. "The Selection, Analysis, and Approval of Federal RICO Prosecutions." *Notre Dame Law Review* 65 (1990): 1035–49.

Conyers, John Jr. "Corporate and White-Collar Crime: A View by the Chairman of the House Subcommittee on Crime." *American Criminal Law Review* 17 (1980): 287–88.

Copeland, Cary H. "National Code of Professional Conduct for Asset Forfeiture." *The Police Chief*, October 1993, pp. 2–3.

Crovitz, L. Gordon. "How the RICO Monster Mauled Wall Street." *Notre Dame Law Review* 65 (1990): 1050–72.

Darmstadter, Henry C., and Leslie J. Mackoff. "Some Constitutional and Practical Considerations of Civil Forfeitures Under 21 U.S.C. Sect. 881." *Whittier Law Review* 9 (1987): 27–53.

Dettelbach, Steve. "Forfeiting the Right to Counsel." *Harvard Civil*

Bibliography

Rights–Civil Liberties Law Review 25 (1990): 201–20.

Dillin, John. *Christian Science Monitor*, series of articles on forfeiture, June 17, September 28, 30, October 1, 4, and 5, 1993.

Dombrink, James, and James W. Meeker. "Racketeering Prosecution: The Use and Abuse of RICO." *Rutgers Law Journal* 16 (1985): 633–54.

Epps, Cheryl Anthony. "DOJ Forfeiture Reform Proposal Ignores Problems." *Washington Digest*, no. 8 (May 1994).

Finkelstein, Jacob J. "The Goring Ox: Some Historical Perspective on Deodands, Forfeitures, Wrongful Death and the Western Notion of Sovereignty." *Temple Law Quarterly* 46 (1973): 169–290.

Fried, David J. "Rationalizing Criminal Forfeiture." *Journal of Criminal Law & Criminology* 79 (1988): 328–436.

Gellhorn, Walter. "The Abuses of Occupational Licensing." *University of Chicago Law Review* 44–68 (1976).

Goldsmith, Michael, and Mark Jay Linderman. "Asset Forfeiture and Third Party Rights: The Need for Further Law Reform." *Duke Law Journal* (1989): 1254–1301.

Hayes, Arthur S. "A Jury Wrestles with Pornography." *The American Lawyer*, March 1988, pp. 96–101.

Herz, Michael E. "Forfeiture Seizures and the Warrant Requirement." *University of Chicago Law Review* 48 (1981): 960–91.

Hollander, Nancy. "Statement on Behalf of the National Association of Criminal Defense Lawyers, before the House Committee on Government Operations Legislation and National Security Subcommitee Regarding the Federal Asset Forfeiture Program," June 22, 1993.

Hughes, William J., with Edward H. O'Connell. "In Personam (Criminal) Forfeiture and Federal Drug Felonies: An Expansion of a Harsh English Tradition Into a Modern Dilemma." *Pepperdine Law Review* 11 (1984): 613–34.

Hyde, Walter W. "The Prosecution and Punishment of Animals and Lifeless Things in the Middle Ages and Modern Times." *University of Pennsylvania Law Review* 64 (1916): 696–730.

Jankowski, Mark A. "Tempering the Relation-Back Doctrine: A More Reasonable Approach to Civil Forfeiture in Drug Cases." *Virginia Law Review* 76 (1990): 165–95.

Kandaras, Kenneth. "Due Process and Federal Property Forfeiture Statutes: The Need for Immediate Post-Seizure Hearing." *Southwestern Law Journal* 34 (1980): 925–39.

Karraker, Cyrus H. "Deodands in Colonial Virginia and Maryland." *American Historical Review* 37 (1932): 712–17.

Bibliography

Kasten, Lawrence A. "Extending Constitutional Protection to Civil Forfeitures That Exceed Rough Remedial Compensation." *George Washington Law Review* 60 (1991): 194–244.

Klaidman, Daniel. "Reshaping the Power to Seize." *Legal Times*, March 28, 1994, pp. 1, 22.

Kurisky, George A. "Civil Forfeiture of Assets: A Final Solution to International Drug Trafficking?" *Houston Journal of International Law* 10 (1988): 239–73.

Lauter, David. "U.S. Seizure of Assets Accelerates." *National Law Journal*, September 6, 1982, pp. 1, 8.

Leibowitz, Arnold H. "Administrative Conference of the United States. Civil Forfeiture: The Issue and Some Recommendations." Draft copy, January 1994.

Lovejoy, David S. "Rights Imply Equality: The Case Against Admiralty Jurisdiction in America, 1764–1776." *William and Mary Quarterly*, 3d ser., vol. 16 (1959): 459–84.

Lynch, Gerard E. "RICO: The Crime of Being a Criminal." *Columbia Law Review* 87 (1987): 661–762.

McCarthy, Michael. "Rendering Illegal Behavior Unprofitable: Vehicle Forfeiture under the Uniform Controlled Substances Act." *Creighton Law Review* 8 (1974): 471–95.

McClellan, John L. "The Organized Crime Act (S.30) or Its Critics: Which Threatens Civil Liberties?" *Notre Dame Lawyer* 46 (Fall 1970): 55–200.

Maxeiner, James R. "Bane of American Forfeiture Law—Banished at Last?" *Cornell Law Review* 62 (1977): 768–802.

Miniter, Richard. "Ill Gotten Gains." *Reason*, August–September 1993, pp. 32–37.

———. "Property Seizures on Trial." *Insight on the News*, February 22, 1993, pp. 10–13, 32–35.

Mintz, Howard. "Inmates' Win in Forfeiture Case Stuns Prosecutors." *Legal Times*, December 12, 1994, pp. 8–10.

National Association of Criminal Defense Lawyers. Forfeiture Abuse Task Force Document, May 2, 1994.

———. "Section-by-Section Analysis of the Department of Justice's Proposed Forfeiture Act of 1994."

Nelson, William Patrick. "Should the Ranch Go Free Because the Constable Blundered? Gaining Compliance with Search and Seizure Standards in the Age of Asset Forfeiture." *California Law Review* 80 (1992): 1309–59.

259

Bibliography

O'Brien, Alice M. "Caught in the Crossfire: Protecting the Innocent Owner of Real Property from Civil Forfeiture under 21 U.S.C. Section 881(a)(7)." *St. John's Law Review* 65 (1991): 521–51.

O'Donnell, John. "RICO Forfeiture and Obscenity: Prior Restraint or Subsequent Punishment?" *Fordham Law Review* 56 (1188): 1101–28.

Palm, Craig W. "Rico Forfeitures and the Eighth Amendment: When Is Everything Too Much?" *University of Pittsburgh Law Review* 53 (1991): 1–95.

Parcels, Susan. "An Analysis of Federal Drug Related Civil Forfeiture." *Maine Law Review* 34 (1982): 435–58.

Petrou, Peter. "Due Process Implications of Shifting the Burden of Proof in Forfeiture Proceedings Arising Out of Illegal Drug Transactions." *Duke Law Journal* (1984): 822–43.

Pianin, Irving A. "Criminal Forfeiture: Attacking the Economic Dimension of Organized Narcotics Trafficking." *American University Law Review* 32 (1982): 227–55.

Piety, Tamara. "Scorched Earth: How the Expansion of Civil Forfeiture Doctrine Has Laid Waste to Due Process." *University of Miami Law Review* 45 (1991): 911–78.

Reed, Terrance G., and Joseph P. Gill. "RICO Forfeitures, Forfeitable Interests and Procedural Due Process." *North Carolina Law Review* 62 (1983): 57–113.

Reed, Terry. "Criminal Forfeiture Under the Comprehensive Forfeiture Act of 1984: Raising the Stakes." *American Criminal Law Review* 22 (1985): 747–83.

Rosenberg, Jay A. "Constitutional Rights and Civil Forfeiture Actions." *Columbia Law Review* 88 (1988): 390–406.

Saltzburg, Damon Garett. "Real Property Forfeitures as a Weapon in the Government's War on Drugs: A Failure to Protect Innocent Ownership Rights." *Boston University Law Review* 72 (1992): 217–42.

Schecter, Michael. "Fear and Loathing and the Forfeiture Laws." *Cornell Law Review* 75 (1990): 1151–83.

Schier, Michael L. "The Bill of Rights Becomes the Latest Casualty in the War on Drugs and Organized Crime—Surprisingly, Forfeiture of Attorney Fees Is Consistent with the Fifth and Sixth Amendments." *Cincinnati Law Review* 59 (1991): 905–56.

Smith, Sean D. "The Scope of Real Property Forfeiture for Drug-Related Crimes Under the Comprehensive Forfeiture Act." *University of Pennsylvania Law Review* 137 (1988): 303–34.

Bibliography

Spaulding, Karla R. "'Hit Them Where It Hurts': RICO Criminal Forfeitures and White Collar Crime." *Journal of Criminal Law & Criminology* 80 (1989): 197–292.

Speta, James B. "Narrowing the Scope of Civil Drug Forfeiture: Section 881, Substantial Connection and the Eighth Amendment." *Michigan Law Review* 89 (1990): 165–210.

Stenton, Doris M. "England. Henry II." In *The Cambridge Medieval History*, edited by J. B. Bury. Cambridge: Cambridge University Press, 1957.

Strafer, G. Richard. "Civil Forfeitures: Protecting the Innocent Owner." *University of Florida Law Review* 37 (1985): 841–61.

Tarlow, Barry. "RICO: The New Darling of the Prosecutor's Nursery." *Fordham Law Review* 49 (1980): 165–306.

Taylor, William W. III. "The Problem of Proportionality in RICO Forfeitures." *Notre Dame Law Review* 65 (1990): 885–995.

Weiner, Edward C. "Crime Must Not Pay: RICO Criminal Forfeiture in Perspective." *Northern Illinois University Law Review* 1 (1981): 225–59.

Williams, Nathan B. "Forfeiture Laws." *American Bar Association Journal* 16 (1930): 572–73.

Winn, Peter A. "Seizures of Private Property in the War Against Drugs: What Process Is Due?" *Southwestern Law Journal* 41 (1988): 1111–34.

Wisotsky, Steven. "Crackdown: The Emerging Drug Exception to the Bill of Rights." *Hastings Law Journal* 38 (1987): 889–926.

Wroth, L. Kinvin. "The Massachusetts Vice Admiralty Court and the Federal Admiralty Jurisdiction." *American Journal of Legal History* 6 (1962): 250–68, 347–67.

Zeldin, Michael F., and Roger G. Weiner. "Innocent Third Parties and Their Rights in Forfeiture Proceedings." *American Criminal Law Review* 28 (1991): 843–61.

Government Documents

Accounting for Federal Asset Forfeiture Funds: A Guide for State and Local Law Enforcement Agencies. Washington, D.C.: Department of Justice, July 1991.

Asset Forfeiture: A Seldom Used Tool In Combatting Drug Trafficking. Comptroller General's Report to the Honorable Joseph R. Biden, U.S. Senate, GGD081-51, April 10, 1981.

Asset Forfeiture: Improved Guidance Needed for Use of Shared Assets.

Bibliography

General Accounting Office, Report to the Chairman of the Government Information, Justice, and Agriculture Subcommittee of the House Committee on Government Operations, GAO/GGD-92-115, July 1992.

Attorneys' Fees Forfeitures. Hearing before the Senate Committee on the Judiciary, 99th Cong., 2d sess., S. Hearing 99-973, May 13, 1986.

Comprehensive Crime Control Act of 1983. Hearings before the Subcommittee on Criminal Law of the Senate Committee on the Judiciary, 98th Cong., 1st sess., 1983.

Comprehensive Crime Control Act of 1983. Report of the Senate Committee on the Judiciary on S. 1762, Senate Report No. 98-225, September 14, 1983.

Comprehensive Criminal Forfeiture Act of 1982. Report of the Senate Committee on the Judiciary, 97th Cong., 2d sess., Senate Calendar No. 749, Report No. 97-520, August 10, 1982.

Comprehensive Drug Abuse Prevention and Control Act of 1970. Report of the House Committee on Interstate and Foreign Commerce, 91st Cong., 2d sess., Report No. 91-1444 (pt. 1), September 10, 1970.

Comprehensive Drug Penalty Act of 1984. Report of the House Committee on the Judiciary, 98th Cong., 2d. sess., Report No. 98-845 (pt. 1), June 19, 1985.

Conyers, John Jr. "A Bill to Reform the Laws Relating to Forfeitures." 103d Cong., 1st sess., H.R. 3347, 1994.

Copeland, Cary H. *Directive No. 93-4.* Washington, D.C.: Department of Justice, Office of the Deputy Attorney General, Executive Office for Asset Forfeiture, January 15, 1993.

Department of Justice Asset Forfeiture Program. Hearing before the Legislation and National Security Subcommittee of the House Committee on Government Operations, 102d Cong., 2d sess., September 30, 1992.

Disposition of Seized Cash and Property. Hearing before the Subcommittee on Federal Spending, Budget, and Accounting of the Senate Committee on Governmental Affairs, 100th Cong., 2d sess., S. Hearing 100-904, June 23, 1988.

Doyle, Charles. *Crime and Forfeiture.* CRS Report for Congress, December 30, 1992. Washington, D.C.: Congressional Research Service, Library of Congress, 1992.

———. *Drug-Related Seizure of Property.* CRS Report for Congress, October 15, 1992. Washington, D.C.: Congressional Research Service, Library of Congress, 1992.

———. *Equitable Distribution and Adoptive Forfeiture.* Report No. 90-538A, November 5, 1990. Washington, D.C.: Congressional Research Service, Library of Congress, 1990.

262

Bibliography

Federal Drug Forfeiture Activities. Hearing before the Subcommittee on Crime of the House Committee on the Judiciary, 101st Cong., 1st sess., Serial No. 55, April 24, 1989.

Federal Drug Forfeiture Activity. Hearing before the Subcommittee on Crime of the House Committee on the Judiciary, 100th Cong., 2d sess., Serial No. 135, March 4, 1988.

Federal Government's Forfeiture Programs: Seized Cash and Forfeited Property Management. Hearing before the Subcommittee on Federal Spending, Budget, and Accounting of the Senate Committee on Governmental Affairs, 100th Cong., 1st sess., September 25, 1987.

Federal Government's Response to Money Laundering. Hearings before the House Committee on Banking, Finance, and Urban Affairs, 103d Cong., 1st sess., Serial No. 103-40, May 25–26, 1993.

"Forfeiture Act of 1994, The." Administration bill, Department of Justice, 1994.

Forfeiture in Drug Cases. Hearings on H.R. 2646, H.R. 4110, and H.R. 5371 before the Subcommittee on Crime of the House Committee on the Judiciary. 97th Cong., 1st & 2d sess., 1981, 1982.

Forfeiture of Narcotics Proceeds. Hearings before the Subcommittee on Criminal Justice of the Senate Committee of the Judiciary, 96th Cong., 2d sess., Serial No. 96-81, July 23–24, 1980.

Forfeiture Portions of the Comprehensive Crime Bill and the Anti-Drug Abuse Act of 1986. Hearing before the Subcommittee on Crime of the House Committee on the Judiciary, 100th Cong., 1st sess., Serial No. 27, March 9, 1987.

Gallagher, Patrick. *The Management and Disposition of Seized Assets.* Washington, D.C.: Department of Justice, Bureau of Justice Assistance, Asset Forfeiture, 1992.

Goldsmith, Michael, and William Lenck. *Protection of Third-Party Rights.* August 1990. Reprint, Washington, D.C.: Department of Justice, Bureau of Justice Assistance, Asset Forfeiture, January 1992.

Guide to Equitable Sharing of Federally Forfeited Property for State and Local Law Enforcement Agencies. Washington, D.C.: Department of Justice, Office of the Deputy Attorney General, Executive Office for Asset Forfeiture, December 1990; rev. 1994.

Handbook on the Comprehensive Crime Control Act of 1984 and Other Criminal Statutes Enacted by the 98th Congress. Washington, D.C.: Department of Justice, December 1984.

House Reports, 91st Cong., 2d sess. Miscellaneous Reports on Public Bills VI. Vols. 1–6, beginning January 19, 1970. Washington, D.C.: GPO, 1970.

Bibliography

Hyde, Henry J. "Civil Asset Forfeiture Reform Act of 1993: A Briefing Paper." Mimeographed handout from the congressman's office, June 16, 1993.

——. "Civil Asset Forfeiture Reform Act of 1993," as introduced by U.S. Rep. Henry J. Hyde as part of *Bill to Reform Certain Statutes Regarding Civil Asset Forfeiture*, 103d Cong., 1st sess., 1993.

Measures Relating to Organized Crime. Hearings before the Subcommittee on Criminal Laws and Procedures of the Senate Committee on the Judiciary, 91st Cong., 1st sess., March 18–26, June 3–4, 1969.

Murphy, T. Gregory. *Uncovering Assets Laundered through a Business*. Washington, D.C.: Department of Justice, Office of the Deputy Attorney General, Executive Office for Asset Forfeiture, 1992.

Myers, Harry L., and Joseph Brzostowski. *Drug Agents' Guide to Forfeiture of Assets*. Washington, D.C.: Drug Enforcement Administration, 1981. Rev. ed., edited by William L. Lenck, 1987.

National Drug Control Strategy. Budget Summary, January 1990. Washington, D.C.: The White House, 1990.

National Drug Control Stategy. Budget Summary, February 1991. Washington, D.C.: The White House, 1991.

National Drug Control Strategy: A National Response to Drug Abuse. Budget Summary, January 1992. Washington, D.C.: The White House, 1992.

Organized Crime Control. Hearings before Subcommittee No. 5 of the House Committee on the Judiciary, 91st Cong., 2d sess., Serial No. 27, May 20–August 5, 1970.

Review of Federal Asset Forfeiture Program. Hearing before the Legislation and National Security Subcommittee of the House Committee on Government Operations. 103d Cong., 1st sess., June 22, 1993.

Section-by-Section Analysis of the Forfeiture Act of 1994. Washington, D.C.: Department of Justice, 1994.

Senate Reports, 91st Cong., 1st Sess. Miscellaneous Reports on Public Bills V. Vols. 1–5, January 3–December 23, 1969.

Troland, Mary. *Asset Forfeiture: Law, Practice, and Policy*. 2 vols. (loose-leaf binding). Washington, D.C.: Department of Justice, 1986.

Index